marketing
ROI

THE PATH TO CAMPAIGN, CUSTOMER, AND CORPORATE PROFITABILITY

James D. Lenskold

 AMERICAN MARKETING ASSOCIATION

McGraw·Hill

New York   Chicago   San Francisco   Lisbon   London   Madrid   Mexico City
Milan   New Delhi   San Juan   Seoul   Singapore   Sydney   Toronto

The **McGraw·Hill** Companies

Library of Congress Cataloging-in-Publication Data

Lenskold, James D.
Marketing ROI : the path to campaign, customer, and corporate profitability / by
James D. Lenskold.
p.   cm.
Includes bibliographical references.
ISBN 0-07-141363-4 (hardcover : alk. paper)
1. Capital investments—Evaluation.   2. Rate of return.   3. Profit.   I. Title:
Marketing 'Return On Investment'.   II. Title.

HG4028.C4L397   2003
658.15'54—dc21   2003001407

4 5 6 7 8 9 0   DOC/DOC   2 1 0 9 8 7 6 5 4

ISBN 0-07-141363-4

McGraw-Hill books are available at special quantity discounts to use as premiums and
sales promotions, or for use in corporate training programs. For more information, please
write to the Director of Special Sales, Professional Publishing, McGraw-Hill, Two Penn
Plaza, New York, NY 10121-2298. Or contact your local bookstore.

This book is printed on acid-free paper.

This book is dedicated to Karen, Bethany, and Meghan for their love and support. I owe you a lifetime of value and many positive returns.

CONTENTS

Acknowledgments   ix
Introduction   xi

PART I UNDERSTANDING ROI PRINCIPLES

CHAPTER 1 PROFIT IS THE GOAL, ROI IS THE
               MEASURE   3

Are We Ready for Marketing ROI?   4
The Power of Marketing ROI   8
Shortfalls in Alternative Marketing Measurements   10
Addressing Profit Pressures   11
Marketing ROI: The Next Wave for CRM   13
Understanding the Key Challenges   14
Yes, the Time Is Right for Marketing ROI   17

CHAPTER 2 GETTING THE ROI BASICS   19

Key Financial Concepts   21
Defining Incremental Value   24
Point-of-Decision Perspective   26
ROI by a Different Name   28

CHAPTER 3 MARKETING ROI IS DIFFERENT   33

Marketing Has Greater Flexibility   34
Incremental Measures Go Further   35

CHAPTER 4 MORE MEASURABLE THAN EVER   39

Technology Simplifies the Measures   42
Privacy Issues   43
Determination Counts   44

CHAPTER 5 MARKETING ROI PROCESS   47

Part I Conclusion   50

PART II BUILDING THE ROI FORMULA

CHAPTER 6 MEASURING RETURN ON INVESTMENT   53

Calculating the Return   54
Calculating the Investment   58
Where ROI Measurements Go Wrong   64
Customer Lifetime Value vs. ROI   66

CHAPTER 7 INVESTMENT AND RETURN PATTERNS   71

Acquisition Marketing Patterns   71
Retention Marketing Patterns   75
A Look at Customer Loyalty   81
Cross-Sell Marketing Patterns   83

CHAPTER 8 PROFIT DYNAMICS AND KEY
PRINCIPLES   87

Retention Marketing and Acquisition Marketing:
A Head-to-Head Comparison   88
Key Principles for ROI   95

Aligning Measures with Decisions   96
Establishing Financial Measures for Strategic Initiatives   97
Accurate and Complete Accounting of ROI   99
Keeping Performance Metrics in Check   100
Taking Residual Value into Consideration   104
Part II Conclusion   108

PART III APPLYING MARKETING ROI

CHAPTER 9 ADOPTING THE MARKETING ROI
                 PROCESS   113
Putting Marketing ROI to Work   115
The True View of Marketing ROI   118

CHAPTER 10 MANAGING CORPORATE-LEVEL
                  PROFITABILITY   125
Executive Responsibilities   126
Standardizing the ROI Formula   127
Setting the ROI Threshold   142
Setting Marketing Budgets   144
Monitoring and Modifying Marketing Budgets   145
Aligning Performance Rewards   146

CHAPTER 11 MANAGING CUSTOMER
                  PROFITABILITY   149
Division Manager Responsibilities   150
Multilevel ROI Measurements   151
Mass-Marketing Measures   156

CHAPTER 12 CUSTOMER PATHING™ STRATEGIES   163
Managing Budgets   170
Research, Development, and Benchmarking   171

CHAPTER 13 MANAGING CAMPAIGN
PROFITABILITY   173

Marketing Manager Responsibilities   175
Preplanning Research and Intelligence   176
Campaign Innovation and Screening   186
Market Testing   189
Results Analysis   191
Strategic Decisions   198
Customer Pathing Checkpoint   205

CHAPTER 14 THE MEASUREMENT PROCESS   209

Insight for Smarter Decisions   210
Types of Measurement Processes   213
Data Integrity   219

CHAPTER 15 STRATEGIC PROFIT MANAGEMENT   223

Customer Segment Investment Strategies   224
Managing the Marketing Investment Portfolio   228
The Marketing ROI Control Panel   233

CHAPTER 16 THE IMPLEMENTATION PROCESS   239

The Cross-Functional Team   242
The Role of Technology   244
Low-Tech Solutions   246
The ROI Champion   247
First Steps to Greater Profits   248
Conclusion   250

Notes   251
Index   257

ACKNOWLEDGMENTS

This book is a milestone on a path that resulted from the encouragement and experience of many intelligent individuals along the way. Thanks go first to Liz Gorski who has kept the clients of Lenskold Group on track over the long period of time in which my attention was diverted. Rich Largman, executive consultant extraordinaire, deserves credit for the initial motivation to get this started. My excellent advisory board of Tom Atkinson, Margaret Barrett, Michael Harp, and Jean Pankow helped set the right priorities and find the balance between developing these new concepts while managing the existing business.

Jim Stanton deserves double credit for providing a solid financial perspective while we were at AT&T together and then coming back into a similar role more than a decade later. Ken Cook was also a major contributor, helping to frame out the publishing proposal and serving as a sounding board throughout the writing process. Thanks to Bob Upham and his team at Chatham Systems Group for giving me the insight into the CRM and campaign management technologies that make it possible to implement many advanced marketing ROI processes.

Sincere thanks go to the individuals who took the time to share their expertise and experience through phone interviews and E-mail dialogues. These people share a similar passion for smarter, more profitable marketing and our conversations were certainly the best part of the entire process. This includes Peter Accorti and Donna DePasquale of Marketswitch Corporation; Bob Boehnlein and Rob McLaughlin of Aprimo, Incorporated; David Bonthrone of Dendrite International; Bill

Cook of the Advertising Research Foundation; Tom Hannigan and Andrew Katz of Chatham Systems Group; Lloyd Lyons of Bank One; James McQuivey and Jim Nail of Forrester Research; George Michie and Alan Rimm-Kauffman of Crutchfield Corporation; Tom Nicholson of Sears, Roebuck and Company; Jim Novo of the Drilling Down Project; Dr. Martha Rogers of Peppers & Rogers Group; Don E. Schultz of Northwestern University; Jim Sterne of Target Marketing of Santa Barbara; Rachele Williams of the American Productivity & Quality Center; and Randy Zeese of AT&T.

Special thanks to Martha Rogers from this group, who not only shared her valuable insights on the topic, but also offered kind words of advice.

I am grateful for the support of Sandra Barry, Ruth Stevens, Pete Lenskold, and Ken Sandler for providing valuable insights and taking the time to review draft materials along the way and to David Marine for contributing his excellent research skills. I appreciate the support provided by the folks at McGraw-Hill and the American Marketing Association. Thanks also to the Dublin Pub in Morristown for the late evening meals, and the Roxbury Library for a place of solitude away from the office and home.

My family and friends deserve many sincere thanks for years of support and encouragement.

INTRODUCTION

The sole purpose of marketing is to get more people to buy more of your product, more often, for more money. That's the only reason to spend a single nickel, pfennig, or peso. If your marketing is not delivering consumers to the cash register with their wallets in their hands to buy your product, don't do it.[1]

SERGIO ZYMAN

I was fortunate to have begun my career at AT&T just as this one-time monopoly was entering the competitive arena. The marketing organization was quite savvy in the decade that followed the split off from the Baby Bells and significant attention was paid to financial analysis. Just five years into my career, I had already helped launch the customer-acquisition group and was then managing a $20 million budget and a team responsible for innovating customer-retention marketing programs. I am a strategist and innovator at heart and could never survive a pure "numbers" job. What intrigued me about marketing return on investment (ROI) was the incredible intelligence that could be captured and applied to the strategy to improve future performance. I had a passion for driving profits. I was also young enough to take ideas from my M.B.A. finance classes and start questioning the measurement and budget management processes.

Initially, my focus was to improve the accuracy of marketing ROI measures so that they better reflected the actual marketing impact. I worked with very, very smart people but when it came to the financials, they never looked deep enough to see the flaws. I revised the way we measured the performance of a weekly campaign targeted to relocating households and then developed a sophisticated model for capturing the true ROI for customer-retention programs. Would you believe that the previous method of measuring customer retention was to compare the money spent on retention marketing programs against all of the profits that stayed with the company? In the early days of telecommunications competition, MCI and Sprint were new to consumers and still experiencing quality issues. AT&T could do next to nothing and still keep 85 to 90 percent of its customers. You can imagine how good the impact of AT&T's retention programs looked when in reality there was really minimal impact. This required a shift to tracking only *saved* customers and aligning the financial benefit with the period in which the save occurred.

I wasn't satisfied with improving campaign measurements and decided to develop and present an approach for maximizing profits at the corporate level. The budgeting process, based primarily on historical budgets and endlessly re-running performance projections, was inefficient and far from optimizing profitability. My proposed solution was presented to senior executives at AT&T. The conclusion was that the new process, which included prioritizing investments based on campaign-level ROI projections, was absolutely valid but required more sophisticated systems and better access to data.

The marketing ROI concepts I had developed never went any further until almost a decade later. It was through a consulting engagement for Chatham Systems Group, a company that implements sophisticated Customer Relationship Management (CRM) solutions, that I discovered how far campaign management technologies have advanced. The improved access to data and marketing automation can now easily support more advanced marketing ROI analysis at the campaign, customer, and corporate levels. While the technology has evolved, it is clear that ROI practices within most corporate marketing departments have not yet changed significantly.

The goal of this book is to serve as a comprehensive guide for effectively using marketing ROI to improve profitability. It covers a broad range of marketing ROI techniques and insights, while avoiding heavily covered topics such as research, modeling, and experimental design. There is no magic formula to convert soft marketing metrics such as awareness and satisfaction into an ROI equation, but there is plenty of direction for making both small and large improvements in profitability. You will find marketing tools and measurement techniques that will facilitate the development of better strategies, especially CRM strategies, which are typically intended to improve profitability. Marketing ROI is essentially a simple formula that can be adapted and used in many ways—when applied correctly.

The tools and techniques presented here apply to even the broadest definitions of marketing. In fact, the proper use of marketing ROI measurements is capable of comparing investment options as diverse as a direct marketing campaign, a dedicated sales force, a retail distribution channel, and an Internet marketing campaign. Marketing ROI analysis can scale from the incremental value of a tag line on an envelope to the implementation of a multimillion-dollar enterprise CRM marketing initiative. It can be used to compare the ROI of a price reduction to a marketing initiative that includes a free offer. The concepts and examples in this book cover marketing communications and the need for more proactive management to connect investments with the incremental returns. For our purposes, marketing is defined as all activities, including sales and advertising, intended to influence customer behaviors toward generating a financial transaction.

The presentation of the marketing ROI concepts is intended to apply across a broad range of industries and applications. There are differences in the way marketing is measured and also differences in terminology (which you may need to watch for when reading the book). The underlying principles should be valid regardless of industry. It should also be noted that there are limitations to the effectiveness of marketing ROI practices. One of the foundations for guiding better marketing investments is that measurements and analysis will be effective at predicting the returns on future investments. Companies that have low-quantity, high-value customers are subject to less predictability. The same applies to marketing initiatives that generate low sales volume. Measuring the value of a single speaking engagement at a conference or assigning a large team to pitch a single client over the course of a year may not be possible. The intention is to improve the measurement of the financial value of marketing investments wherever possible and recognize that other decisions will still need to be subjective or rely on nonfinancial value.

Another key assumption underlying the principles of marketing ROI is that companies will be able to obtain the data necessary to complete the ROI analyses presented. Companies do not have perfect knowledge of the financial activity surrounding marketing initiatives, but by understanding the benefits that are possible with marketing ROI techniques, it may be easier to justify the actions necessary to improve knowledge in this area. Some ROI concepts will not be effective for certain companies based on their lack of access to the right information. The goal is to identify what can be implemented in your current environment and how you can make improvements to support further implementation of the marketing ROI process.

There is tremendous opportunity to have an impact on profitability at the campaign, customer, and corporate levels. The information presented here will provide insight to executives, marketers, financial managers, and research analysts. For those readers who want to easily gather the insight necessary to unlock the profit potential in their company, I suggest you just glance over the formulas and calculations. Those who want to understand the logic behind the concepts or want to implement specific tools and techniques should be attentive to the calculations. Part I establishes the rationale for marketing ROI and introduces some key principles. Part II covers the ROI formula, how to get it right, and how different profit patterns are reflected in the calculations. Part III gets into the strategic applications that are possible, as well as the roles necessary to plan and implement more effective marketing measurements.

The concepts presented here should advance the knowledge and understanding of marketing ROI throughout the industry. This is one more step in establishing more effective marketing measurements by building on the insights and experience of many quality sources. While writing this book, I have evolved my own concepts significantly. Hopefully others will take these concepts even further and continue to forge the path to better profits.

PART I

UNDERSTANDING ROI PRINCIPLES

PROFIT IS THE GOAL, ROI IS THE MEASURE

Investment or expense? How a company manages its marketing budget drives not only how well the marketing organization can perform, but also how well the company can perform. Shareholders expect the company to maximize profits so they can achieve the highest possible returns from their investments. The company maximizes profits by maximizing sales revenues, minimizing overhead expenses, maximizing gross margins, and managing its own investments to an appropriate level of risk and expected returns.

Let's face it, the ultimate purpose of marketing is to generate profitable sales, and it is to the benefit of shareholders, executives, and marketers to manage the budget as an investment. Consider that return on investment (ROI) is calculated for large capital expenditures and technology implementations where the profits from productivity and incremental sales are much more difficult to estimate and measure. Marketing, including the communications, advertising, sales, and distribution functions, is directly responsible for driving profits into the company by selling to customers and there is no longer room for excuses. As Sergio Zyman, former chief marketing officer of Coca-Cola, clearly summarized in his book, *The End of Marketing As We Know It*, the "sole purpose of marketing is to get more people to buy more of your product, more often, for more money."[1] Every strategy and tactical decision should be intended to increase profits. It is completely reasonable, and highly beneficial, to expect a return on investment for each incremental marketing dollar spent.

Companies must maximize profits over the long term and marketing investments must do the same. Goals are set by the company to provide common vision and purpose. Measurements are then aligned with the goals to track actual performance relative to the goals and to provide feedback that can help guide future decisions. While profits are necessary to stay in business and to satisfy shareholder expectations, executives must have a vision and purpose that goes beyond just profits to maintain the company's success. Ultimately, their broad goals for quality, customer satisfaction, new product development, and employee satisfaction should all lead back to sustaining and growing long-term profits.

With profits as the goal and the marketing budget managed as an investment, ROI must emerge as the primary marketing measurement. The advanced concepts around marketing ROI can provide significant financial control to corporate executives while also empowering marketing managers. The marketing ROI process can be used to provide a subjective view of long-debated issues such as the prioritization of retention versus acquisition marketing. Modeling criteria can be refined to drive more profitable analysis. Customer Relationship Management (CRM) strategies can be refined to improve profitability and companies that are not ready to adopt CRM can use Customer Pathing™ concepts to manage customer profitability (presented fully in Chapter 12). The budgeting process can be streamlined and modified to truly deliver profit optimization. You'll find no better way to tap into missed profit opportunities than to move farther down the path of marketing ROI measurements.

Are We Ready for Marketing ROI?

It is an interesting time with respect to the adoption of ROI measures within marketing. Marketers have always had a strong interest in measures of success and have been focused on improving sales and profits. At some point in history, the challenges of measuring the actual sales driven by specific advertising and brand-marketing expenditures shifted measurement criteria, such as awareness, perception, and purchase intention to the forefront. Marketing placed such strong emphasis on creative and entertainment value, which would score high on awareness and perceptions, that it lost touch with its primary purpose of generating profits. Removing the direct connection between marketing initiatives and profits led to a corporate mentality that marketing was more of an expense than an investment. Lord Leverhulme, whose company Lever and Kitchen eventually became Unilever, is credited with the widely known quote "Half the money I spend on advertising is wasted. The trouble is I don't know which half." (This has been repeated so frequently that the quote is also attributed to John Wanamaker, Henry Ford, and a host of other business executives).[2] Marketers have had some strange pride in repeating this proclamation instead of putting it to rest. Executives know that their R&D department is working on new products or production processes that will only succeed in a small percentage of their attempts, but they trust that overall the returns from the few successes will greatly exceed the overall investment. The difference in investments is further demonstrated in the financial treatment of investments where product development and R&D expenses are capitalized as assets based on their future value, while customer-acquisition marketing is immediately expensed without accounting for future customer value as an asset.[3] Recent rulings by the Financial Accounting Standards Board officially declared marketing as an expense for accounting purposes, but this should not deter companies from intelligently managing the marketing budget as an investment with the expectation of healthy returns.[4]

The tide is shifting toward greater accountability and stronger measurements for marketing. However, this trend is not being driven by marketing, where resistance still persists, or from the CEOs. Financial managers are looking more closely at how marketing budgets are being allocated. Chief information officers (CIOs) and information technology managers, drawn into the marketing process by sales force automation, CRM technologies, and electronic marketing channels are also increasing their involvement in marketing measurements. Overall, the typical champions for increased attention on marketing ROI tend to be senior managers who are analytical by nature, regardless of their job titles.[5]

In 1990, Frederick Reichheld and Earl Sasser Jr. demonstrated the financial value of customer loyalty in their *Harvard Business Review* article that presented the frequently cited quote, "Companies can boost profits by almost 100% by retaining just 5% more of their customers."[6] The economics of customer loyalty were subsequently detailed in Reichheld's book *The Loyalty Effect*. This potential to increase profits through better customer loyalty sparked the growth of CRM—a practice that is still making inroads into corporate business models today. The insight demonstrated through Reichheld's retention model is exactly what better measures of marketing ROI offer as a guide to more profitable decision making.[7]

Recent research shows that marketing ROI is both a priority and a challenge for most companies. In Accenture's survey of marketing executives in the United States and the United Kingdom, 68 percent reported difficulty measuring the ROI of their marketing campaigns. This was determined to be the most severe challenge faced by marketers. Lacking information on customer profitability was also listed as a top challenge.[8] James McQuivey of Forrester Research cites a combination of company culture and access to data as a key barrier to marketing ROI measures. Consumer-product companies have significant data-availability issues based on their distance from the consumer. One of the key needs is to apply more sophisticated segmentation practices that guide channel decisions toward improvements in customer value.[9]

The best-practice report *Maximizing Marketing ROI* prepared by the American Productivity and Quality Center (APQC) in conjunction with the Advertising Research Foundation (ARF) presented the following findings:

- The pressure is on marketing to demonstrate a quantifiable return and on CEOs to deliver value to their stockholders and business alliance partners.
- ROI-based marketing is sought by more marketers.
- ROI process works best with ongoing programs and interdisciplinary teams.
- ROI-based models encourage decision makers to challenge and revise the budgeting process.
- Leveraging suppliers adds competitive advantage.

This study found that the best-practice companies gained a competitive advantage and increased profitability through the application of marketing ROI measurements and modeling. These benchmark companies are now able to quickly compare and prioritize alternative marketing options, more easily make informed decisions, and effectively spread learning companywide from the common framework that exists. ROI measurements allowed company executives, financial managers, and marketing managers to speak the same language in terms of performance expectations. Using common terms and standard measures in place of marketing metrics that were not clearly aligned with financial value enabled marketers to gain more executive support for additional funding requests.[10]

Increasing the use of marketing ROI is only going to result in increased profits if the calculations are done properly. The term *marketing ROI* has been used to represent much more than profit generation, leading to a certain level of confusion. Yes, the word *return* could be construed to mean every benefit the company gains from the investment, including soft measures such as awareness and customer satisfaction, but *ROI* is a financial term in the business world where "return" represents a financial gain. The worst abusers of the *ROI* term are those who present return on investment based on revenue in place of profits. A number of E-mail marketing companies offer prospective customers ROI calculators that are based on revenue, which then show positive ROI for investments that would clearly be losing money. It could be an honest mistake that resulted from confusion in the marketplace since the mistake has been repeated by reputable marketing organizations. For those companies using ROI to sell their solution, intentionally using this inaccurate ROI calculation borders on scamming the customer.

Perhaps the question isn't whether companies are ready for marketing ROI, but can companies wait any longer? When Kevin Clancy and Robert Shulman of the consulting firm Yankelovich Clancy and Shulman published *The Marketing Revolution: A Radical Manifesto for Dominating the Marketplace* more than a decade ago, they made it clear that marketing must become more accountable for delivering profitable returns. They presented a fresh perspective on marketing that justified greater attention to marketing measurements that would guide better strategies and investments.[11] Companies that have taken action based on this insight have surely benefited, but the industry as a whole has made little progress. Clearly, billions of wasted marketing dollars leak out of the corporate till and the only companies benefiting are those selling the advertising and marketing.

Keep this very important fact in mind—even without ROI measures in place, marketing investments are generally profitable. Successful companies are currently generating profitable sales and managing their marketing expense effectively. However, transitioning to ROI as the primary marketing measure offers the opportunity for improvements in campaign, customer, and corporate profitability. Unprofitable marketing investments will be cut and budgets will be increased where clear profit potential can be demonstrated. With more than $231 billion in advertising and marketing expenditures in 2001[12] and with continued growth being projected, it should be of some concern that 68 percent of the companies reported difficulties in measuring marketing ROI. Money is being left on the table and that's profit that can be going directly to the bottom line.

The Power of Marketing ROI

The most powerful and useful marketing measure is return on investment, a measure that can relate the total investment made to the total return generated from that investment. ROI can be modified to reflect the relative importance of short- or long-term profits and is one of the few marketing measurements that can be used to measure and compare diverse marketing efforts with consistency across large organizations. Above all, accurate ROI measures, along with clear corporate guidelines, can be relied upon to steer the optimal marketing decisions.

Think of ROI measures as intelligence that can be used in strategic and tactical development of marketing initiatives. Marketers rely on all forms of intelligence: customer needs, market conditions, competitive activities, and campaign performance history to improve marketing effectiveness. ROI projections can serve as intelligence into the profit potential. It provides insight into the value that an initiative, strategy, or investment can deliver.

Marketers who can embrace these key principles of marketing ROI have much to gain.

- *ROI is the ultimate measure for guiding marketing investments.* Many other measures provide tremendous insight and intelligence and are critical for making strategic and tactical marketing decisions. Decisions such as improving customer relationships and loyalty, maximizing customer lifetime value, increasing customer satisfaction, or decreasing acquisition costs cannot effectively guide each marketing investment and maximize profits without incorporating the ROI measure.
- *Marketing ROI is unique.* The standard ROI measure could not be simpler. It comes down to how much more money you end up with (your return) compared to what you invested. Unlike typical large capital investments, marketing investments are made up of many small investment decisions. This means that decisions are not just for selecting marketing programs but also for determining how each incremental dollar should be invested.
- *Marketing ROI must be a primary measure used by companies and organizations to remain competitive.* Applying these techniques to guide marketing investments and marketing strategies will benefit every organization. Each organization has a finite marketing budget and should apply these principles to generate the greatest return on its investment. Those organizations that have a greater purpose than maximizing profits, including nonprofit companies and select for-profit companies, must still pay close attention to ROI to best guide investments that will ensure financial survival.
- *Marketing ROI is most beneficial with executive level involvement.* The benefits of ROI analysis and planning extend to all levels of a company; however, the major impact on profits can only come with a corporate level commitment. Company executives can improve profits by using ROI in the budget allocation process. They also can set expectations, define standards, and empower their marketing team to drive the right decisions on how marketing investments are made.

The corporate mind-set has already begun to shift from treating the marketing budget as an expense to treating it as an investment. Additional effort is needed to manage this investment in such a way to best sustain and grow the business. Improving the return-on-marketing investments can be accomplished by using the ROI measure as a tool for planning, measuring, and optimizing marketing strategies.

Shortfalls in Alternative Marketing Measurements

Marketing measurements other than ROI show only a piece of the total picture. These measurements often present great insights that can lead to better marketing strategies; however, these are typically not complete enough for guiding marketing investment decisions toward the greatest profits.

Common marketing measures, such as cost per sale, sales conversion rates, and customer value, are each missing either expense or return information that make these poor choices for critical marketing decisions. Cost-per-sale and sales conversion rates do not take into consideration that different marketing efforts may attract customers with different value. Setting customer value as the primary measure independent of an ROI analysis does not take into account the marketing expense and the fact that pursuing the highest-value customers is not always the most profitable form of marketing.

The term *customer lifetime value* (CLV) is used differently in different industries. ROI is dependent on capturing the future stream of profits that result from a specific investment, which will be referred to as *incremental customer value* (ICV) throughout this book. The most accurate references to CLV capture the entire flow of current and future investments and profits. This measure works much like the ROI calculation for an aggregated set of campaigns. Some industries, such as book clubs, use very consistent marketing and can rely on CLV measures that already incorporate ROI calculations. However, for most companies the use of this form of CLV does not align with the decision-making process since decisions for each campaign are made independently of one another instead of as a preset series of marketing activities for each customer.

The key to using marketing measurements effectively is to understand how the measurements relate to one another. Figure 1.1 shows the marketing-measurement hierarchy as outlined in the article "Marketing ROI: Playing to Win," published in the May/June 2002 issue of *Marketing Management*. Tier 1 includes marketing ROI as the measure to align with the goal of maximizing company profits. Many commonly used marketing measurements such as sales conversion rates and revenue-generated cost per sale are based on the three Tier 2 measures, which include customer value, number of customers, and marketing expense. These Tier 2 measures feed into the ROI equation. The Tier 3 consists of *performance indicators* that are inferior in terms of prioritizing campaigns but provide very valuable information that can be used to provide feedback necessary to modify strategies and indicate what is driving a campaign's level of success.[13]

The Accenture research study found that four marketing performance measures were used most commonly—response rate (79%), revenue generation (78%), customer retention (69%), and profit generation (66%). Each measure is important and all are essential in generating ROI measures. As demonstrated throughout this book, the ROI measure provides marketers with tremendous decision-making and planning capabilities.

Addressing Profit Pressures

In both good and bad economies, companies make extensive efforts to generate greater profits, which are increased by decreasing expenses, increasing sales, or improving margins. Implementing or improving your use of ROI to guide marketing investments can strengthen your profit potential without increasing your marketing budget.

When the economy was booming, Internet companies spent huge marketing budgets to very quickly build market share. Granted, there was not a historical precedent for the true value of quickly building market share, however, more prudent ROI analysis in the planning stage could have made it clear to many of those failed companies that their expectations for generating future profitable returns were never realistic given their customer-acquisition costs.

Figure 1.1 Marketing Measurement Hierarchy

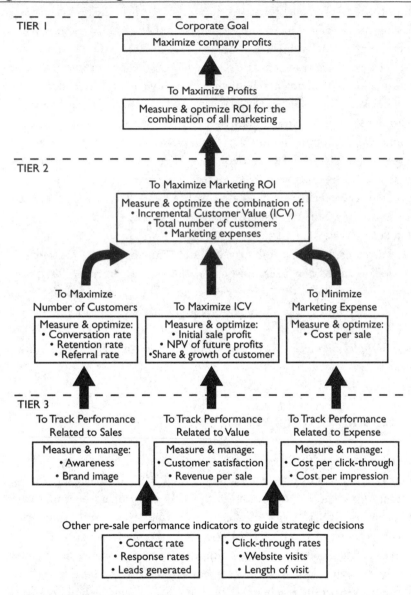

TIER 1

Corporate Goal

Maximize company profits

To Maximize Profits

Measure & optimize ROI for the combination of all marketing

TIER 2

To Maximize Marketing ROI

Measure & optimize the combination of:
• Incremental Customer Value (ICV)
• Total number of customers
• Marketing expenses

To Maximize
Number of Customers

Measure & optimize:
• Conversation rate
• Retention rate
• Referral rate

To Maximize ICV

Measure & optimize:
• Initial sale profit
• NPV of future profits
•Share & growth of customer

To Minimize
Marketing Expense

Measure & optimize:
• Cost per sale

TIER 3

To Track Performance
Related to Sales

Measure & manage:
• Awareness
• Brand image

To Track Performance
Related to Value

Measure & manage:
• Customer satisfaction
• Revenue per sale

To Track Performance
Related to Expense

Measure & manage:
• Cost per click-through
• Cost per impression

Other pre-sale performance indicators to guide strategic decisions

• Contact rate
• Response rates
• Leads generated

• Click-through rates
• Website visits
• Length of visit

Source: James D. Lenskold, "Marketing ROI: Playing to Win," reprinted with permission from the American Marketing Association (*Marketing Management*, Volume 11, Number 3, May/June 2002).

The economic recession that followed the boom triggered the common reaction to scale down expenses, including advertising and marketing. Highly respected management gurus consistently indicate that cutting back on marketing investments that drive future profits is a costly mistake. On the verge of the holiday season of 2001, Kmart implemented a strategy shift that included cutting its advertising budget by roughly 50 percent. This cost-savings measure was intended to support a lower pricing strategy but it backfired and sales were dismal. Kmart could not recover and by January 2002 the company had filed for Chapter 11. With a solid process for planning and monitoring marketing investments using ROI analysis, companies can have greater insight into prioritizing budget cuts and knowing the impact of those cuts on both short-term and long-term profits.

Marketing ROI: The Next Wave for CRM

Corporate CRM initiatives can significantly benefit by integrating more advanced marketing ROI measurements and tools. CRM technology has been a major expense at many large corporations and most of these companies are struggling to see the payback. The next wave of activity around CRM will come from efforts to leverage the existing technology to generate profits. There are many synergies between CRM strategies and ROI measurement practices. CRM systems often contain critical information necessary for improving ROI measures and ROI analysis can be used to guide CRM marketing efforts.

ROI contributes to the advancement of CRM initiatives in the following ways:

- Spending limits can be established at the customer level based on projected value.
- The value of retaining incremental customers through customer-loyalty programs can be assessed and aligned with the appropriate level of investment.
- The ROI measure provides the necessary insight to balance retention and acquisition spending.

- Aggregated ROI analysis can be used to support greater integration between marketing programs using the Customer Pathing strategies (a concept covered in Chapter 12).

CRM initiatives can support ROI measurements in the following ways:

- Customer-based marketing strategies can be optimized by maximizing customer profitability.
- Modeling efforts to project CLV for targeting can also be used for ROI measurements.
- Marketing campaign history may be a valuable source for analysis that establishes benchmark values for select forms of marketing activities and customer behavior.

Understanding the Key Challenges

Measuring ROI does have its challenges as confirmed by the high percentage of marketing executives reporting difficulties in the Accenture survey. The major challenges that face companies working toward more accurate and useful ROI marketing measurements are:

- *Generating reliable future value projections.* Customer behavior is not always predictable in the fast-changing markets of today, and marketers need to make quick decisions that do not allow time for tracking actual purchase behaviors. Some companies capture only immediate purchase value for their ROI analysis. More and more companies are developing some form of CLV but that may not always align with the measure necessary for an ROI analysis of a specific marketing investment.
- *Getting access to data.* The total value generated from a marketing investment could include immediate purchases, future purchases, future customer service expenses, retention rates, and referrals. Marketing organizations do not always have access to this information, leaving gaps in the analysis.

- *Standardizing measurements, values, and practices.* Corporate standards for ROI calculations, values, and practices allow for greater accuracy and consistency between marketing groups across the organization. Without corporate standards in place, each marketing group is likely to create its own version of an ROI formula that best suits its needs and success criteria, without regard for maximizing corporate profits.
- *Establishing cost-effective measurement processes.* While experimental tests and research studies may be effective forms of capturing critical values, the reality is that the cost to measure performance must be a worthwhile investment as well. This means that certain marketing efforts will have gaps when the measurement cost is not justified.
- *Establishing valid control groups.* Measuring the impact of marketing campaigns on behaviors and transactions often requires a control group to serve as a comparison against the pattern of behaviors without the marketing campaign. Many marketing efforts such as those broadcast in mass media make it impossible to establish valid control groups.
- *Matching results back to the appropriate marketing initiative in multichannel marketing environments.* Marketers rely on multiple contacts to generate sales, and customers rely on multiple channels for information, service, and transactions. Measuring the ROI on a specific marketing investment within multichannel campaigns can be quite complex.
- *Allocating expenses.* Marketing expenses such as creative or development costs need to be captured but must not deter investment into development of new marketing programs and innovations.
- *Understanding residual value.* Those marketing investments that have an impact on the results of future marketing activities do not fit in the standard ROI measurement process. This value must be identified and understood to drive the best investment decisions.
- *Organizational barriers such as compensation structures.* The existing processes and internal culture include many barriers to the effective use of ROI measurements. Organizational barriers are presented in detail later in this chapter.

- *Total sum approach.* When calculating results, marketers tend to identify and assume profits that show up in other marketing programs or sales channels, without ensuring that those same results are not double-counted. The sum of individual campaign returns and investments should net fairly close to the total profits and budget when marketing ROI measurements are managed properly.

So how do you address these challenges to use ROI more effectively? It is necessary to understand the degree of impact that each challenge could have for your environment. The goal is to gain greater insight for making strategic decisions and prioritizing marketing investments, so the first checkpoint must be on the reliability of the ROI analyses. Once the process can be trusted to provide good information, there can be further development for continued improvement.

Most of these challenges can be managed by technology, best practices, and behavior shifts. Technology is helping companies move past many of the data and analysis challenges and will only get better as users of ROI marketing measures define their needs to the information technology (IT) organization. Best practices for improving ROI measures continue to be introduced and this book presents approaches for many of the challenges listed. Behavior shifts from marketing campaign managers all the way to senior executives will take time but will happen if supported with tools, training, and incentives.

Organizational Barriers

Improving marketing measures using a more thorough approach to ROI can provide marketers with greater insight and empowerment, but this will not be enough to overcome the organizational barriers to adopting the process. From the company perspective, ROI practices offer the potential to maximize profits generated with the marketing budget available. From the employee perspective, the culture and reward system of the company often do not align with behaviors that contribute toward maximizing corporate profits.

The key organizational barriers around adopting ROI as the primary marketing measure include:

- *Rewards and recognition.* Compensation, recognition, and career advancement tend to motivate short-term gains over long-term gains and individually driven gains over collective corporate gains.
- *Lack of financial skills.* Marketing managers may be limited in their financial analysis capabilities and ROI is more sophisticated than most other marketing measures.
- *Truth in results.* Marketing managers risk losing credit for sales that actually result from previous marketing investments.
- *Risk of hard measures.* The performance of some individuals is based more on creativity or concepts than hard measurable numbers. This is not only a threat to the company's assessment of the individual, but also a threat to the individual's flexibility to maintain creativity as his or her primary objective.
- *Budget allocation power.* Executives and senior marketing managers will rely less on nonfinancial considerations in the budget-allocation process when the majority of marketing investments are associated with a projection for ROI. The shift in budgets tends to be associated with a shift in power.
- *Fear of change.* Some of the resistance will simply be associated with the fear of the unknown.

There are solutions to all of these barriers, although the challenge to implement these cannot be underestimated. Just as CRM initiatives require organizational change, so will any corporate-wide change. Fortunately, ROI marketing measures can be adopted on a small scale and expanded over time.

Yes, the Time Is Right for Marketing ROI

Marketing ROI measures have the potential to increase profits and improve marketing performance, so how could it not be the right time? Companies are demanding that every department work smarter and marketing must step up to the plate and motivate change. You can't afford to fall behind the competition in the use of marketing ROI measures when profits are at stake. The current age of marketing is bringing companies closer to the individual customer and each relationship must be managed to maximize customer profitability. The process of setting marketing budgets based on previous year budgets is terribly inefficient and outdated. Companies benchmarked in the APCQ/ARF study, including Kraft, Colgate-Palmolive, AT&T, and Minute Maid are proving that attention to marketing ROI is essential. The ability to make better marketing investment decisions can lead to more precise targeting, stronger strategies, and increased effectiveness to win a greater share of the most profitable customers and sales. The more profitable a company can be, the more firepower it has for improving products, service, and marketing presence.

CHAPTER 2

GETTING THE ROI BASICS

If leaders truly care about creating value for their long-term investors, they must incorporate into their calculations a reasonable interest charge for their use of equity capital. Profits in excess of this hurdle rate can then be considered to have created investor value.[1]

FREDERICK F. REICHHELD

Return on investment (ROI) is a financial measurement. ROI analysis is used to assess and guide many different forms of corporate and personal investments. However, as mentioned in the previous chapter, ROI is frequently used incorrectly and inaccurately. Before getting into the specific ways ROI is customized for use in marketing, let's first establish a foundation of understanding around the ROI formula by starting with the very basics.

This is the ROI formula in its most basic format:

$$ROI = \frac{Return}{Investment} = \frac{Gross\ Margin - Marketing\ Investment}{Marketing\ Investment}$$

ROI is presented in the form of a percent so that a positive number indicates a financial gain from the investment and a negative number indicates a financial loss. When the gross margin is equal to the marketing investment, the ROI is 0 percent and the investment is considered to be breakeven.

The marketing investment includes all of the expenses that are put at risk to market the product, service, or company. The return is all of the financial gain beyond the initial investment that is attributed to that investment. It basically represents the present value of the inflow of revenues and outflow of expenses that result directly from the investment made.

The term *gross margin* is used to represent the present value of incremental profits and expenses in the calculation of return. More detail will be provided on how gross margin is calculated for marketing measurements in Chapter 6. In general, the term represents the contribution made to company profits prior to deducting the marketing investment.

If you have had limited exposure to ROI calculations, it may be easy to understand the basic concept by considering an example based on a personal investment. Let's say that a person purchases 100 shares of stock at $40 each for an initial investment of $4,000. Add to this the cost of the transaction, which was $25. There is a risk that all of the $4,025 will be lost. This is the person's true investment amount. If all shares are sold the next day for $45, the income is $4,500. Deducting the initial $4,025 investment from the $4,500 income received nets $475, which represents the total return. The return on investment is $475 divided by $4,025, which equals 11.8 percent.

$$\text{ROI} = \frac{\$4,500 - \$4,025}{\$4,025} = \frac{\$475}{\$4,025} = 11.8\%$$

Now consider an example of the ROI calculation for a basic marketing investment where all profits are generated immediately (to temporarily avoid an explanation of net present value). A company has developed a new product and will need to generate sales through marketing. The marketing campaign requires a total budget of $100,000. This is the total investment at risk, i.e., the amount that will be lost if no sales are generated from the marketing campaign. Let's say the marketing generates $500,000 in product revenue, which has a cost of goods of $250,000 and additional expenses of $100,000 related to sales. The gross margin is $500,000 − $250,000 − $100,000, which equals

$150,000. The cost of goods and the expenses related to sales are deducted from the return and not considered investments, since these costs were not at risk.

The return on investment is calculated as follows:

$$\text{ROI} = \frac{\$150,000 - \$100,000}{\$100,000} = \frac{\$50,000}{\$100,000} = 50\%$$

The marketing campaign earned 50 percent above the initial investment. The calculation of ROI for marketing campaigns and customer profitability is much more comprehensive than this simple example.

Key Financial Concepts

For those who could use a refresher in finance 101, the following key financial concepts are essential for ensuring that the ROI measures established for your company will align with the right marketing investment decisions. This is not an attempt to turn marketers into financial experts but to present perspectives on how customer behaviors driven by marketing investments translate into profits for the company.

Net Present Value

Net present value (NPV) is very important for reflecting the time value of money. Since the ROI measure will ideally capture the full impact of a marketing investment, it may need to include profits and expenses that extend over time. Profits generated in future time periods are not as important or even as valuable to a company as profits delivered immediately. This future cash flow can be discounted on a monthly, quarterly, or annual basis, depending on how much relative value a company places on cash in current versus future time periods.

The NPV calculation discounts future profits to a value the company would determine to be equitable if received today. For example, if the NPV of $1,000 received next year was calculated to be $800, the company would prefer to have an amount equal to or greater than $800 today instead of the $1,000 next year.

The gross margin within the ROI equation is based on the NPV of the stream of profits and expenses that result from the marketing investment. This creates an accurate view and an equitable comparison between marketing campaigns that generate returns over different time periods. In the examples presented in this book, NPV calculations discount cash flow on an annual basis unless otherwise specified.

Gross Margin

Gross margin represents the financial contribution coming back to the company once the marketing investment has been made. It is the sales revenue, minus the fully loaded cost of goods to produce the product or service, minus any costs incurred related to the sale. Since this flow of income and expenses will occur over a period of time, the gross margin must be converted into NPV. The basic formula is:

Gross Margin = NPV (Revenue − Cost of Goods − Incremental Expenses)

Cost of goods sold captures fixed costs and variable costs such as materials, manufacturing, labor, and overhead costs, which are allocated based on a percentage of revenues. Incremental expense represents variable costs specific to the sale or set of new customers acquired such as order processing, fulfillment, and customer service. The actual marketing expense is not deducted from the gross margin so the gross margin represents all of the profits generated, including recovery of the marketing investment. Gross margin can also include additional financial contributions such as cost savings and profits generated from customer referrals as shown in Part 2.

Discount Rate

The discount rate is used within the NPV calculation. It is the rate by which the future profits and expenses are discounted to represent a comparable present value. In the example above, a 25 percent annual discount rate was used to equate $1,000 of next year's profits to $800 of this year's profits ($1,000 was divided by the sum of 1 plus the discount rate, so $1,000 was divided by 1.25, which is $800).

Too often, marketers using ROI set this rate without much consideration. It will vary by company and really requires input from the finance department. The discount rate is a reflection of the rate at which the company can borrow money and the risk associated with that company's performance expectations. Large, established companies with good credit history will use a lower discount rate than newly formed ventures that could be considered high risk. Strategically, the discount rate can be used to align the ROI measure with the company's priority for short-term or long-term profits.

Incremental Customer Value and Customer Lifetime Value

Since the term *customer lifetime value* (CLV) is used so differently within the industry, the term *incremental customer value* (ICV) will be used in this book to represent the net present value of the income flow generated by a customer (or segment of customers) as a result of the specific marketing investment being measured. For purposes of calculating ROI, it is critical that ICV include only the stream of profits and expenses that a customer or segment of customers will generate for the company without additional investment beyond the investment being measured. The ICV must be matched with the incremental investment.

CLV will be used to represent the total of all investments made and the total of all returns generated over the course of that customer's lifetime. Individual marketing campaigns may show that some investments do not generate enough ICV to be considered profitable but that the entire flow of campaigns to a customer are profitable as measured by the CLV.

Don Peppers and Martha Rogers, leading consultants on one-to-one relationships and building customer value, define customer lifetime value (also referred to as "actual value") as the NPV of gross margin that the company expects to realize from a customer. They use the term *poten-*

tial value to represent the total NPV of gross margin the customer can spend with the company by earning 100 percent share of the customer and growing the customer's total spending. The actual value is most relevant to ROI measurements of past performance. The potential value of a customer, which is very significant to the development of profitable marketing strategies, can influence the ROI projections based on the potential profits that can be earned by different customer groups.[2]

ROI Threshold or Hurdle Rate

The ROI threshold, also known as the "hurdle rate," is the minimum ROI level for which a company will make investments. For example, if a company's ROI threshold is 25 percent, funding will be provided for any investment opportunity that exceeds that level and rejected for any investment opportunity below that level. Theoretically, the ROI threshold should be equal to the discount rate, both of which should represent the company's cost of securing capital. However, this is not a practical expectation since the ROI threshold may need to be adjusted higher for such purposes as accounting for a margin of error in the calculations, protecting against potential overlap, and recovering general marketing expenses. Companies may choose to set multiple ROI thresholds based on the level of risk anticipated for the marketing investment or based on the stages of strategic development.

Defining Incremental Value

Ideally, ROI calculations measure the incremental return generated by the incremental marketing investment. Marketing investments can be broken down into very small incremental levels, from the addition of a marketing channel or offer to the addition of one more targeted prospect. Incremental return is subject to more discretion by the company, depending on the data available and the approach that the finance department would like to take. This impacts the way gross margin is measured.

Producing products and services requires a combination of fixed costs and variable costs. General business expenses must also be allocated appropriately and covered within the cost of goods sold. Any incremental expenses specific to a sale are included in the gross margin calculation so that the return truly captures just profits (prior to deducting the marketing investment).

There is discretion in determining how to allocate both general business expenses and fixed costs when calculating incremental value. In a detailed discussion with Jim Stanton, CFO of AT&T Consumer Local Service, he explained how the estimated cost of an incremental minute on the AT&T communications network is very different when viewed as a pure incremental expense compared to a fully loaded expense. The company wants to motivate investments that drive incremental minutes since that does add profits to the company, but it must also ensure that all fixed and general business expenses are covered. In most companies, the cost to produce each incremental product or service will generally decrease as volume increases. Financial management can get quite complex when the same product has different cost values for each marketing initiative. Managing ROI projections based on dynamic cost of good values would also be complex and require advanced procedures and sophisticated technologies.

Consider a company's profit and loss statement, but just for a subset of 1,000 customers, assuming all returns come in the first year to avoid discounting for net present value.

	Total	Per Customer
Revenue	$1,000,000	$1,000
Cost of goods sold (50%)	$ 500,000	$ 500
General and administrative costs (excluding marketing)	$ 300,000	$ 300
Gross margin (EBITDA—earnings before interest, tax, depreciation, and amortization)	$ 200,000	$ 200

Using an approach that considers fully loaded costs, the incremental customer value would be considered $200. This is necessary when guiding the core marketing investments that are delivering 1,000 customers and $200,000 worth of gross margin. At the other end of the spectrum is a purely incremental view that considers only variable costs. If a marketing investment could generate one incremental customer in the scenario above, the cost to goods to produce the additional products for this one customer may only be $250 (instead of the $500 average shown). It may require no additional general or administrative costs to handle one additional customer so the pure incremental customer value in this case would be $750 ($1,000 in revenue less $250 in cost of goods). The first example may be underestimating the ICV while the second example is overestimating ICV since it does not take into consideration that as incremental sales grow, there will need to be new machinery, more staff, and more administrative costs.

There are many positions between these two extremes based on consideration of the fixed and variable costs. The goal is to lead the decision-making process toward driving additional profits so the closer the definition for customer value can be to truly incremental, the better profits can be maximized.[3]

Point-of-Decision Perspective

Marketing ROI is intended to help guide the best decisions for marketing investments. To drive the right decisions, the calculation of ROI will differ for strategic planning and for performance measurement. Strategic planning occurs prior to a marketing investment and the performance measure occurs after, changing the perspective for decision making.

To maintain the objective of maximizing profits, it is important that investments are directed toward the best opportunities available at the time. This requires a *point-of-decision* perspective where investment decisions of the past do not influence the investment decisions of the present. The marketing budget must constantly be allocated or reallocated to generate the best possible return.

The key distinction is that ROI projections in the planning stage can exclude previous investments to support the point-of-decision perspective, while ROI analyses for performance measurement should be inclusive of all historical costs ensuring that each investment decision stands on its own merits.

It is very possible that marketing initiatives already underway may lose funding using this approach. In certain situations, market conditions change the initial assumptions, additional requirements are identified, or better investment opportunities come along. With a point-of-decision perspective, new investments are not made to justify previous investments, and poor investment decisions of the past may still be leveraged to provide profitable returns from future investments.

A brief example will help convey the point-of-decision perspective. A company that has invested $500,000 in a customer modeling initiative must make a decision on spending an additional $500,000 to implement the marketing campaign. The company had originally projected $1,300,000 in gross margin, which would have generated a 30 percent return on the initial $1 million investment. New projections estimate only $950,000 in gross margin; however, the customer modeling has already been developed.

The initial ROI projection was as follows:

$$\text{ROI} = \frac{1,300,000 - 1,000,000}{1,000,000} = \frac{300,000}{1,000,000} = 30\%$$

The revised ROI projection for the entire initiative based on new assumptions is:

$$\text{ROI} = \frac{950,000 - 1,000,000}{1,000,000} = \frac{-50,000}{1,000,000} = -5\%$$

The company's choices are to either continue the marketing initiative or cancel it. The $500,000 modeling investment has been made and is not recoverable. Using a point-of-decision approach to the ROI analysis, the company would progress as follows for this example:

- Prior to the initial investment, the ROI projections showing 30 percent ROI would be compared to the company's ROI threshold. At an ROI threshold of 20 percent, the company made the decision to proceed with the investment.
- The company invested $500,000 to complete the customer modeling technology.
- New information on customer response and profitability was completed to show a lower profit potential for the initiative.
- At the point between the modeling investment and the campaign investment, the company would assess the ROI potential on just the remaining $500,000, knowing that it had the option to invest that budget into other marketing initiatives. The revised ROI analysis showing the loss of 5 percent is not relevant at this time. The investment of $500,000 into the marketing campaign that leverages the customer modeling technology can generate a return of $950,000 for an ROI of 90 percent. This investment exceeds the ROI threshold of 20 percent and should therefore be pursued.

The revised ROI analysis for the entire marketing initiative is used for measurement purposes and is completed at the conclusion of the project. Assuming that the actual gross margin was $950,000, the ROI for the entire $1 million investment would be a $50,000 loss. The company can then use that measurement to assess whether the projections were off, the market conditions changed, or the project was mismanaged.

The point-of-decision ROI analysis would maximize the profit potential, or in this case, minimize the loss. Had there been a change in the expected cost of the marketing campaign from $500,000 to $850,000 instead of a change in projected return as outlined in the example above, the ROI potential would have been only 12 percent and the decision would have been to halt the additional investment so the budget could be used to fund better alternatives above the ROI threshold.

ROI by a Different Name

It does not have to be called ROI or look exactly like an ROI equation to serve the same purpose and follow the same fundamental principles of managing marketing investments toward greater profitability. Many lifetime value calculations are fundamentally capturing the same information as an ROI calculation, taking into consideration the net present value of the investment and the subsequent profit stream over time. George Michie, marketing analyst at the consumer electronics catalog retailer Crutchfield Corporation, presented a comprehensive process for measuring customer-acquisition profitability at the 2002 DMD New York Marketing Conference. This is a perfect example of how measurement standards that are unique to certain industries can be customized to capture the key elements necessary to manage profitability.

Crutchfield Analysis

The marketing team at catalog and Internet retailer Crutchfield Corporation has a passion for profitability and it has paid off well in terms of incremental profits. The measurement and analysis methodology was led by vice president Alan Rimm-Kauffman and supported by a marketing team that included marketing analyst George Michie.

In the catalog industry, customer-acquisition strategies frequently involve a combination of product advertising to generate an initial purchase followed by catalog mailings to motivate repeat purchases. Winning the repeat purchase is necessary to make the customer acquisition profitable. Cost per new buyer (CPNB) is the metric that is compared to first-year customer value to assess customer profitability. Crutchfield's analysis took into consideration all costs necessary to represent the series of two investments (advertising and catalogs) and the same gross margin value that would be used in an ROI analysis. Expenses and profits were assessed in a one-year view.

Consider first the scenario being measured (the numbers have been changed to protect Crutchfield's proprietary sales information).

Advertising cost = $2,000
Sales revenue of initial sale = $3,000
Cost of goods of initial sale = $1,500
Variable costs of initial sale = $500
Number of new buyers = 50

The CPNB metric is relevant to this industry because it is safe to assume that the cost invested will outweigh the profits returned. The formula and calculations follow:

$$\text{CPNB} = \frac{\text{Advertising Costs} - \text{Margin from First Order}}{\text{Number of New Buyers}}$$

$$\text{CPNB} = \frac{(\$2,000) - (\$3,000 - \$1,500 - \$500)}{50} = \$20$$

The ROI equation considers the entire investment relative to the entire return so the number of buyers is not necessary. This same analysis for the advertising campaign alone would be:

$$\text{ROI} = \frac{\text{Gross Margin} - \text{Investment}}{\text{Investment}}$$

$$\text{ROI} = \frac{(\$3,000 - \$1,500 - \$500) - (\$2,000)}{\$2,000} = \frac{-\$1,000}{\$2,000} = -50\%$$

This shows a negative return on investment as was expected for this initial advertising campaign. The next analysis is on the customer value generated over the course of the first year. This measurement is done on the entire base of repeat purchasers and is not limited to the new buyers generated from the specific ad being measured. While it would be better to calculate the value of buyers for the specific ad, this is a reflection of the reality that every piece of information is not always worth the cost to measure. The numbers used in the analysis:

Catalog cost = $20,000
One year sales = $120,000

One year cost of goods = $60,000
Number of total new buyers = 5,000
Number of repeat buyers = 2,000

Since the catalog campaigns are expected to achieve positive returns, this campaign is analyzed to calculate 1st year value. The gross margin is only generated by the 2,000 repeat buyers, but the value must be assigned based on the total number of new buyers. This is necessary to formulate an analysis that combines the CPNB with what represents the value per new buyer.

$$\textbf{1st Year Value} = \frac{\textbf{1st Year Margin from Repeat Buyers} - \textbf{Catalog Costs}}{\textbf{Number of Total New Buyers}}$$

$$\textbf{1st Year Value} = \frac{(\$120,000 - \$60,000) \quad \$20,000}{5,000} = \$8$$

If Crutchfield's analysis were completed using just this information, it would be considered unprofitable since the CPNB of $20 exceeds the 1st year value of $8. The ROI analysis for this catalog campaign alone would result in an ROI of 200 percent based on a $20,000 investment that could generate a return of $40,000. Analyzing the two campaigns together would result in an ROI of −27 percent, which is consistent with the conclusion that this is unprofitable.

Crutchfield's measurement process went beyond this point based on analysis that showed that not all sales from advertising could be tracked. The marketing team established benchmark values to adjust the results, factoring in nontracked sales. This calculation added an "extra credit" of .5 sales for each sale tracked, which resulted in an additional $19 beyond the $8 value per customer for a total of $27 of 1st year value. The $27 in 1st year value exceeds the $20 CPNB, so the acquisition campaign is considered profitable.

The corresponding ROI analysis would factor this into the initial advertising campaign to show 75 new buyers instead of 50 new buyers, changing that ROI to −25 percent. The ROI analysis of the second campaign would be measured based on just the 75 new buyers (not the entire base of 5,000) that nets to a 200 percent ROI. The combined ROI totals 4 percent, which is positive and, since Crutchfield criteria is to invest in positive returns, the ROI analysis leads to the same conclusion that the acquisition campaign should be funded.

The comparison shows that this measurement process can be used much like the ROI calculation to guide marketing decisions. In isolated situations like this where the measurement process is effectively serving its purpose, there is no need for change. As you will see from the information presented in the remainder of this book, shifting to an ROI measurement approach creates many additional benefits and opportunities.

The information the Crutchfield team generated with this analysis led to the cancellation of advertising channels that were not profitable, and renegotiation of advertising rates that were close to profitable. Did the increased attention on marketing measurements make a difference? According to Michic, "We project the addition of roughly $1.8 million to the bottom line in just one year." It's clear that there are profits to be gained with each incremental step toward better marketing measurements and this means added value for both shareholders and customers. Rimm-Kauffman indicates that "it is important for Crutchfield to manage our advertising budgets effectively. We place the bulk of our energy into providing exceptional customer service and support. This customer focus pays off in the long run from repeat business and customer referrals."[4]

CHAPTER 3

MARKETING ROI IS DIFFERENT

R OI is a measure used by the financial managers of a company to guide the company's major investment decisions. To understand how marketing ROI is different from ROI analyses completed in other areas of a business, it makes sense to look at capital investments where ROI is a standard part of the decision-making process. For example, a financial manager may evaluate an expansion opportunity for the business that requires new machinery. Several pieces of machinery may be considered, each at different price points with different operating and maintenance expenses and different capabilities. All of the future incremental profits and expenses will be discounted to calculate a net present value. The projected net returns will be compared to the investments and the best ROI that meets the company's minimum ROI (hurdle rate) and strategic goals will be selected. In another example, the ROI may be used to assess a new technology for Customer Relationship Management (CRM). The expenses to install and operate the CRM system would be compared to the expected returns generated from changes to customer-retention rates, customer profitability, productivity gains, and customer service savings. The projected ROI could be used to both justify an investment and select the best choice.

Marketing investments are prioritized and selected much differently than capital investments, requiring a different approach to ROI analysis and allowing for more creative use of the ROI calculation. First of all, the number of marketing investments, the frequency of investments, and the relatively small increments in which investments can be made create an incredible number of decision-making possibilities, while capital investments are typically limited to infrequent, large-scale investments. Also, the assumptions that go into marketing ROI measurements are subject to change on a regular basis as competition, customer needs, and marketing channel expenses change. Based on this, marketing ROI measurements must be

1. Flexible
2. Dynamic
3. Focused on each incremental investment

Marketing Has Greater Flexibility

Marketing is very scalable compared to capital investments where, for example, it is unlikely that an investment will be made in 50 percent of the needed machinery or CRM system. Marketers must consistently make decisions on how much advertising is required, how many contacts to reach with direct marketing, how frequently customers should be marketed to, and the ideal point for customer modeling. Each marketing campaign can be composed of a wide range of channel combinations, packaged with a wide range of offer values, and scaled to a wide range of prospect populations and be viable at a wide range of investment levels. Marketing investment decisions are more complex than a decision to invest or not invest and go beyond a decision to select the best investment choice from a pool of alternatives.

> The ROI analysis becomes a powerful tool not only to determine which programs should be funded, but also to determine to what level each program should be funded.

In the following example, a simple question is posed on the scalability of an existing marketing campaign. If a current campaign that costs $500,000 generates a 35 percent ROI for a net return of $175,000, what

does the same campaign generate at $400,000 or $600,000? The change
in investment level can be reflected in many ways such as changing the
target market reached by the campaign, the offers value, or the number of marketing channels. The projections reported in the next chart
show that a decreased investment level of $400,000 generates a 37 per-
cent return while the increase to a $600,000 investment generates a
33 percent return.

Investment	$400,000	$500,000	$600,000
Gross margin	$548,000	$675,000	$798,000
Return	$148,000	$175,000	$198,000
Net ROI	37%	35%	33%

This view of ROI at multiple investment levels provides marketing
managers and executives with better information but is not in a form
where a clear decision can be made. The marketer has the option to
increase profits by choosing to increase investment to the $600,000 level
or to increase ROI by dropping to the $400,000 level.

The key to optimizing profits from marketing investments is to view
each incremental investment independently and continue to make additional investments that exceed the ROI threshold. This approach is ideal
for prioritizing investment opportunities for marketing, which can
include many different tactical elements, each of which can be scaled to
different levels.

Incremental Measures Go Further

ROI measurements can improve profitability by assessing the incremental value of each incremental investment. This is more advanced
than comparing total returns from investments at $400,000 and
$500,000—it requires looking at the stand-alone value of the incre-
mental return from the $100,000 difference and then breaking that
down further if necessary.

The appropriate investment level for the incremental scenario can be
determined once the company's ROI threshold is established. In this

example, the ROI threshold will be set at 25 percent. In most cases, the company will have a number of alternative investment opportunities that can generate ROI above this threshold of 25 percent.

Starting with the information available, the three investment levels can be broken down to show the ROI for each incremental investment. Marketing investments are not completely scalable since there could be a minimum development cost or a fixed population for some marketing initiatives. It is assumed that $400,000 is the minimum investment for this campaign, which can then be increased to any investment level up to $600,000. The next chart shows the ROI calculations for each of the two incremental $100,000 investments.

Investment	$400,000	$500,000	$600,000
Gross margin	$548,000	$675,000	$798,000
Return	$148,000	$175,000	$198,000
Net ROI	37%	35%	33%
Incremental investment		$100,000	$100,000
Incremental gross margin		$127,000	$123,000
Incremental return		$ 27,000	$ 23,000
Incremental ROI		27%	23%

The analysis begins with the lowest investment level possible and then considers each incremental investment separately. The $400,000 investment meets the ROI hurdle rate. The next $100,000 investment generates an incremental $127,000 in gross margin, which represents an incremental return of $27,000 and a 27 percent return on that incremental investment.

The next incremental investment of $100,000 brings the total to $600,000. The investment generates only an incremental $23,000 return, which at a 23 percent ROI, is below the minimum 25 percent ROI threshold. Figure 3.1 shows the incremental ROI. At a point between $400,000 and $600,000, the last incremental dollar invested meets the 25 percent ROI threshold. The ROI analysis would continue at smaller and smaller increments of investments until this point is identified. This is shown in Figure 3.1 as an investment of $512,500. Modeling can be used to accomplish the same optimal investment point as

Figure 3.1 Incremental ROI for Scalable Marketing Campaign

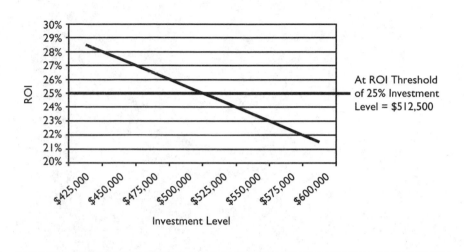

At ROI Threshold
of 25% Investment
Level = $512,500

was manually completed here but must incorporate calculations that measure ROI at incremental investment levels.

The increase in profits just from making decisions based on incremental investment levels can certainly add up. In a straight ROI analysis, the $600,000 investment would have been made since the total ROI exceeded the ROI threshold. That investment would generate $198,000 in profit return. A $600,000 investment that was split between the optimal point in this campaign—$512,500—and another campaign that generated the minimum ROI of 25 percent would generate $200,000. An additional $2,000 in profit was possible on a single campaign just from taking a smarter approach to guiding marketing investments. This is a profit that goes directly to the bottom line. The total value of more precise measurements can be quite significant across a large number of marketing investments.

Measuring incrementally is only one source of increased profits from adopting marketing ROI measures. Companies that have explored marketing ROI techniques in the past but found barriers to effectively implementing the new measures should look again. Improved measurability and more clearly defined ROI guidelines specifically for marketing have opened up new possibilities.

CHAPTER 4

MORE MEASURABLE THAN EVER

Marketing, no matter what practitioners thought in the past, is more science than art. It is no longer necessary to rely on hunch, hope, mythology, and experience or on creative breakthroughs and divine illumination. The data and tools currently exist to dramatically improve a company's marketing programs for new and established products and services. All that's required is the will to use them.[1]

KEVIN J. CLANCY AND ROBERT SHULMAN

Marketing is becoming more measurable based on the advancements of technology and the growth in electronic marketing channels such as E-mail marketing and Web advertising. Direct marketing has a history of being fairly measurable while mass advertising has been more challenging to measure. Test marketing has been a primary measure for gauging the impact of marketing and advertising by using controlled comparisons between segments of the market exposed to the marketing to those not exposed. Marketing measurements are based on a combination of actual behaviors, quantitative testing, and educated assumptions.

Marketing contained entirely on the Internet is among the easiest to track. Not only can results be measured in terms of sales but also in the interim behaviors such as open rate of E-mail, click-stream patterns of Web pages viewed, and repeat visits. In fact, the abundance of data actually becomes as much a challenge as it is a benefit. With the proper data in hand, it's much easier in online marketing to understand the behaviors of both customers and prospects and, in real time, make strategic decisions for modifying the marketing to improve results.

The reality is that most marketing initiatives are multichannel, combining Internet marketing with traditional marketing and retail channels. Customers want relationships where multiple channels can be used throughout the communication and transaction experience. This significantly adds to the tracking complexity and requires the integration of information from many sources to provide a comprehensive picture at a campaign or customer level. The key is to gain access to the data, test assumptions, understand the limitations of the information available, and make constant improvements in the decision-making process.

The trend of measurement capabilities is likely to further increase over time. Available technology can take current measures of individual exposure to advertising and individual behaviors within existing channels much further than it is today. Along with these new capabilities questions arise as to both the economic feasibility of implementation and the social issues of individual privacy.

Here are some ways that marketing measurements are being improved or could potentially become available in the marketplace in the future, based on the level of customer support, industry support, and industry's ability to profit from offering additional measurement services.

- Advanced enterprise technology for enterprise resource planning (ERP) and CRM initiatives offer data flow to and from the many customer sales and marketing channels, which allows for improved measurements and integrated transaction information.
- Modeling for targeting high-value customers often contains predictive information on customer lifetime value, which is beneficial in improving ROI measures.
- Retail data is getting more sophisticated and more comprehensive.
- Mass media channels, such as television advertising, have been among the most difficult to measure. Cable TV companies are upgrading the wired connection between the house and the point of distribution to allow for two-way communications. Technology can be

implemented to identify viewership of advertisements to the household level.

- Radio will be approaching a similar level of measurability if Internet radio or satellite subscription radio increases and more Internet-enabled entertainment appliances are introduced. Individuals currently have the ability to personalize their own radio station programming through solutions such as MSN Entertainment or Yahoo!'s Launch.com. So not only could there be measurements of advertisements delivered at a household level, but also at the listener level as each household member gains the ability to personalize their advertising preferences as well as their listening preferences.
- Advertising on mobile devices and interactive cell phone technology will begin to accelerate, offering the same measurement and response tracking capabilities as the Internet.
- Taking the concept of mobile device tracking to an extreme, cell phone technology will eventually be capable of determining your exact physical location through Global Positioning Systems (GPS). Privacy issues aside for the moment, this technology could be evolved to the point where an individual's exposure to outdoor ads and retail visits could be tracked based on knowing the person's physical location.

Will all this extreme level of tracking come into the mainstream of marketing in the near future? Not likely, but tracking capabilities will certainly increase as the technology is adapted to provide more personalized interactions and customer relationships. The expansion of new advertising and marketing channels, combined with the explosive clutter of messages coming at consumers will motivate increased use of advertisement filtering technology (for example, the capability provided by personal video recorders such as TiVo or ReplayTV, which skip over television commercials). This filtering technology can also be the basis of personalization, so a win-win approach to matching company offers with customer interests is likely to evolve. As personalization technology evolves, so too will come increased measurability.

The advancements in marketing measurements will allow:

- More accurate return on investment measurements
- Allocation of mass media costs down to an individual/household level
- Understanding of the customer behaviors through the sales cycle as measured by performance indicators, which can be used to identify points of marketing weakness that need improvement
- Profiling best customers or responders based on integration with demographic information and outside data
- Increased segmentation of the target audience into groups based on common needs or behaviors
- Increased intelligence in customer-lifetime-value measurements, projections, and modeling

This all results in smarter marketing from more informed decisions. Real-time, customer-level measures allow for more responsive, quality decisions. Where complete information is not available, assumptions can be used. Best practices must be put in place to improve the quality of assumptions over time and to ensure consistency across a corporation.

Technology Simplifies the Measures

Determining ROI, incremental customer value, and profit optimization requires aggregating lots of data, modeling the information, and then running calculations. This has traditionally required the support of statistical modeling experts who would spend weeks running analyses that may or may not meet the marketers' needs and would often require more time for additional analysis. Technology is placing more of the data analysis and modeling capabilities into the hands of the end users. Data queries can be run in real time and any additional analysis that is needed can be completed instantly, greatly reducing cost and turnaround time. Marketers do not need to be experts in modeling, financial analysis, or even basic math, if the right tools and training are provided.

Technology has advanced in the form of campaign management, business intelligence, executive reporting, and sales force automation. Companies such as Aprimo (aprimo.com) are automating the process to capture marketing expenditures at a much more detailed level as well as manage the entire marketing process through planning, implementation, and results. Other companies such as Marketswitch (marketswitch.com) offer specific marketing functionality such as profit and ROI optimization to support the selection of target customers, offers, and channels. Campaign management tools, both stand-alone and incorporated into CRM systems, are becoming more robust as tools to support marketers and are also providing executives with better insight into marketing performance.

Point-of-sale data combined with the right software applications can be a valuable tool for improving profitability as well. Chip Hoyt, director of consulting for Bristol Technology, published an article, "The Software Side of Marketing," in which he states, "For example, the largest and most profitable spirit and wine company in the world, Guinness/UDV, uses software technology to identify incremental profit opportunities and develop strategies aimed at exploiting them. Like many companies, profitability for Guinness products varies widely by account, geography, seasonality and other factors. Planners need to understand which product attributes generate the most volume and profit on account, regional, or seasonal bases. Brand, sales, and trade marketers are able to target funds precisely where they will earn the greatest return."[2]

More data and more processing power allow for more advanced levels of measurements. The industry is hungry for more accurate financial models for marketing that can increase profits and guide strategic decisions. Some of the new measurement approaches presented in this book are more advanced and are dependent on technology for practical use within corporate marketing departments. As technology continues to advance in terms of campaign-management applications, real-time measurement tools will enable companies to make better real-time decisions.

Privacy Issues

Measurements will continue to improve in accuracy as behaviors can be tracked down to the individual or household level. As with personalized marketing in general, there is a fine line in terms of consumer benefit versus consumer privacy. Marketers can build a case that tracking a customer's behavior over time in exchange for personalizing the experience has a win-win outcome. When the tracking of behaviors is done specifically to increase profitability and measure marketing strategies, the argument does not hold up as well. The goal is to integrate the two purposes so that the consumer does get value from personalization while the company increases profitability through more targeted offers.

Determination Counts

Technology provides advanced tools that simplify the process but the real driver of profitability measures is the determination to uncover a realistic picture of results as demonstrated by individuals such as Tom Nicholson, director of public relations for Sears, Roebuck and Company. While so many in the marketing and advertising industry raise concerns that financial measures will stifle creativity, Nicholson was creatively designing measurements to understand the value of investments into advertising and public relations initiatives. He wrote an excellent article covering an in-depth case study in, "What Every CEO Wants to Hear from Communications: Objective Measures Essential to More Effective Communications Planning," published in the 2001–2002 issue of the *Journal of Integrated Communications* (jiconline.com).

Sears's measurement initiatives covered a number of different forms of communications, including print and broadcast ads, public relations placements on "The Oprah Winfrey Show" and "The Rosie O'Donnell Show" and a single fashion article in the *New York Times*. These communications initiatives can be considered among the most difficult to isolate and capture the incremental value generated. Achieving reliable measurements required a combination of structured market tests, modeling of sales and media data, and applying a number of reasonable assumptions. As Nicholson states in his article, "we were interested in measuring programs, not in measuring the effectiveness of individuals." This approach allows the measurement process to offer greater objectivity and a focus on what's best for the company.

A number of valuable conclusions resulted from the measurements conducted by Sears. First, traditional PR and advertising measurements of gross rating points (GRPs) and audience profile are not enough to assess return on investment. The ROI analysis of public relations placements on two programs showing similar audience numbers indicated that one program generated twice the ROI. Next, Sears was able to determine the impact of a store opening on brand equity and link this back to identify the channels responsible for generating the most value. Additionally, the measurement of a single article in the *New York Times* provided not only the actual return generated but also new insight into the strength of certain types of media that had been previously assumed to have limited value.

According to Nicholson, "one of the key challenges in the analysis process is integrating information from multiple databases. In addition, we had an abundance of information and had to filter it down to just the key data points. On the expense side, we track expenses for public relations at a project level to manage our investment strategies." Nicholson indicated that it is not feasible to conduct such extensive analysis on every investment but it is justified for larger initiatives. They seek to track the impact of PR and advertising to at least the level of awareness and intentions to purchase, two leading indicators of consumer behavior, which are then converted to estimates of actual purchases through internally derived assumptions. In some cases, such as the placement of the fashion footwear article in the *New York Times*, they are able to track incremental purchases attributed directly to the public relations placement.

"The goal is to establish measures that can be trusted to make future decisions more predictable. That is what guides better strategies and increased profitability," said Nicholson. Measurements based on assumptions should be validated where possible and tested under different market simulations to ensure quality.

The details provided in Nicholson's case study make it clear how measurement and analysis has dramatically shifted future strategies and investments. The priority of communications channels has shifted for certain initiatives. Certain media channels once perceived as insignificant are now understood to have high value and the incremental value of PR combined with advertising campaigns is known. Marketing investments are now directed toward greater profitability and continued measurements will be used to monitor and adjust strategies as necessary.[3]

Throughout the industry, marketing effectiveness measures are being improved through a combination of increased access to data, more advanced technologies, and through the innovation of marketing, research, and financial professionals determined to make a difference. There will rarely be the right conditions for measurements that are 100 percent accurate, but understanding what makes for an ideal environment establishes a benchmark for continuous quality improvement.

CHAPTER 5

MARKETING ROI PROCESS

So let's take a look at what the entire marketing ROI process would encompass in an ideal world. The concepts presented in the remainder of this book may not fit every company nor be easily implemented into every corporate environment. If you are able to understand the key principles and the potential value, you should then be able to determine the best way to adapt the concepts into your own environment.

As a brief preview of what will be presented, let's walk through the process at a very high level. The marketing ROI process is implemented at the campaign, customer, and corporate level to maximize company profits. Marketing ROI will be used in the planning of campaigns to run projections that help guide marketing strategy development. The campaigns will be implemented and the results tracked. These results will be used to complete the ROI analysis that then serves as input into the marketing strategy for modifications and new developments (see Figure 5.1). Additional profits can be gained by looking beyond performance at the individual campaign level. Customer profitability will be maximized by measuring the ROI of a number of combinations of marketing campaigns that are delivered to the customer. At the corporate level, the ROI projections for each possible marketing investment will be captured and subsequently prioritized for budget allocation.

Figure 5.1 Marketing ROI Process Overview

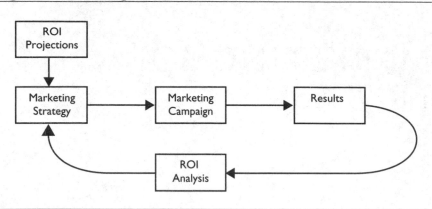

Here is a vision of how the process can be managed within a company that has fully implemented the marketing ROI process:

- A standardized ROI formula will be used as the primary marketing measure. All marketing investment opportunities could then be easily compared and prioritized.
- An ROI threshold will be established by the financial organization and management will generally fund the optimal mix of marketing opportunities that could exceed the ROI threshold.
- Budget allocation will be based on maximizing corporate profits with an appropriate balance between short-term and long-term profits. Marketing investments will be managed like an investment portfolio, which has risk diversification factored into the planning for profit optimization. A portion of the budget will be set aside for development and emerging strategies to support innovation and allow time for performance improvement.
- Marketing activities will be designed, measured, and managed to maximize customer profitability, which in turn will maximize corporate profitability.
- The expense of measuring ROI and customer value will be kept cost effective by using benchmark studies, modeling, and research studies.
- Complex analysis and ROI calculations will either be automated or performed by analytical experts to keep marketers focused on their

core competency of developing and implementing high-impact strategies that will motivate customer behavior and generate additional profits.

- ROI measures will be properly aligned with strategic decisions. Accuracy of ROI projections and practices will constantly be validated and improved upon.
- ROI projections and measures will be as close to an incremental view as possible.
- Executives will have the capability to instantly view the impact on the entire marketing budget and expected return when variables are changed (such as the ROI threshold or discount rate) or assumptions must be modified to reflect such global activities as competitive activity or increased channel costs.

Why will companies make the effort to implement such significant change within their organization? Consider the many benefits that are possible:

- Faster, more accurate decision making that is possible with a standardized process for assessing investments and estimating returns (a benefit mentioned by best-practice benchmark companies in the APQC/ARF report *Maximizing Marketing ROI*)[1]
- Better crisis management through greater intelligence on the impact of shifts in strategies, competitive actions, or budget resources
- Improvement in shareholder value as marketing budgets are directed toward greater profit opportunities
- Opportunity to fuel growth with greater generation of profits
- Better learning from organization-wide success and failures that is made possible with the use of standardized measures (another benefit of benchmark companies in the APQC/ARF study)[2]
- Growth in both top-line sales and bottom-line profits that can be generated with the same budget through a smarter prioritization process
- Demonstration of measurable value for marketing; helping to shed the image of a discretionary expense
- Improvements in measurement and management processes that will last

Part I Conclusion

When it comes to marketing measurements, only return on investment provides a complete picture of both incremental profits and investments and aligns with the primary purpose of the company. There is a recognized shortfall in the quality of existing marketing ROI measurement processes as demonstrated through numerous industry research studies, meaning millions and millions of marketing budgets are being poorly invested and corporate profits are not reaching full potential. Customer Relationship Management (CRM) initiatives have a greater chance of success when combined with marketing ROI to manage customer profitability. With ever-increasing competition and constant pressure on companies to deliver more profits, better management of marketing budgets is a necessity.

Part I has covered the key challenges faced on the path to effective marketing ROI measurements and the basic financial concepts required as a foundation on which to build. The uniqueness of ROI for marketing has been established, showing the potential for carefully managing the profitability of marketing investments.

Part II goes much deeper into the ROI formula. It covers each element of the return side of the calculation as well as the investment side, highlighting specific areas where the most common errors occur. Examples are provided in progression from basic principles to more complex concepts, showing some common patterns for acquisition, retention, and cross-sell marketing investments. Typical profit dynamics found in marketing are put into an ROI perspective and common issues that are raised as limitations of marketing measures are addressed.

The key principles of marketing ROI presented in Part II will then lead into the more strategic applications presented in Part III.

BUILDING THE ROI FORMULA

CHAPTER 6

MEASURING RETURN ON INVESTMENT

It is better to be vaguely right than precisely wrong.[1]

SUNIL GUPTA AND DONALD R. LEHMANN

Marketing ROI should be used by marketing managers to compare and prioritize investment opportunities in the planning stage and to measure the actual performance relative to expectations in the analysis stage. It is a powerful financial tool that can guide strategies and investments toward greater profits for a company. Misunderstanding or misapplying the ROI formula creates plenty of room for error. Data quality and availability will be challenging enough so every effort should be made to ensure the calculation is accurate. Knowing the intricacies of the formula as presented here will certainly help.

The bottom line is that ROI is a financial measure based on using clearly defined pieces of information. The "return" represents the financial gain beyond the initial investment. The "investment" is the total of all the expenses that were put at risk for the purpose of generating the return. In general, each marketing investment is expected to contribute to the generation of profits as customers are influenced to purchase more. You not only want to earn all of your investment back but also have extra profits, since that is the company's primary goal.

ROI is presented as a percentage, calculated by dividing the return by the investment.

$$\text{ROI} = \frac{\text{Return}}{\text{Investment}} = \frac{\text{Gross Margin} - \text{Investment}}{\text{Investment}} = \frac{(\text{Revenue} - \text{Cost of Goods Sold}) - \text{Investment}}{\text{Investment}}$$

Figure 6.1 shows the relationship between revenue, gross margin, and return.

The ROI value will be a positive percentage, a negative percentage, or zero. A positive ROI indicates you've earned more than enough profits to cover your investment. If the ROI is negative, you've lost money. Zero ROI is your income-based break-even point. The ROI value will generally be measured against company objectives or used in comparison to other ROI values for decision making.

Calculating the Return

Removing the investment value from the return portion of the equation leaves the gross margin, which is driven almost entirely by the cus-

Figure 6.1 Relationship Between Revenue, Gross Margin, and Return

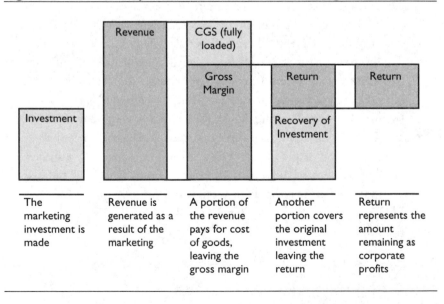

tomer value generated. The gross margin should capture the net present value of the incremental income flow relative to the expected income flow without the investment. Financial value can also come from customer referrals that link back to the original investment and from cost savings based on changes in customer behaviors. Costs that must be deducted from the gross margin include the Cost of Goods Sold (CGS) (production and delivery of products and services including overhead expenses), promotional discounts and offers tied to the sale, and the expenses necessary to support the customer. The value of the initial sale is often captured when ROI is measured, but it is also important to capture the present value of future activity, which may drive more profitable decisions. The gross margin formula is broken down as follows:

Gross Margin = Net Present Value of Revenue and Expense Income Flows

This is equal to the NPV of:

- Incremental customer value
    - Revenue (including initial sale, repeat sales, recurring revenue)
    - Less cost of goods sold (product/service cost, returns, and uncollected revenue)
    - Less direct sales expenses (special offers, order processing and fulfillment costs, post-sale customer service, incremental staff costs)
- *Less* incremental customer expenses (any service costs not included in the cost of goods sold figure above)
- *Plus* incremental savings (any cost reductions that result from the marketing investment)
- *Plus* gross margin of referrals (referrals can be generated from customers or third-party influencers reached by the marketing initiative)

In addition to these income flows, marketing investments can drive changes to awareness and perceptions, contribute to future loyalty, or result in the collection of valuable customer intelligence. These outcomes don't have an immediate financial value but will positively or negatively impact the financial value generated by future investments. This future financial impact, referred to here as *residual value*, is not included in the standard ROI formula since additional investments are required but must certainly be factored into the decision-making process as presented later.

Incremental customer value (ICV) must not be confused with customer lifetime value (CLV). An existing customer will have an expected set of behaviors and value, and the ROI measure should capture just the incremental customer value driven by the marketing investment being measured. The time period over which the ICV is captured will be driven by the expected duration of impact on behavior changes. Limiting the ICV to the initial sale may be appropriate for some businesses but will neglect significant value for many other businesses. The ICV for newly acquired customers must not include future or potential lifetime value that requires additional marketing investments. Yes, increasing the base of customers does have financial benefit to future investments but this is another form of residual value that must be measured separately. When ROI is measured for all investments made against a customer over his or her lifetime, the gross margin will capture all incremental value and the result should be comparable to a customer-lifetime-value measure.

The CGS should capture all of the costs associated with producing the product or service. Companies will take different approaches to this value ranging from a pure view of incremental expenses to a fully loaded view where all direct and indirect expenses are captured. Direct sales expenses that result from the marketing activity, including everything from order processing and special offers to incremental sales support expenses, must be deducted from the revenue to net to the product/service profit.

The incremental customer expenses category is intended to capture the cost of maintaining new customers generated from the marketing investment being measured. This is most relevant when the marketing investment generates long-term purchasing relationship or recurring revenue. Many costs such as billing or customer service may typically be included in the cost of goods.

Cost savings must be captured as a return when appropriate. Some marketing investments may be designed to partially or entirely achieve a financial return based upon changing customer behaviors in such a way that reduce expected costs. An example would be a marketing initiative that migrated existing customers into a special program where customer service activities could be done online instead of by phone. Success with this effort will include reduced expenses as part of the return.

Referral value is especially important for marketing activities that generate new customers who are likely to remain active customers for a long period of time. This also includes referrals from *third-party influencers* such as the media or leaders of credible organizations that are reached by the marketing investment and in turn generate additional sales.

Challenges Associated with Gross Margin Measurements

Capturing the incremental customer value is by far the greatest challenge associated with marketing ROI measurements. Measurements and decisions must be made promptly, so there is no time to track actual customer value over an extended period of time. The challenges in determining the gross margin measures include:

- The decision timing requires that estimates be made, in some cases based on limited information.
- Customer value is subject to fluctuate with time based on customer, market, and competitive conditions. Estimates are likely to have some variance from actual value.
- Customer data must be accurate and accessible, which is often not easily done. The data required will need to come from different sources, be aggregated, and then maintained.
- Incremental customer value for a particular investment may require special tracking methodologies to link customer actions to specific marketing investments.
- Both the measurement process and modeling can be expensive and must be justified.

Gross Margin Data

The data necessary to project gross margin will come from a variety of sources that can provide both actual and estimated values. These include:

- Sales and pricing information
- Financial data
- Marketing metrics (nonfinancial customer actions) that can be used to estimate financial value
- Internal benchmark values that can be used as assumptions (such as the average customer referral rate)
- Modeling and profiling data that project future behaviors

Calculating the Investment

When using ROI to guide decisions toward greater profitability, investment is defined as "the expense at risk" and does not include expenses related to delivering sales, which are actually factored into the gross margin. An expense belongs under investment if it will be incurred when absolutely no sales are generated. Those expenses related directly to sales are simply deducted from the revenue in the gross margin calculation and are not included in the investment. Marketing expenses such as the development and implementation of advertising, direct-mail, or point-of-purchase promotion may have costs which are clearly identified as the investment. Look hard at other expenses that must be incurred as part of the marketing initiative such as the training of the sales staff or modifications to the corporate website.

The marketing investment represents the expenses that are put at risk. It does not include expenses related to delivery of the sale, which are deducted from the gross margin.

Both the up-front and variable expenses can make up the investment. Inclusion of some expenses will be subjective, depending on how the organization wants to manage investment decisions. Some expenses benefit multiple marketing campaigns and need to be treated carefully in the measurement process to ensure that ROI measures align with decisions in the planning stage and capture a comprehensive view in the analysis stage.

Investment = NPV of the sum of all at-risk marketing expenses

This is equal to the NPV of:

- Marketing expense at risk
    Up-front development costs (creative, systems, channel preparation)
    Variable expenses (mass media, direct to consumer, sales support material)
- *Plus* long-term expense commitments
- *Plus* staff resources required for development and implementation (sales, marketing, advertising, research, customer contact channels)
- *Plus* allocations of multicampaign investments (not to be included in projections for planning, strictly for post-implementation analysis)

The up-front and variable expenses may include the following:

- Creative development of marketing and advertising promotions
- Production and printing of materials
- Incremental distribution channel expenses
- Media and delivery expense
- Marketing lists
- The cost of promotional giveaways that are not sales-driven
- Database and system development to support the specific marketing campaign
- Research directly related to a specific campaign
- External strategic planning resources for the campaign
- Cost for staff time for marketing, sales, project management, executive and administrative support (if tracked as part of the

investment, these expenses should not be included as overhead in Cost of Goods Sold)

- Channel promotions and preparation (i.e., training prior to the campaign start)
- The cost of inquiries or service through contact channels beyond sales processing (the investment may require an expense budget to handle high-contact volume that does not convert to sales)
- Measurement systems and research studies
- Allocated expenses for general marketing support

Long-term expense commitments will apply only to select marketing investment decisions such as a loyalty program or special media purchases that include a contractual commitment. When these expenses are included in the ROI calculation, all expected financial returns from these future expenses should also be included.

Challenges Associated with Investment Data

Marketing expenses that go into the investment figure are typically easy to predict. The challenges are primarily in keeping the investment values aligned with the point of decision. Expenses associated with higher-level investments that will be made regardless of the decision to proceed with the marketing initiative to be measured should not be included in that ROI for planning purposes. The approaches presented in Part III can be very effective in providing the insight necessary to make the most profitable decisions.

Investment Data

The investment is typically easy to accurately estimate prior to committing to the marketing initiative. The required data will come from:

- Budget projections
- Actual expenses
- Expense allocation models

Recovering Development Costs

Creating a new marketing initiative or adapting an initiative for a new channel or strategy will require an up-front cost for development. The cost for this development certainly must be part of the investment decision. More elaborate and expensive campaigns should have higher expectations for profit returns in order to achieve comparable ROI. In some cases, the development cost is initially associated with a small-scale market test and the ROI measure must be viewed at the level of a large-scale rollout. In other cases, the high-development cost for the initial marketing channel is then leveraged for lower-cost development in other channels, or it is reused for future marketing investments over a long period of time.

The ROI analysis must be adjusted to drive the right decisions. The goal is to apply the expense in a way that will be most appropriate. Here are three ways up-front costs can be treated based upon the situation and practices of the company.

1. *Absorb the development costs immediately.* If the marketing campaign is a one-time campaign or the expectation for future use of the development investment is unknown, 100 percent of the development costs should be included in the ROI investment decision.
2. *Base the decision on the ROI projection for a full-scale rollout.* For marketing campaigns that will be test marketed prior to rollout, the campaign should be developed with a full-scale ROI projection in mind. If the projected ROI for the full-scale program is expected to meet the company's ROI threshold, the decision will be to make the investment.

    Projecting all test marketing at a rollout level will leave many investment dollars unaccounted for since not all campaigns test marketed proceed to a rollout stage. This can be accounted for in two ways. First, allocate test marketing expenses as overhead or second, manage a portion of the budget for emerging campaigns where the ROI expectation is lower.
3. *Assess incremental and allocated investments.* Some development costs benefit multiple campaigns, such as purchasing a prospect

mailing list or improving website functionality. This may be driven by one initial marketing initiative even though the benefit applies to many. The ideal approach is to assess the ROI of this special investment on its own—what is the incremental return generated from the incremental investment.

Another approach is to determine the campaigns where this investment has an impact and allocate the expense in such a way that drives the best decisions (for example, this can be allocated based on an even spread or one based on the proportion of expected value). At the planning stage, the cost would be factored into the many different campaigns and then compared to the new expected returns for each. A $250,000 investment may result in $50,000 in incremental investment expense for five marketing programs. These programs should be able to show an incremental return that exceeds this investment.

Keep in mind how the ROI analysis needs to be different in the planning stage and in the measurement stage. These options can be used in either stage as long as the use in the planning stage is based on the future investments and is not burdened with the allocation of expenses from past investment decisions.

Broadscale Marketing Support Expenses

A number of marketing investments are intended to have broad impact on many marketing campaigns. Websites, CRM initiatives, and brand advertising can fall into this category for some companies. The three options presented in the previous section for development costs can also apply to these types of expenses. In Part 3, some strategic concepts will be presented which may be applied when making investment decisions for broadscale marketing support initiatives.

The following list are a number of expenses that fall into this category. These contribute to the success of marketing campaigns and need to be considered when completing ROI analyses.

- Brand communications to support broad sales and marketing efforts
- The website, its content, and its valuable links across the Internet

- Customer intelligence collection through customer contact channels
- Marketing databases and systems
- Marketing research not directly related to a campaign
- CRM initiatives

Decisions to pursue these initiatives are made with the expectation that incremental value will be generated by specific marketing campaigns. The process of allocating expenses across multiple channels and marketing programs is a challenging one, primarily because of the subjectivity. A corporate or marketing organization decision needs to be made for the allocation process, and then the organization must make a commitment to follow that process consistently.

Some forms of allocation methods are as follows:

- Proportioned against those initiatives that coincide with the same target audience
- Proportioned based on the expected lift for each channel/program (more easily applied if some test marketing has provided insight into the differences)
- Proportioned based on relative marketing budget
- Proportioned based on any of the above but applied only to the core campaigns from which the company generates the bulk of its gross margins. This leaves the expense burden off of smaller or developing marketing programs that can very well bring incremental profit to the company

While some forms of mass advertising are intended to generate immediate sales, a level of brand advertising can create emotional connections and brand preferences that last over a very long period of time and may even have implications on how the stock market values the company. It is not realistic to force investment decisions for this type of branding into a standard marketing ROI equation, since the incremental value will be impossible to identify for each investment. For purposes of managing other investments using the marketing ROI process presented here, this form of advertising would be considered as overhead expense. From there, it can be managed using brand equity calculations, which are better geared for this form of investment measurement.

Allocating Staff Expense

Most marketing measurements do not factor in staff expenses at the campaign level but do this at a department or corporate level. This is acceptable if most marketing investments require comparable staff resources. Where marketing investments are providing leads that are handed off to a sales force, the expense for sales staff should also be considered here. Any marketing initiative that requires significantly more or less staff should be compared to other initiatives with this expense factored into the investment portion of the ROI equation.

Certain campaign management technologies have automated this process so that the view of each campaign includes complete expenses and staff resources. This improves the decision-making capabilities and the ROI analysis. Using an ROI analysis that incorporates staff expense into the decision process is much more precise and can improve profitability. It is also more accurate, especially since campaigns require different levels of staff resources. Without including staff expenses at the decision level, those marketing investments that barely meet the ROI threshold and require a higher than average amount of staff time are most likely draining profits from the company.

Where ROI Measurements Go Wrong

A number of common errors can be made in ROI calculations, several of which have been discussed earlier in this chapter. The errors presented here may seem fundamental but you would not have to look far to find real-life examples. Many of these have been made by well-respected, leading companies and consultants, so check your own internal measurements carefully. A slightly different version of this checklist was shared with Internet guru Jim Sterne who published it in his book *Web Metrics*.[2]

- *Error #1: Revenue is used in place of gross margin.* In the English language, "return" could be construed to mean everything gained back from an investment, but in financial language, return is equal to the gross margin (net present value of profit stream) minus the original investment. It is the amount that goes to the bottom line, not the top line. Overestimating the profit contributions of marketing investments can be extremely harmful to the company's financial stability. A positive ROI based on revenue is misleading and has a very good chance of losing profits for the company.

- *Error #2: The investment is overstated with cost of sales.* You will have marketing expenses that go toward generating profitable sales and then expenses associated with delivering those sales. The investment portion of the equation represents only the marketing expenses that are put *at risk*. It should not include discounts, special offers, or fulfillment costs that are sales driven.

- *Error #3: Only immediate profit is counted, neglecting future value.* The return generated by marketing programs is sometimes restricted to the profit from an immediate sale without taking into account the future value of that customer. This may be based on limited data, the need to make decisions promptly to replicate the performance of a marketing program, or a priority on short-term profits over long-term value.

- *Error #4: The total customer lifetime value is counted in place of incremental profits.* Here we have the opposite problem where too much value is counted instead of too little. It is important that all of the profits generated directly from this investment are captured no more, no less. Some companies identify the total lifetime value, defined as all of the future profit stream of a customer, and use that as the value of each new customer. However, typically the amount of profit a customer is expected to generate over the course of their lifetime with the company is dependent on additional marketing investments.

- *Error #5: The ROI analysis is not aligned with the decision to be made.* The ROI analysis should be different when measuring past performance or future investments. Expenses already incurred are not important when choosing between possible marketing investments; however, these expenses are very important when measuring the performance of a marketing program as a benchmark for future decisions or measuring the performance of decision makers for rewards and recognition.

- *Error #6: The ROI analysis is neglected in favor of* **strategic value.** It is sometimes claimed that certain *strategic* business objectives must override the financial analysis that would guide marketing investments toward the greatest profit. Strategic decisions could include customer satisfaction, employee satisfaction, or service quality. However, since businesses exist for the purpose of generating profits, there is typically some financial benefit that is expected to be derived in the future from these objectives determined to be strategic and possibly determined to have an unmeasured value. Developing assumptions as to the incremental value of these decisions, or running an ROI analysis to determine the results necessary to justify the strategic decisions, will lead to better, fact-based investments from the marketing budget.
- *Error #7: Total ROI is calculated in place of an incremental ROI.* Using the power of ROI as a planning tool for marketing, leads to a better understanding of the expected value for each investment so the budget can be effectively allocated to maximize the total return. Each investment decision should be made comparing the incremental investment to the incremental return.
- *Error #8: Positive ROI is used as the funding threshold.* In certain strategic situations, a small positive return on investment (such as a 1 percent ROI) is enough to justify funding. However, achieving positive ROI is not enough if the corporate budget is being managed prudently. Investments must generate enough return to show annualized ROI in excess of both the cost of capital and alternative investment options.

The key to successfully using ROI in marketing is establishing a standard formula that is accurate, aligns with strategic decisions, and can be used consistently throughout a company for a fair comparison to guide investments.

Customer Lifetime Value vs. ROI

Once again it is important to note that the term *customer lifetime value* (CLV) is used inconsistently. A number of articles have been published that claim that a certain level of increase in CLV is more valuable than the same percent decrease in customer-acquisition costs. In the example presented here, the CLV term is meant to represent net present value of the future stream of profits following the customer-acquisition cost (which is also the "return" in this case). For marketers that attempt to use CLV measurements in place of ROI, the following analysis will demonstrate the need to consider the combination of dollars invested and incremental value generated.

The example is based on a published article that claimed a 20 percent increase in revenue had more value to a company than a 20 percent decrease in acquisition costs based on the improvement to CLV. Increasing the revenue per customer does correlate with increasing customer lifetime value, but is this enough to guide your marketing investments? Let's see how a decision based on an accurate assessment of CLV stands in terms of generating profits for the company.

The analysis was based on a marketing program that generated $2,000 in revenue per customer and $400 in gross margin per customer, which resulted from an acquisition campaign that had a cost of $800 per customer. The following chart shows the initial calculations of customer lifetime value:

	Baseline
Annual revenue per customer	$2,000
Annual costs per customer (80%)	$1,600
Annual net profit per customer	$400
Average customer lifetime (years)	5
Customer lifetime value[3]	$2,000
Acquisition cost	$800
"Net CLV" (= return)	$1,200

The comparison of a 20 percent decrease in acquisition cost to a 20 percent increase in revenue resulted in the following:

	Baseline	20% Decrease in Acquisition Cost	20% Increase in Revenue
Annual revenue per customer	$2,000	$2,000	$2,400
Annual costs per customer (80%)	$1,600	$1,600	$1,920
Annual net profit per customer	$400	$400	$480
Average customer lifetime (years)	5	5	5
Customer lifetime value	$2,000	$2,000	$2,400
Acquisition cost	$800	$640	$800
"Net CLV" (= return)	$1,200	$1,360	$1,600
Change in net		13.3%	33.3%

The conclusion is accurate in the form it is presented. The 20 percent increase in revenue provides a much more significant increase in CLV than a 20 percent decrease in acquisition cost. So what would you do as a marketer with this information? If you had two marketing programs with the results shown in these two scenarios, the conclusion certainly would guide you toward choosing the program that increases customer value. That would be a costly mistake. At the corporate, customer, and campaign level, it is critical to maintain the focus on making investments where the highest return is possible.

Here is what the missing ROI analysis shows:

	Baseline	20% Decrease in Acquisition Cost	20% Increase in Revenue
Return = "Net CLV"	$1,200	$1,360	$1,600
Investment = acquisition cost	$800	$640	$800
ROI	150%	213%	200%

Both changes relative to the baseline campaign show an increase in ROI. However, the program that requires a lower investment has the greater ROI. The second program does offer more profit to the company but that reflects the fact that a higher investment was made into that version of the campaign. There is budget remaining for the campaign in which acquisition cost was decreased and it can be used to increase the scope of this marketing campaign or to fund other profitable marketing programs.

View the two opportunities in terms of a $100,000 budget where all of the investment was placed into each respective campaign.

	Baseline	20% Decrease in Acquisition Cost	20% Increase in Revenue
Investment	$100,000	$100,000	$100,000
Acquisition cost	$800	$640	$800
Number of customers acquired (= Investment ÷ acquisition cost)	125	156	125
CLV (not discounted) (Annual revenue per customer × average lifetime)	$2,000	$2,000	$2,400
Total return to company (Number of customers × CLV)	$250,000	$312,500	$300,000

The ROI analysis is the better method for maximizing the profit from the company's investments in marketing. The campaign with the lower acquisition cost not only generated more profits but also more customers, which can be beneficial for future marketing initiatives.

Managing CLV is certainly critical to maximizing company and customer profitability. Doing this requires that the marketing initiatives used to improve customer lifetime value are prioritized based on ROI potential.

CHAPTER 7

INVESTMENT AND RETURN PATTERNS

In the marketplace, constant references are made to the fact that customer retention is more profitable than customer acquisition. This may be accurate most of the time but will not always be the case based on the marketing environment and the investments required to change customer behaviors. Different types of marketing activities have different patterns of income flows. The measurement of retention marketing in particular can be unique depending upon the company's business model. The information presented here is intended to show some possible patterns to highlight the dynamics of marketing investments and provide a visual demonstration of where new strategies can drive different profit outcomes.

Acquisition Marketing Patterns

Acquisition marketing involves making investments into a campaign or series of campaigns to prospective customers to generate first-time purchasers. For acquisition marketing in particular, care must be taken to capture customer value accurately because the company will have very limited information on a new customer. The value of the initial sale may be known quickly but future value will need to be estimated to make timely decisions on further investment into the same campaign. If at least some portion of the new customers is likely to make repeat purchases with the company as a result of this initial acquisition-marketing investment, then counting just the profit from the initial sale would be underestimating the return. The goal is to capture all incremental value generated from the investment.

Accurately capturing the investment amount must be done carefully as well. It generally takes a number of impressions, from a number of marketing campaigns to convert a prospect to a customer. The principle that the return must be aligned with the investment decision is at the core of the marketing ROI process. The profits are generally going to be attributed to the final campaign that converts the new buyers. Where possible, analysis should be done to understand which previous campaigns and mass-marketing efforts contributed to the campaign results so the series of marketing initiatives can be managed more effectively. Acquisition marketing can benefit from Customer Pathing strategies that move prospects progressively through the sales cycle to achieve more successful results.

Some possible patterns of profit flow over time are shown in several figures (see 7.1, 7.2, and 7.3). Actual patterns for an acquisition campaign will vary by industry, company, and product. Figure 7.1 is based on making a marketing investment (shown as negative profit per customer), which is then followed immediately by a single purchase (with the profit representing the average net profit per customer generated from the sale).

Figure 7.1 Acquisition ROI for a Single Sale

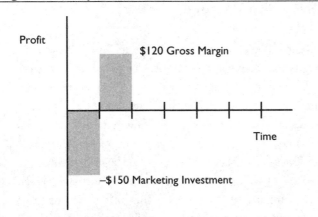

The return is the difference between the profit and the investment. The profit shown in Figure 7.1 is actually smaller than the investment, showing that this acquisition investment is not profitable on its own. The ROI equation that accompanies Figure 7.1 is as follows:

Period (years)	I	2	3	4	5
Gross margin	$120	0	0	0	0
Discount rate = 15% per year	1.00	1.15	1.3225	1.5209	1.749
Discounted GM	$120	0	0	0	0
NPV of gross margin	**$120**				
Marketing investment	$150				
Return	$30				
Return on investment (ROI)	−20%				

It is not uncommon to incur a loss during customer acquisition. An ROI analysis of this campaign, integrated with a series of additional ones that demonstrate an overall profitable investment, would be required to obtain funding.

Figure 7.2 Acquisition ROI for Recurring Margin

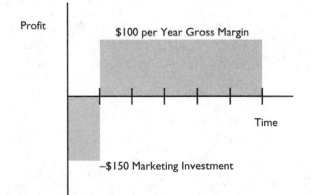

The next acquisition pattern shown in Figure 7.2 is based on a steady recurring revenue stream where 100 percent of the customer base is retained. The ROI equation that accompanies Figure 7.2 is as follows:

Period (years)	1	2	3	4	5
Gross margin (GM)	$100	$100	$100	$100	$100
Discount rate = 15% per year	1.00	1.15	1.3225	1.5209	1.749
Discounted GM	$100	$86.96	$75.61	$65.75	$57.18
NPV of gross margin	**$385**				
Marketing investment	$150				
Return	$235				
Return on investment (ROI)	157%				

This profit pattern where no defection occurs is not realistic. It does show the process of discounting future profits to calculate the net present value.

Figure 7.3 portrays the profit patterns where the initial sale is followed by additional sales in future time periods. A decline in profits is shown over time based on the assumption that without future investments into retention marketing campaigns, competitors will draw a portion of customers away each period. The ROI equation that accompanies Figure 7.3 is as follows:

Period (years)	1	2	3	4	5
Gross margin (GM)	$120	$100	$70	$40	$10
Discount rate = 15% per year	1.00	1.15	1.3225	1.5209	1.749
Discounted GM	$120	$86.96	$52.93	$26.30	$5.72
NPV of gross margin	**$292**				
Marketing investment	$150				
Return	$142				
Return on investment (ROI)	95%				

Figure 7.3 Acquisition ROI with Customer Defection

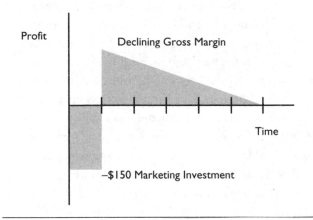

This shows how the rate of customer defection and discounting the value of future profits leads to less contribution in each subsequent year. Keep in mind that even though the value is decreasing, the decision to fund the investment depends on capturing the future value that is projected.

Other patterns of customer acquisition exist as well. With some acquisition campaigns, the pattern would show a long series of marketing investments prior to generating the first sale. Some companies will show an upward profit trend following customer acquisition in place of the downward trend shown in Figures 7.1 through 7.3. This requires low defection rates and a pattern of repeat purchases that are, on average, more profitable than the initial sale.

Retention Marketing Patterns

The purpose of retention marketing is to sustain the existing profit stream from current customers, in effect decreasing the expected trends of customer defection. The nature of retention marketing varies on the basis of the business model used. For example, companies that provide services such as cable television, telecommunications, or credit card services expect that for the majority of acquired customers, a recurring revenue stream will continue with minimal additional marketing investment. Conversely, many consumer product companies operate in a highly competitive and dynamic sales environment. Additional marketing investments are critical to influence both their valuable, brand-loyal customers who must be protected from the competition and their other less loyal customers who will only continue purchasing their product with marketing reinforcement. For some companies and industries, customer loyalty and retention are driven primarily by the customer's experience with the company and by the actual competitive advantages that exist. However, in industries in which consumers perceive little competitive differentiation, marketing can often make the difference in customer retention and loyalty.

Measurements to capture ROI for retention marketing must compare the actual profit stream (post-marketing) with the originally expected profit stream (ideally validated through a control group) to calculate the incremental value. Companies with existing customer relationships expect a future stream of profitable business to be transacted. The expected profit stream reflects the current level of customer spending, adjusted to reflect the attrition rate, or the percentage of business lost to the competition over time. Shown in light gray in Figure 7.4,

Figure 7.4 Retention ROI with Steady Impact

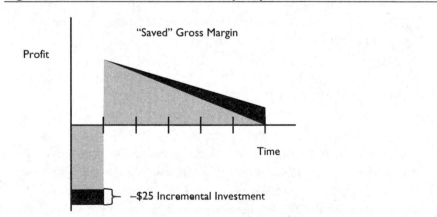

the initial investment leads to a profit pattern in which each period (which could be represented in months, quarters, or years) will show a decline in profits from existing customers, based on the assumptions that no additional marketing investments are made.

In Figure 7.4, the black shaded area represents the incremental investment and the incremental profit stream. This particular marketing investment has increased the retention rate (decreasing the attrition rate) with a steady impact over time.

The incremental profit stream from retention marketing is much different from the profit stream from acquisition marketing. Where acquisition marketing generally results in a spike in profits from an immediate sale followed by a flow of additional sales over time, the impact of retention marketing occurs slowly over time from the improved rate of profit retention. After all, a steady annual defection rate of 12 percent translates to just 1 percent defection per month—and that's the base from which profits can be retained.

The numerical representation of this graph and the ROI calculation that follows are based on an average customer value of $100 profit per year. That profit level should translate into an annual revenue value in the range of $200 to $1,000, depending on the gross margin rate, which varies significantly by industry and product segment. This would typically be analyzed in months or quarters but is done here in years for simplicity in discounting future value. As the numbers demonstrate, the greatest impact comes in future periods, which is discounted back to a present value.

Period (years)	1	2	3	4	5
Existing gross margin projection	$100	$75	$50	$25	$0
Discount rate = 15% per year	1.00	1.15	1.3225	1.5209	1.749
Discounted gross margin	$100.00	$65.22	$37.81	$16.44	$.00
NPV of gross margin	**$219.46**				
New gross margin with retention marketing	$100	$80	$60	$40	$20
Discount rate = 15% per year	1.00	1.15	1.3225	1.5209	1.749
Discounted gross margin	$100.00	$69.57	$45.37	$26.30	$11.44
NPV of gross margin	**$252.67**				

Incremental gross margin	$33.21	($252.67 − $219.46)
Marketing investment	$25.00	
Return	$ 8.21	
ROI	32.8%	($8.21 ÷ $25)

One significant challenge with single retention marketing campaigns is making enough of an impact on customer behavior to create a lasting change in customer defection rate over long periods of time (five years in the example above).

For the next example, Figure 7.5 shows the pattern of a marketing investment that has a short-term impact on customer retention.

The customer behavior in this example represents a postponement of defection. The marketing activity convinced a portion of potential defectors to continue spending with the company for some additional time, but then the defection accelerated to result in the same end point (zero spending) as the original projection. In this example, the short-term retention impact is not enough to produce a positive ROI as shown in the calculation:

Period (years)	1	2	3	4	5
Existing gross margin projection	$100	$75	$50	$25	$0
Discount rate = 15% per year	1.00	1.15	1.3225	1.5209	1.749
Discounted gross margin	$100.00	$65.22	$37.81	$16.44	$.00
NPV of gross margin	**$219.46**				
New gross margin with retention marketing	$100	$80	$60	$30	$0
Discount rate = 15% per year	1.00	1.15	1.3225	1.5209	1.749
Discounted gross margin	$100.00	$69.57	$45.37	$19.73	$.00
NPV of gross margin	**$234.66**				
Incremental gross margin	$15.20	($234.66 − $219.46)			
Marketing investment	$25.00				
Return	−$9.80				
ROI	−39.2%	(−$9.80 ÷ $25)			

The next example shows how retention marketing profitability is greatly improved when the investment can be targeted to more vulnerable customers, that is, those who are more likely to defect. Consider Figure 7.6, which shows the incremental retention value for a segment of customers experiencing a very high defection rate.

Figure 7.5 Retention ROI with Short-Term Impact

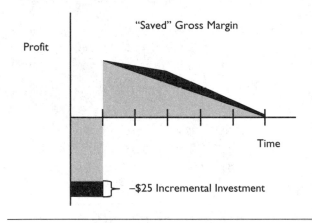

Figure 7.6 Retention ROI on Highly Vulnerable Customer Segment

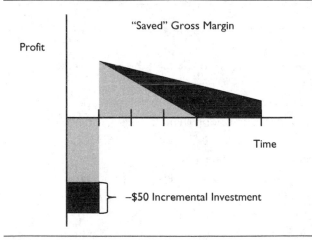

There is certainly high ROI potential for marketing investments that can change the defection rate of highly vulnerable customers to match that of the standard customer population. The calculations shown in the next chart demonstrate how a high ROI can be achieved even with an increase in the marketing investment cost relative to the other examples.

Period (years)	1	2	3	4	5
Existing gross margin projection	$100	$50	$0	$0	$0
Discount rate = 15% per year	1.00	1.15	1.3225	1.5209	1.749
Discounted gross margin	$100.00	$43.48	$.00	$.00	$.00
NPV of gross margin	$143.48				
New gross margin with retention marketing	$100	$80	$60	$40	$20
Discount rate = 15% per year	1.00	1.15	1.3225	1.5209	1.749
Discounted gross margin	$100.00	$69.57	$45.37	$26.30	$11.44
NPV of gross margin	$252.67				
Incremental gross margin	$109.19	($252.67 − $143.48)			
Marketing investment	$ 50.00				
Return	$ 59.19				
ROI	118%	($59.19 ÷ $50)			

As a quick recap of key points from the past three examples:

- Customer retention impact grows in each incremental period when marketing delivers a consistent improvement to a constant defection rate.
- Discounting of profits in future periods to net present value partially negates the increasing value of each incremental period.
- Marketing activities that have short-term impact must have significant impact to achieve acceptable ROI.
- Targeting highly vulnerable customer segments greatly improves the potential for profit improvements.

A Look at Customer Loyalty

Now let's tread into the sacred ground of customer loyalty to understand the challenges that can make it so difficult to achieve profitability with retention marketing. Customer loyalty analyses have shown that a significant increase in profits can be attained when a company retention rate is shifted from 90 percent to 95 percent per year. Improving customer loyalty is a solid strategy that should be part of every business plan. Ideally, customer loyalty will come from the customer experience or the uniqueness of the product offered. However, if the company expects loyalty to result from marketing activity, the question is how much will it cost to achieve the desired shift?

This next example examines the financial dynamics of shifting the retention rate from 90 percent to 95 percent per year, including the investment side of the equation in addition to the commonly viewed profit side. It demonstrates the challenge in achieving profitable retention marketing for a generally loyal customer base. Figure 7.7 graphically shows the incremental gross margin that is anticipated from the retention improvement.

These examples use the average values at a single customer level, so as the retention rate for the customer base moves from 90 percent to

Figure 7.7 Retention Rate Improvement from 90 Percent to 95 Percent

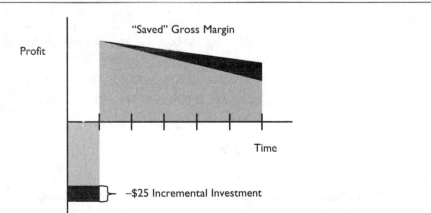

95 percent, the average value per customer increases. Looking at the increased value per customer that results from the improvement in retention, it is possible to determine the maximum investment in marketing that can be made to achieve this improvement.

First, the gross margin of the average customer when the retention rate is 90 percent must be calculated:

Period (years)	1	2	3	4	5
Gross margin without defection	$100	$100	$100	$100	$100
Original retention rate	0	90%	90%	90%	90%
Adjusted gross margin	$100.00	$90.00	$81.00	$72.90	$65.61
Discount rate = 15% per year	1.00	1.15	1.3225	1.5209	1.749
Discounted gross margin	$100.00	$78.26	$61.25	$47.93	$37.51
NPV of gross margin @ 90% retention	**$324.95**				

Second, the gross margin is calculated for the average customer at a 95 percent retention rate:

Period (years)	1	2	3	4	5
Gross margin without defection	$100	$100	$100	$100	$100
New attrition rate	0	95%	95%	95%	95%
New gross margin	$100.00	$95.00	$90.25	$85.74	$81.45
Discount rate = 15% per year	1.00	1.15	1.3225	1.5209	1.749
Discounted gross margin	$100.00	$82.61	$68.24	$56.37	$46.57
NPV of gross margin @ 95% retention	**$353.79**				

The difference between these two values is $28.84, an 8.8 percent gain in NPV of gross margin over the original expected NPV of

$324.95. This is certainly a sizable gain when multiplied out to an entire customer base, but only if it can be attained without a major investment.

The marketing investment that generates a 20 percent ROI when the return is $28.84 is $24.03 (calculated by dividing $28.84 by 1 + 20%). The final checkpoint on the ROI calculation is

Incremental gross margin	$28.84	($353.79 − $324.95)
Marketing investment	$24.03	
Return	$4.81	
ROI	20%	($4.81 ÷ $24.03)

This means that for a targeted customer base with an average lifetime value of $325 and a 10 percent defection rate, *a retention marketing program is limited to a $24.03 investment per customer to cut the defection rate in half over an entire five-year period.* Keep in mind that $24.03 is the total NPV of all investments, not an annual investment, and that the NPV of $325 in profits represents somewhere between $200 and $1,000 per year in revenue (depending on profit margins). It would take a pretty creative and highly effective marketing strategy to deliver results at this level with such a limited investment.

The barrier to achieving profitability in this scenario comes as a result of making an equal investment of $24.03 into every customer, while in reality 90 percent of those customers will continue their purchase behaviors without the marketing. The financial return can come only from changing behaviors of the 10 percent that are expected to defect. If you do not know which customers are likely to defect, the only choice will be to invest retention dollars into all of them. However, as demonstrated in the previous examples, the more investments can be focused on vulnerable customers, the greater is the profit potential.

Cross-Sell Marketing Patterns

Marketing to existing customers generally produces better results than marketing to new prospects. There are an infinite number of profit patterns for the lifetime flow of investments and profits from a customer.

Two patterns are presented here. The first is a pattern based on a single cross-sell marketing overlaid on an existing customer's profit projection. The second pattern shows a cumulative view of a series of marketing investments and profit impact for a customer over time.

The investment shown in Figure 7.8 generates an immediate sale and an increase to the future profit stream. The ROI calculations for just the incremental impact shown in this pattern are as follows:

Period (years)	1	2	3	4	5
Incremental gross margin	$0	$35	$30	$25	$20
Discount rate = 15%	1.00	1.15	1.3225	1.5209	1.749
Discounted GM	$0.00	$30.43	$22.68	$16.44	$11.44
NPV of gross margin	**$80.99**				
Marketing investment	$50.00				
Incremental gross margin	$80.99				
Return	$30.99				
ROI	62%				

The previous examples have shown the impact of one or two campaigns while in reality customers typically receive an ongoing series of campaigns. It is through this series of marketing campaigns and repeat

Figure 7.8 Incremental ROI of Cross-Sell Campaign

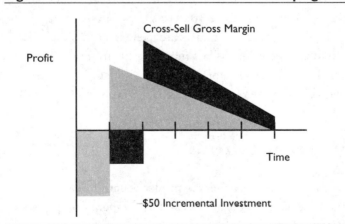

Figure 7.9 Campaign Series Leading to Loyalty

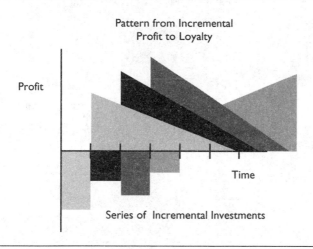

purchases that companies can build knowledge and customize the relationship to improve loyalty. The profit pattern shown in Figure 7.9 represents the dynamic where each new campaign generates incremental profits and finally customer loyalty is earned. Profits can then increase and marketing investments can decrease.

Marketers can improve customer profitability by developing a series of marketing investments that are greater in value when integrated instead of delivered independently. This is the foundation of the Customer Pathing concept to be presented in Chapter 12. The *aggregated* ROI calculation for this series of investments is shown in the next chart.

Period (years)	1	2	3	4	5
Incremental gross margin:					
Acquisition campaign	$100	$75	$50	$25	$0
Cross-sell campaign #1	$0	$35	$30	$25	$20
Cross-sell campaign #2	$0	$0	$35	$30	$25
Cross-sell campaign #3	$0	$0	$0	$40	$80
Total gross margin per period	$100	$110	$115	$120	$125
Discount rate = 15%	1.00	1.15	1.3225	1.5209	1.749
Discounted GM	$100.00	$95.65	$86.96	$78.90	$71.47
NPV of gross margin	**$432.98**				

Marketing investment acquisition campaign	$150	$0	$0	$0	$0
Cross-sell campaign #1	$0	$50	$0	$0	$0
Cross-sell campaign #2	$0	$0	$100	$0	$0
Cross-sell campaign #3	$0	$0	$0	$40	$0
Total marketing investment per period	$150	$50	$100	$40	$0
Discount rate = 15%	1.00	1.15	1.3225	1.5209	1.749
Discounted GM	$150.00	$43.48	$75.61	$26.30	$0.00
NPV of marketing investments	**$295.39**				
Incremental gross margin	$295.39				
Marketing investment	$432.98				
Return	$137.59				
ROI	47%				

The patterns of investments and returns are unlimited, but the principles and process should be applicable to all forms of marketing. Chapter 8 explores the profit dynamics that can drive priorities between acquisition and retention marketing and summarizes the key principles that are essential to accurately establish a standard ROI formula.

CHAPTER 8

PROFIT DYNAMICS AND KEY PRINCIPLES

Because its purpose is to create a customer, the business enterprise has two—and only two—basic functions: marketing and innovation. Marketing and innovation produce results; all the rest are costs.[1]

PETER DRUCKER

In the examples of investment and return patterns shown in the previous chapter, situations arise in which acquisition marketing will not generate enough profits to cover the initial investment and retention marketing will require shifts in long-term retention rates that are unreasonable to achieve an acceptable profitability level. Strategically, growing the customer base and improving retention rates are both highly critical to increasing company profits so marketers must use ROI tools to help guide the right decisions. This chapter covers the marketing dynamics that influence profitability.

The ROI of marketing campaigns can be improved by a number of obvious outcomes, such as:

- Acquisition or retention of higher value customers, achieved through better targeting, more appropriate offers, or a stronger customer focus
- Higher sales-conversion rates, achieved through better targeting, better timing, matching offers to customer needs, and more effective communications
- Increased purchase volume and increased purchase frequency, achieved through targeting offers and communications based on customers total potential spending instead of on current spending

- Improved customer retention, achieved through acquisition of the appropriate customers, better customer relationships, loyalty programs, and a carefully managed stream of communications
- Decreased marketing expenses, achieved through better targeting, optimizing the marketing channel mix, and carefully managing development and production expenses

Developing marketing strategies to achieve increased profits can be further improved by understanding the differences in retention and acquisition marketing, the benefits of a true incremental perspective, and the key principles of marketing ROI. One underlying aspect of profit improvements in each of these areas is that the more precise the information used in the analysis, the better the decisions can be managed. Gaining access to customer-level information will provide much more actionable insight than using values based on average customers, average costs, or general assumptions. Detailed information is not always possible so each company must do the best with what is available while periodically exploring the possibility, cost, and value of improving access to customer-level data.

Retention Marketing and Acquisition Marketing: A Head-to-Head Comparison

Retention marketing and acquisition marketing each has its own profit dynamic that influence where a company places greater attention. Although companies and industries have unique patterns of retention and acquisition that require very different approaches to the development of marketing strategies, the challenges of increasing ROI for each will generally be consistent.

What Drives Retention Marketing Profits?

Retention marketing generates profits through "saved" customers, which means keeping the profit stream of customers who would have otherwise changed their decision to continue purchasing from the company. The key drivers of retention profitability include

- Customer vulnerability
- Customer value
- Lasting impact

Customer Vulnerability. Profitable retention marketing is dependent on defining the highly vulnerable target market. The population of vulnerable customers likely to defect is the only source of saved revenue, and investments applied to loyal customers can result in no profit returns (marketing that also motivates incremental spending is not considered here in order to show just retention marketing dynamics). The more vulnerable a target audience is, the more that can be invested per prospect, and consequently, the greater potential to generate a positive behavior change. In some industries, the majority of customers are vulnerable and they make purchase decisions with no brand loyalty. In that situation, targeting retention marketing is less of a concern, but creating a positive impact is a much greater issue.

Customer Value. Customer loyalty strategies generally intend to protect the company's most valuable customers. Reaching higher-value customers also allows for a higher marketing investment, which may be necessary to effectively retain customers. In the early 1990s, AT&T Consumer Marketing was experiencing customer defection at a relatively slow pace, so modeling to provide a value-vulnerability rating for each customer was essential to improve retention profitability.

Lasting Impact. Recall from the profit patterns for retention marketing shown previously that customer defection happens slowly over time, creating two challenges in terms of "lasting impact" for retention marketing. Consider that a customer segment with an annual defection rate as high as 60 percent experiences a monthly defection rate of just 5 percent. A retention marketing communication may save a portion of those customers from defecting in the same month as the contact, but how effective can that marketing effort be at changing the defection rate for each successive month? Marketing strategies designed to have impact over an extended period of time have a greater potential for retaining incremental profits.

The second challenge with the lasting impact of retention is how long a saved customer will stay with the company. Some retention marketing—in particular immediate promotional offers or discounts that do not address the reasons for a customer's decision to defect—will only delay the defection by a short period of time. Retention initiatives that change the defection rate steadily over several years generate greater profit returns each successive year. Short-term retention impacts are extremely difficult to prove out financially.

Customer loyalty programs have the potential to be profitable for companies that experience high defection rates. These programs are designed to have lasting impact, they can be structured to provide the highest rewards to the most valuable customers, and they can contribute value by motivating incremental spending per customer.

Targeting special offers only to vulnerable customers has strategic implications that might also have financial implications, especially if the offer is made at the time a customer is informing the company of his or her decision to end the relationship. When loyal customers become aware of special offers made to defecting customers, the level of trust and the relationship with the company diminishes. This requires that retention marketing with special offers be carefully delivered through controlled channels such as direct marketing or customer contact channels. The message surrounding the offer must also be carefully crafted to be sensitive to the perceptions of loyal customers. Impacts on customer loyalty should be carefully monitored and reflected in the ROI calculations where appropriate.

What Drives Acquisition Marketing Profits?

Acquisition marketing is attractive to companies because of the immediate boost in revenue and growth in customers, both of which are metrics highly valued by the investment community. The key drivers of acquisition marketing profitability include

- Customer needs
- Customer value
- Customer retention

Customer Needs. Information on purchase patterns and the needs of prospective customers is typically not available or is very limited. Demographic information and insight into general interests, determined in some cases by the source of the prospect list, can be used to target marketing initiatives toward prospects more likely to have a need for the product or service being offered. Acquisition marketing is more like a broadcast of a message as opposed to the dialogue that can exist with an existing customer.

Customer Value. Access to customer value information is also limited for acquisition marketing. Modeling of available data and structuring offers toward higher-value segments of prospects can improve the profits generated.

Customer Retention. Acquisition marketing must be designed not only to generate high sales conversion rates or high-value, short-term purchases but also to bring in customers who will continue to purchase with the company. The long-term income flow generated from the acquisition marketing investment should be incorporated into the ROI measure, and the "residual value" that results from bringing in more responsive customers to benefit future marketing initiatives should be included in the prioritization of investments.

The high cost of customer acquisition is often enough to make acquisition marketing unprofitable on its own. The ideal approach is to integrate acquisition campaign strategies with the subsequent marketing campaigns that generate additional profits from the same set of customers to ensure that an acceptable ROI is being achieved.

Acquisition marketing can also have an impact on customer loyalty. Very often, companies make attractive offers limited to new customers only through mass media channels that reach loyal customers. If the company does not justify this offer, this may motivate customers to defect to become *new* again or give a negative impression that results strictly in customer defection. The financial losses must be reflected in the ROI calculation for this marketing activity.

Summarizing the Differences

Marketers and executives who have been approached with the question as to why their strategy favors retention over acquisition marketing, or vice versa, can benefit from understanding the differences in the dynamics driving profitability. Table 8.1 summarizes the differences.

The challenge of targeting an unknown set of vulnerable customers within a total customer base, which can put retention marketing at a disadvantage relative to acquisition marketing, is shown in Figure 8.1. Marketing campaigns that have an equivalent impact in terms of the response rate generated from the targeted audience nets to a much lower save rate than an acquisition rate. The investment to influence the target audience for acquisition must be managed relative to the value generated by the 2.5 percent response, whereas the investment for retention is managed relative to a net impact of .5 percent response (2.5 percent of the 20 percent defecting that could be saved).

Figure 8.1 Response Dynamic of Acquisition vs. Retention Marketing

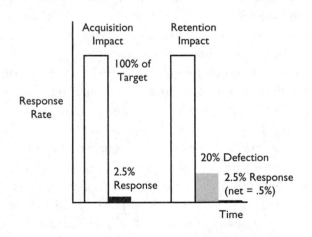

Table 8.1 Comparison of ROI Measurement Capabilities for Retention Marketing and Acquisition Marketing

	Retention Marketing	Acquisition Marketing
Future customer value	Access to customer-level information improves retention ROI potential.	Depends on modeling to improve value of acquired customers
Customer needs	Greater predictability and ability to collect information during customer interactions should improve targeting of offers and sales rates.	Depends on modeling to improve sales conversion rates
Vulnerability	The ability to predict vulnerability using existing data is essential to achieving retention profitability.	Acquisition marketing initiatives that are measured on short-term sales or contribution to future marketing efforts are less dependent on vulnerability, however modeling to target more loyal customers can improve ROI.
Duration of impact	Predicting the duration of impact for saved customers is similar to that of newly acquired customers; however the duration has a greater impact on retention since profits from an improved retention rate grow over time.	The generic profit patterns are based on an initial value followed by diminishing returns. The length of time a customer continues to make purchases will depend on the business model for customer acquisition.
Short-term measurability	Retention is at a huge disadvantage because the short-term save rate measures represent a very small portion of the total profit contribution and the lasting impact is difficult to predict.	Acquisition marketing tends to generate more profits in the short term, and certain types of behaviors (the monetary value of the initial purchase, the timing of the second purchase) can be good predictors of future value.
Reliability of measures	Projected value for saved revenue can have a high margin of error as a significant percentage of the total value comes in later years and is subject to more fluctuation in market conditions.	Projected value will be subject to less fluctuation when most profits are realized in the near term.

Not All Customers Are Created Equally

Too often, the values used to calculate ROI are based on an average of all customers, regardless of the value of actual customers saved or acquired, and this may miss a significant profit dynamic in support of retention marketing. Profitability will increase as measures more accurately reflect the reality that customers can become more profitable over time. The profit rate of a customer can be improved over time on the basis of the decreasing costs associated with increased purchase volume, lower servicing costs, and better price points. Because customer profitability and value tend to increase the longer customers stay with a company, the difference between the ROI potential for a saved customer compared with an acquired customer may require more in-depth analysis. The following example reflects the difference in customer value that may be possible over time. Recall that *potential value* is the total revenue of a customer across all competitors.

Period (years)	1	2	3	41
Total potential value (revenue)	$1,000	$1,000	$1,000	$1,000
Share of potential value	40%	60%	80%	95%
Customer revenue per year	$400	$600	$800	$950
Profit rate	10%	12%	14%	16%
Gross margin	$40.00	$72.00	$112.00	$152.00
Discounted gross margin	$40.00	$62.61	$84.69	$99.94
Base NPV of new customer (base value in first four years @ 15% discount rate)	$287.24			
Referral rate	0	1%	3%	5%
Incremental gross margin (referral rate applied to NPV of a new customer)	$0	2.87	8.62	14.36
Spend growth rate	0	5%	10%	25%
Incremental gross margin	$0	$6.00	$14.00	$40.00
Total gross margin	$40.00	$80.87	$134.62	$206.36
Discounted gross margin	$40.00	$70.32	$101.79	$135.69
Total NPV for customer years 1–4 (@ 15% discount rate)	**$347.80**			

Period (years)	4	5	6	7
Total gross margin (held constant at year 4 value)	$206.36	$206.36	$206.36	$206.36
Discounted gross margin	$206.36	$179.45	$156.04	$135.69
Total NPV for customer years 4–7 (@ 15% discount rate)	$677.53			

In this case, losing a customer who has been with the company for four or more years will certainly have a greater financial impact than losing a newly acquired customer. This reinforces the notion that marketing decisions can become much more effective as information and analyses improve.

The conclusion that should be drawn by this insight into retention and acquisition marketing is that the general statement indicating that it is better to retain current customers than to acquire new customers certainly applies to most business strategies but should not be assumed for marketing. The nature of a company's marketing environment, customer loyalty patterns, and marketing effectiveness will determine which has the greater ROI potential (and it will not always be retention marketing). Careful analysis into the financial impact of customer defection must be completed to create accurate ROI measures. With respect to customer-acquisition marketing, it is a safe assumption that the greatest profitability can result from strategies that incorporate an integrated plan for how to retain those newly acquired customers.

Key Principles for ROI

The following key principles are essential to effectively using ROI to guide marketing investments and strategies. These are also covered in the remainder of this chapter.

- **Measures should be aligned with decisions.** This not only applies to point-of-decision analysis but also to situations where interdependencies exist between multiple campaigns. Multiple levels of measurements can be used to align decisions and measures.

- *Financial values are necessary for all* **returns.** Company objectives generally have some connection to profits and marketing investments are intended to influence customers in such a way that leads to profits.
- *Returns and investments should be complete, accurate, and fit a total sum* **model.** If the returns from all marketing investments were added together, the total sum should result in a realistic aggregated ROI projection. This can be done if calculations are inclusive of all investments and returns without double counting.
- *Performance metrics should be used to estimate financial value but cannot be converted to financial value.* There are marketing initiatives where initial performance metrics can serve as an indication of the actual behaviors that are likely to continue through the sales cycle. From these metrics, an estimated financial can be estimated and used in the decision process. Those marketing initiatives that are intended to result in improvements of nonfinancial metrics will not have an independent ROI since future campaigns are required to generate profitable sales. Performance metrics such as awareness or website visits cannot be translated into a financial value to be used in ROI measures.
- *Residual value should be viewed with caution.* The additional value that marketing investments have on future investments does not belong in the standard ROI measure but cannot be neglected. Strategic decisions should be made with a complete understanding of both the expected return and the impact one investment may have on future investments.

Aligning Measures with Decisions

The ROI measure, used for both planning and performance analysis, is intended to guide strategic decisions. The first point of alignment is to match the investment with the returns. The intricacies of marketing and marketing measurements can be quite complex. At any given time, a large corporation will have multiple campaigns underway, each with multiple contacts and multiple offers delivered through multiple touch points. Measuring the connection between a specific marketing investment and the profit generated can be complex when the cause (marketing investment) and effect (gross margin) cannot be tracked independently from other marketing activity.

The ideal situation is where the profit impact of each investment can be measured at the lowest level possible and aligned with the decisions to be made. Some investment decisions can be effectively tested and measured down to the level of the quality of paper used in a direct mail campaign. Other investment decisions such as the impact of a billboard or a single ad impression in a multichannel campaign are almost impossible to measure with reliable precision.

In some cases, the alignment is improved by aggregating the analysis, running the analysis on multiple levels, or allocating investments. Take, for example, an approach to measuring the impact of a mass advertising investment. The ROI analysis and decision can be based on an integrated campaign that combines the mass advertising with the direct marketing initiatives that would leverage the advertising to generate sales. If the total campaign is not profitable but the direct marketing initiatives are, advertising dollars are being wasted. The ads are either not generating enough awareness and support to convert incremental sales in the direct marketing channels or are generating more awareness that can be converted through the direct marketing channels, meaning overspending on ads or underspending on direct marketing channels.

Establishing Financial Measures for Strategic Initiatives

Not all marketing investments are made for the expressed objective of profits, posing an issue in terms of standardizing ROI as a marketing measure. Marketing investments are sometimes claimed to have a strategic value that does not have a measurable ROI. These types of investments will either have some impact on profits, even if in the distant future, or they will not. Based on the expected impact on profits, these strategic initiatives can be treated as follows:

- *Option A: no anticipated impact on profits.* This could include a goodwill donation or a communication required by legislation that is drawn from the marketing budget. It could also include advertising targeted to the company's shareholders to influence the stock price. Without the goal of generating profits, this cost should not be considered a marketing investment but a general business expense, ultimately captured by the ROI equation in the cost of goods.
- *Option B: indirectly contributes to profits.* Marketing investments such as brand advertising, corporate sponsorships, and customer-service improvements may not have a clear connection to direct sales. In some cases, a different objective and measure may appear to take priority over profits, such as building market share or increasing awareness. These investments and objectives are intended to generate profits but potentially over a longer time than the company's traditional period of measure. It is safe to assume that if ROI projections were made for those strategic initiatives and accurately showed that these investments could not generate an acceptable ROI, those investments would be rejected.

One approach to assessing investments that are difficult to measure is to complete a reverse analysis on the ROI. If a certain investment must meet an ROI threshold, how much in gross margin is required? To reach the gross margin, what quantity of products must be sold through which channels? Is this projection of incremental sales attainable from this investment? This process helps to align the investment with likely sources for the return.

Take for example, a corporate initiative to improve customer satisfaction through guaranteed 24-hour issue resolution. Intuitively, executives can determine that response time is important to customers and that increased satisfaction will generally lead to better customer retention. However, the level of investment for systems, training, staff availability, and internal processes cannot be gauged intuitively. A reverse analysis could be used to translate the estimated investment into a target for incremental profits needed. A $250,000 investment would require $300,000 in profit gain to net a 20 percent ROI. If the average customer's net present value is $600, the company can determine if 500 additional customers can be retained. (The timing of the *save* would also need to be factored into the financial analysis.) In place of saved customers, a reverse analysis can translate an investment into other values related to profits such as incremental product sales or incremental savings.

Using reverse analysis or basic assumptions is necessary to build the connections between strategic investments and the ROI generated. Without establishing financial estimates for strategic initiatives, companies have no standard for comparing marketing investments and they run the risk of consistently making poor investment decisions.

Accurate and Complete Accounting of ROI

The perfect environment for maximizing profits using marketing ROI is one where all of the investments made into programs and all of the returns generated from programs add up, respectively, to represent the complete marketing budget and the total profits generated for the organization (adjustments would be made to reflect net present value calculations).

It's a safe assumption that any organization with any reasonable number of marketing initiatives cannot put a quality check on the *total sum* of ROI without serious guidelines and most likely some form of automation. It's a safe prediction that most companies using ROI measures would find that the return is likely to be overstated and the investment is likely to be understated. It's not entirely intentional, just human nature. Marketers, executives, and agencies are all motivated to work hard to uncover missing value but are not as driven to locate missing costs or overstated results.

Identifying where marketing investments contribute additional value to future investments is a valid and necessary step. If a company were to complete an ROI analysis for mass marketing that was based on converting an awareness value into a financial value, based on the realistic assumption that an increase in awareness improves the results generated by other marketing and sales activities, then the financial value assigned to the mass-marketing investment must be subsequently deducted from the marketing and sales activities that benefit from the mass marketing.

When ROI is measured and monitored at a corporate-wide level, double-counting is more likely to be controlled. Conversely, in organizations where independent marketing groups develop and measure ROI independently, overlap is likely.

ROI projections can also be incomplete if marketing programs use different measures instead of standardizing on ROI as the measure. Without standardization, there is no way to ensure that all costs get captured and all returns are properly assigned to the appropriate investment. Using ROI consistently ensures that all investments are linked to returns so that the best decisions can be made on strategies and investments.

Keeping Performance Metrics in Check

Researchers, consultants, and marketers have been trying for decades to uncover the connection between performance metrics such as awareness, satisfaction, and loyalty to ROI. Some believe that a percentage point of awareness will somehow translate to a financial value of "X" dollars. So many variables are unique to each company, advertising approach, and market condition that it is safe to say this puzzle will never be solved.

Here is everything you'll need to know about the stand-alone value of awareness (or any other performance metric you want to substitute): The short-term financial value of awareness = $0.

Write this down, remember it and it can save you thousands of dollars on future analysis. The value is equivalent to having half of a dollar bill—unless you get the other half—your portion is worthless.

Does this mean that awareness is not important or that it should not be measured? Absolutely not. It means that measuring awareness or managing marketing efforts that generate awareness without an integrated view of the complete sales cycle will most likely lead to lost profits. The same goes for performance metrics such as Web visits, advertising recall, or changes in perceptions. Each action is one step closer to a profitable sale but requires some other marketing activity to make it happen.

The greatest value of performance metrics is in the ability to guide strategies, not investments.

Jim Sterne, who runs Target Marketing of Santa Barbara (target ing.com) and is an internationally recognized speaker and Internet marketing strategist, developed a graphic representation of "The Customer Life Cycle Funnel" (shown in Figure 8.2) in conjunction with Matt Cutler of NetGenesis. These graphs show performance metrics at each stage in the sales cycle.[2] This is an excellent tool for identifying bottlenecks in the sales process that need attention.

There is a method to establish an estimated stand-alone value of performance metrics using the customer-sales cycle. This value should not be used in the ROI analysis but can be useful in guiding strategic decisions. Let's walk through an example of this process to help clarify how this analysis can be used effectively.

Estimating Financial Value of Performance Improvements

This example shows the financial value that results from a single incremental website registration. It is based on data available for various metrics within the sales cycle that begins with the marketing contact that drives website traffic and continues through to a completed sale. Keep in mind that the financial value assigned to this change in a single metric is dependent on future marketing activity. To calculate the value of this performance metric, a customized version of the ROI formula is used.

In this example, Marketing Program A requires a $30,000 budget and its objective is to generate registrations at the website. On average, it must generate 10 website visitors to generate 1 registered user. The registration process includes a request for permission to send E-mail communications. Marketing Program B is an E-mail marketing program delivered to the website registrants at a cost of $4,000 regardless of the quantity. The combination of the two programs generates $50,000 in customer gross margin and nets a $16,000 return.

Figure 8.2 The Customer Life Cycle Funnel

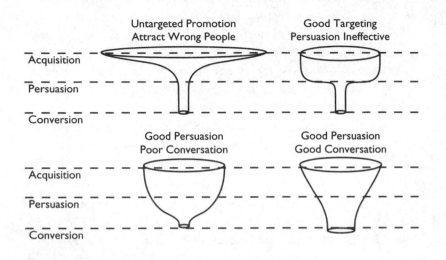

Source: Jim Sterne and Matt Cutler, *Web Metrics: Proven Methods for Measuring Website Success*. Reprinted with permission from John Wiley & Sons.

Following are the key metrics within the sales cycle (also shown in the sales cycle funnel in Figure 8.3).

Conversion rate of Web visits to registered participants	10%
Conversion rate of registered participants to sales	20%

Figure 8.3 Sales Cycle Funnel

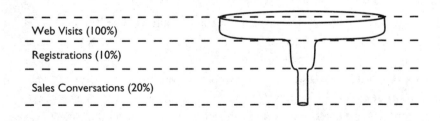

Source: Adapted from Sterne and Cutler Customer Life Cycle Funnel (see Figure 8.2 note)

The goal of this analysis is to understand the value of one incremental website registration. This simplified view assumes the budget can be increased proportionately to increase the quantity of prospective customers flowing through the sales cycle funnel without changing the shape of the funnel.

	Base Assumptions	Revised Assumptions	Increased View
Marketing budget A	$30,000	$30,030	$30
Total website visits	10,000	10,010	10
Conversion rate of visits to:			
Registrations	10%	10%	
Total registrations	1,000	1,001	1
Cost per registration	$30	$30	
Marketing budget B	$4,000	$4,000	
Conversion rate registrations to sale	20%	20%	
Total sales	200	200.2	.2
Customer value per sale		$250	$250
Total value	$50,000	$50,050	$50
Total investment	$34,000	$34,030	
Return	$16,000	$16,020	
Return on investment	47%	47%	

The revised assumptions show the changes necessary to lead to one incremental new registered website visitor. Based on the average expenses shown in the base view, an incremental investment of $30 is required to generate 10 additional website visitors and 1 additional registered user. That registered user increases the target audience for Marketing Program B, which has a proven conversion rate of 20 percent. The analysis shows that a fraction of a sale is recorded (representing an average value, not a partial customer) and that each new registration should be worth $50. This can be taken a step further to work back to the value of an incremental website visitor, which is calculated to be $5 ($50 per 10 visitors).

The benefit a marketing manager can gain from running this type of calculation is establishing a benchmark value to use in the planning for generating additional website visitors or registered visitors. New marketing initiatives that can achieve results at lower costs (using investment limits described in Part III) should be considered and tested to determine actual ROI.

Running these calculations poses a danger that comes into play based on two significant risks of using assigned values that can be costly to the company. First, the assigned values depend on future marketing activity so the investment decisions cannot be made independently from the marketing programs that will actually generate the profit. In the example above, the company would not want increases in Marketing Program A to generate additional registered users if this was not coordinated with Marketing Program B to close sales.

The second risk is in double-counting results. If this analysis was completed and shared within a marketing organization, the marketing team responsible for Program A may include the value of $5 per website visitor into their ROI, while the E-business team might claim $50 per registered user for converting Web visitors to registered users, and the marketing team for Program B could claim another $50 for the actual conversion of the sale. ROI measures must be managed properly to remain accurate.

Taking Residual Value into Consideration

Residual value—defined as the impact one marketing investment has on the performance of future investments—can be one of the most challenging aspects of marketing ROI measurements. Marketers generally have a hunch that customers are influenced by the series of communications they receive over time. CRM strategies are intended to organize contacts with customers so consistency and quality of those contacts can result in greater profit returns. When relationships between independent campaigns can be identified, there is not only an opportunity to measure the impact of one campaign on another, but also an opportunity to strengthen marketing strategies through Customer Pathing tech-

niques as presented in Part III. At this point, however, a solid understanding of how to treat residual value will be established.

Here's the challenge that throws a wrench into an otherwise smooth-
running ROI process of measurements leading to smarter investment
decisions. Maintaining an accurate ROI measure requires that the
return be matched with the investment being measured and exclude any
value that requires additional investment. This is consistent with the
premise that measures should be aligned with decisions and should not
be dependent on future decisions. This measurement approach may be
accurate but it is not necessarily complete. The residual value creates a
gap in capturing the complete value of an investment given that marketing programs often have a residual effect that impacts future marketing efforts and value. When a marketing investment that has an
unmeasured residual value is rejected based on an insufficient ROI projection of its own, the results of the future investments will change.
This is much like an opportunity cost where there is a loss incurred
(when the residual value is positive) from not making a decision to invest
in a particular marketing initiative.

Residual value could exist when a marketing program generates a new
customer, a customer contact, or the communication of a message. For
example, it generally costs more to generate business from a new customer than from an existing customer so the marketing program that
generated the new customer has made all future marketing activities
easier and more profitable. If the customer-acquisition costs are too high
and the marketing program is considered unprofitable on its own, it may
not be funded. Assessing the value based on making future marketing
efforts more profitable may change this decision. Residual impact can
be negative as well. Imagine how two outbound telemarketing campaigns within a week will affect the results of a third outbound telemarketing campaign that shortly follows. The sidebar shows the
dynamics of residual value.

The ROI measurement can be modified to create two approaches for
capturing residual value in such a way that leads to reasonable accuracy
and better decision making. The first approach is to measure an aggregated set of marketing programs. The second approach is to assign values to performance metrics that demonstrate *interim* progress toward
financial benefit, as was shown in the previous example.

THE BASIC CONCEPT BEHIND RESIDUAL VALUE

The following example will explain the residual impact on future marketing efforts. It is based on a series of four campaigns to the same set of customers over a three-month period.

Campaign A   Acquisition marketing
Campaign B   Cross-sell product X
Campaign C   Customer loyalty retention program
Campaign D   Cross-sell product Y

The marketing team for Campaign C makes an effort to dig deeper into their marketing measures to assess their residual value. They analyze Campaign D results and determine that the sales rate for customers reached with Campaign C marketing is much higher than the results for the population not reached by Campaign C. The total Campaign D measure of 48 percent ROI breaks down to 90 percent ROI for customers receiving Campaign C and 30 percent ROI for all other customers. The Campaign C team knows their investment had impact and wants to adjust their own ROI to include the incremental value.

Here is where the complexity comes in. If adjustments are to be made to include residual value, it must be complete. Campaign C has added value to Campaign D, but it may owe some of its value to Campaign A or Campaign B. Let's say the investment into Campaign A increased the base of customers and improved the ROI for Campaign C. Also, the marketing in Campaign B actually had a negative impact on the results from Campaign C based on the aggressive sales approach. All of this information is extremely important to maximize profits, but the measurement process must be simplified and must remain aligned with the decision process.

Important steps at this point are:

• Determine if the residual impact makes enough difference to be worth measuring. You need to justify the cost of analysis and measures to dig into the complexity.

- Align the ROI measures with the investment decisions. The ideal approach is to aggregate the ROI measures and the decisions of the series of campaigns that deliver greater profits together than each does independently. This ensures that separate campaigns are not measured, prioritized, and selected separately.
- If the multiple campaigns cannot be combined into a single measure and decision, the residual value must be shown in conjunction with the campaign's own ROI measure. This can be tracked in many ways but the easiest way to manage it may be to show current results along with the impact of that investment. The investment into Campaign C does not have any impact on Campaigns A or B, just on Campaign D. So Campaign C may be tracked in the budgeting process as 35 percent ROI plus RV of 60 percent lift in Campaign D ROI. With this information, any decision to accept or reject Campaign C is operating with complete information. If it is rejected, profits generated for Campaign D will be lost. The same process would apply to the other campaigns so that Campaign B, which had a negative effect, might be tracked as 25 percent ROI plus RV of 20 percent decrease in Campaign C ROI. The decision to fund Campaign B can now consider the profits lost as well.

Aggregated ROI Measurements

The best approach to capture the costs and profits from interdependent marketing programs is to aggregate the multiple marketing activities into a single view. This approach combines the results analysis and planning of one marketing program with others where residual value could exist. For example, an initial acquisition-marketing program would be measured with the marketing programs that follow in order to capture the benefit gained from the cross-sell and up-sell of these new customers. The total value from all marketing campaigns is assessed against the total marketing expense. The residual value is not measured independently but is captured within the combined measurement. This ensures that a complete marketing strategy is in place and that investment decisions are linked to the return. The ROI of the aggregated marketing programs can be compared to the ROI of individual programs, incremental investments, or alternative investments.

Guide Strategies with Two-Part Measurements

The second approach, which may be necessary when independent campaigns cannot be combined into an aggregated measurement and decision, is to guide investment decisions based on a two-part measurement. The standard ROI measurement for a marketing investment would be used in conjunction with a "profit opportunity" measure, which shows the residual value as profits at stake if changes are made to this marketing investment.

The standard ROI measurement must represent the core investment and return that is used for corporate planning in order to avoid double-counting the return that will also be included in the ROI measure of the future investment. The profit opportunity is used to understand the incremental return that could be lost if either the initial marketing initiative is not made or if the connection between the initial and future marketing initiatives is not maintained.

Part II Conclusion

Some core principles are necessary to apply marketing ROI accurately, but in several areas, the approach must be customized to the unique environment of each company and, in some cases, each marketing activity. Once corporate guidelines can be established, the marketing organization should be in a position to apply marketing ROI consistently and more objectively. Whenever doubt exists as to the structure of the guidelines, the checkpoint should be to assess whether the measurements will lead to the most profitable decisions.

Part II framed out the data needed and identified key trouble areas where inaccuracies might occur. It is not always possible or practical to implement marketing ROI measures as desired. With a better understanding of the fundamentals, you are prepared to create the best possible practices that equip the marketing team for setting strategies.

Part III will guide you through making the decisions to standardize the use of marketing ROI at the campaign, customer, and corporate levels. ROI tools for campaign management are introduced. A technique for managing customer profitability, with or without implementation of CRM, is presented. Strategic applications of marketing ROI extend from the basic measures up through executive management, including a proposed control panel that can be automated to allow real-time management of marketing investments to maximize corporate profitability.

PART III

APPLYING MARKETING ROI

ADOPTING THE MARKETING ROI PROCESS

Most companies launch reward programs without assessing their own needs and the economies of cause and effect. They haven't thought through the links between the value delivered to customers and the value created for the company. A rewards program should not give something for nothing: the profits will be illusory, but the costs will be real.[1]

LOUISE O'BRIEN AND CHARLES JONES

A company exists to maximize profits. Companies deliver many other great outcomes but for the most part, all the work that is done to create superior products and services and expand the base of satisfied customers at the lowest expense are ultimately measured by how well the company increases profits. In Parts I and II, the foundation of the ROI calculation was laid out to prepare you to collect and organize the right data for more accurate use. Now it is time to take this information and put it to work. In this Part, the focus becomes much more strategic. Specific responsibilities are provided to manage profitability at the corporate, customer, and campaign level and steps are outlined to effectively customize and apply the marketing ROI process.

Even at this point, it is safe to assume that not everyone is comfortable with the intense focus on profits. You don't like to think that you are in business just for the money. Your company generates great products and services that people love and need. You invest heavily into employee satisfaction or product quality because that is what leads to high levels of customer satisfaction. You might even have concerns that if you put all your focus on profits, eventually neither employees nor customers will be satisfied.

This emphasis on maximizing profits is not at all in contradiction with customer or employee satisfaction. First of all, the tools and concepts are geared toward improving long-term profits for the company while also managing short-term profit goals. Company management is well aware that it is not possible to lose sight of either employee or customer satisfaction and still expect to remain profitable in the long run.

The goal is to effectively prioritize your marketing investments so that the finite budget you have to work with is directed toward generating the greatest return. Applying the marketing ROI process can create a distinct competitive advantage, allowing you to make smarter decisions on whom to target, how to reach them, and how much to invest. The more the competition wastes their marketing budget on unprofitable efforts, the less share of the market they can earn.

What does increasing corporate profits do for you? By applying these processes, you should end up with benefits such as more customers, better customers, lower costs per sale, stronger customer relationships, and increased customer loyalty—all because you focus your marketing where it has the greatest impact. You still need great business and marketing strategies but you are now more equipped to develop, measure, and refine those strategies.

There is opportunity for customer and employee satisfaction to benefit as well. Generating the best return on your marketing investment provides more financial resources to reinvest in such ways that will increase customer satisfaction and employee satisfaction. It increases the stability of the company and strengthens the company's viability during uncertain economic times. Ultimately, it should fatten the bonus checks for employees and dividend checks for stockholders, both of whom want to be rewarded for making smart investment decisions of their own.

Putting Marketing ROI to Work

So are you ready to champion the marketing ROI revolution for your company? In so many areas within an organization, simple changes in the use of ROI tools and an increased focus on ROI can contribute to the growth of company profits. CEOs and senior marketing executives can shift from running endless iterations within the budgeting process to a streamlined marketing investment prioritization process. Marketing managers can improve their campaign strategies with increased intelligence and measures. Managers of marketing divisions can play a stronger role in aligning the optimal series of campaigns and programs targeted over a customer lifetime.

The next three chapters will go into the details of applying marketing ROI to improve corporate-level profitability, customer profitability, and campaign profitability. Before getting into those chapters, the following overview will put the key responsibilities for each level of the company into context. Not all aspects of the marketing ROI process need to be adopted at once or in a specific order to be effective. And even though the executives at the corporate level should be setting key financial parameters, there are ways to work around this if necessary. If you are going to be the marketing ROI champion for your company, go in with the mind-set that you'll be able to benefit from new insights, regardless of how widespread the marketing ROI process is adopted. You can find areas within your responsibilities to achieve initial success and then motivate others to expand upon that success.

Corporate-Level Responsibilities

Ultimately, the most significant decision the executive team needs to make is to what degree the company will adopt marketing ROI as a way of doing business. If the company is prepared to fully move forward with the marketing ROI process, then top marketing executives, along with the company's financial executives, have the following responsibilities:

- Establish the standard measure of ROI to be used consistently across the organization.
- Set a minimum ROI threshold above which all marketing activities can be funded.
- Where applicable, conduct research to establish standard values to be used in ROI calculations to capture the full future impact on profits or expenses.
- Use the marketing ROI process to set and adjust marketing division and program budgets.
- Align compensation and recognition with the corporate goal to maximize marketing ROI. Mobilization of the organization is just as important as building the tools and capabilities.
- Ensure that the company has access to financing to fund marketing activities that exceed the minimum ROI threshold.
- Monitor and modify the process as needed.

The ROI formula can empower marketing staff when standards are in place for creating projections and making decisions. If the company is willing to begin implementing the marketing ROI process at a campaign or customer level only and *not* at the corporate level, the corporate executives should at least set the minimum ROI threshold that the company expects from its investments. Marketers can judge on their own that a negative ROI is not good but cannot do much to evaluate a positive ROI without having a threshold set by the company. Even choosing the better investment out of two campaigns requires an ROI threshold to make a decision. For example, how could a marketer determine if a program generating 15 percent ROI for a total of $1 million in gross margin is better than a program generating 30 percent for a total of $500,000 in gross margin? The threshold also establishes a reference point for a marketing organization with promising new opportunities to make requests for additional budget.

Division-Level Responsibilities

The division is defined, for our purposes, as the organization that has control over the majority of marketing activities for a specific set of customers and can manage customer profitability. In some companies, this may be a distinct business unit or line of business. In other companies, the organizational structure is set more by product line or functional area than by customer segment. For the latter type of companies, the marketing ROI process and tools can still work very effectively; however, certain strategic planning will need to be made by the cross-division team that can represent a complete view of the overall marketing relationship with the customer segment.

Division management should assume the following responsibilities when implementing the marketing ROI process for profit maximization:

- Measure multiple levels of ROI performance to capture the value of the independent campaigns, incremental options, and aggregated campaigns.
- Establish a methodology to measure mass marketing and investments contributing to a broad number of campaigns.
- Establish a Customer Pathing process for strategically managing marketing efforts at a higher level for maximum profits.
- Manage budgets dynamically to maximize ROI at the corporate level.
- Support marketing ROI measures with research, development, and benchmarking.
- Evaluate and implement systems to track and manage customer profitability.

Campaign-Level Responsibilities

The marketing managers responsible for developing and managing campaigns and promotions can use the marketing ROI process in many ways for both measuring and planning. Responsibilities at this level are as follows:

- Develop marketing ROI tools such as investment limits and marketing allowable charts for easy reference as a checkpoint in the initial planning stage.
- Streamline campaign innovation by applying ROI projections to compare potential campaigns against performance requirements.
- Design market tests to effectively maximize learning and effectively project profitability of large-scale rollouts.

- Strategically identify the most profitable campaign marketing mix by applying marketing ROI principles within marketing channel optimization modeling.
- Apply marketing ROI principles for results measurements to maximize campaign profitability.
- Strategically set the most profitable target market profile by applying marketing ROI principles within targeting and marketing mix optimization modeling.
- Coordinate Customer Pathing based on division-level strategies.

The remainder of this chapter is used to establish one of the cornerstone concepts of marketing ROI, which is to use the incremental ROI measurement process. The following three chapters will then expand on the responsibilities outlined previously for managing profitability at the corporate, customer, and campaign levels.

ROI analysis should be made at the lowest level that strategic designs can be made. Each decision for incremental investment should be measured against its associated incremental return.

The True View of Marketing ROI

It is common practice in marketing organizations to test multiple campaigns and make comparisons based on the ROI generated from each. The incremental marketing ROI measure presented here is a more sophisticated process for measuring the ROI of marketing programs. Briefly introduced in the initial chapters of this book, the general concept behind this new process is to break down each incremental investment opportunity and measure ROI at that level. This is perhaps one of the simplest and most significant advances in measurements that a company can choose to adopt. It offers a great opportunity to see an immediate impact on corporate profits by making only slight shifts from the current standard measurements of marketing programs. This measure can be applied at the campaign, customer, and corporate levels. Marketing results and decisions can be surprisingly different using this very simple enhancement for measuring ROI.

Examples of Incremental Measures

As the following examples show, the typical process of testing campaign variations and selecting a campaign based on the total ROI measured for each can lead to lost profits. These two examples consist of a very basic comparison between a standard direct-mail campaign and the same campaign with a bonus offer.

A direct-mail campaign is tested with and without a financial offer. Assume that the campaign without the financial offer has been the proven performer, achieving a return on investment that exceeds the company's minimum ROI threshold of 20 percent. The marketer tests the same direct-mail campaign with and without a $25 offer that is paid out for each new sale. The market test is done with a sample from the prospect base and the decision must be based on the best campaign to reach the total base of 500,000 prospects.

The results of the market test and the costs are projected out for the two campaigns based on reaching the total prospect base, shown in the table below:

	Direct Mail	Direct Mail +$25 Offer
Number targeted	500,000	500,000
Sales conversion rate	1.0%	1.6%
Number of sales	5,000	8,000
Marketing investment	$290,000	$490,000
Cost per sale	$58	$61
Incremental customer value (ICV) per sale	$75	$75
Net profit	$375,000	$600,000
Net ROI	29.3%	22.4%

The incremental customer value (ICV) is assumed to remain consistent between the two campaigns to simplify the example. It is likely that a promotional offer such as this would attract a different type of customer with a different value than the standard direct-mail campaign, but that will not be considered at this point. As a note, the ICV here represents the net present value of current and future gross margin.

What are some observations that a marketer would make on these projections?

- The sales conversion rate increases 60 percent by adding the $25 offer, which is quite significant. Companies relying on the sales conversion rate (also referred to as the response rate in some industries) would use this as the key measure for the rollout decision.
- The marketing investment would need to increase significantly since the $25 offer must be paid out on all sales.
- Even with the significant jump in the total budget, the cost per sale will increase by only a very small amount, roughly 5.6 percent.
- The addition of the offer can bring in $225,000 of additional profit from the same population of 500,000 consumers.
- The ROI of the direct mail with the offer is lower than the direct mail without the offer, however at an ROI of 22.4 percent, it does exceed the 20 percent minimum ROI threshold set by the company.

What decision should a marketer make? Companies that are not yet using ROI thresholds might make a choice based on the cost-per-sale value, which shows that the addition of the $25 offer will not beat the cost per sale of the standard direct-mail package. Without an ROI analysis, however, there is no accurate way to judge if a 5.6 percent increase in cost per sale is worth the additional profit generated. Had the ICV varied between campaign responders, an analysis based on cost per sale would have been even less valid. A cost-per-sale comparison has little meaning when the value of the *sale* is different between the two campaigns being compared.

Other companies may consider the fact that the campaign with the $25 offer exceeded the company ROI hurdle rate of 20 percent and generated additional profits. This appears to be a logical decision but it is where the decision process can go wrong.

Here is how the incremental ROI measure provides a more accurate view and leads to increased profits. Consider the breakdown of the investment decisions possible within the campaign. The direct-mail campaign can be done on its own or with the $25 offer. The $25 offer cannot be done without the direct-mail campaign. The company has the option to invest $290,000 into just the original direct-mail campaign. The company has a separate decision to make on investing an incremental $200,000 into the $25 offer for this campaign to gain the incremental return projected. Keep in mind that the 20 percent ROI threshold implies that the company has alternative investment options for that $200,000 that can generate at least that rate of return.

The following chart shows the projections in terms of the incremental cost and value.

	Direct Mail	Direct Mail + $25 Offer	Incremental View
Number targeted	500,000	500,000	
Sales conversion rate	1.0%	1.6%	
Number of sales	5,000	8,000	3,000
Marketing investment	$290,000	$490,000	$200,000
Cost per sale	$58	$61	$67
Incremental customer value (ICV) per sale	$75	$75	
Net profit	$375,000	$600,000	$225,000
Net ROI	29.3%	22.4%	12.5%

It becomes clear through the analysis that the incremental investment should not be made. The incremental $200,000 investment into the $25 offer would generate an incremental gross margin of $225,000—a net return of $25,000. The ROI on this investment is merely 12.5 percent. With alternative marketing campaigns available to generate at least 20 percent ROI (i.e., netting a $40,000+ return on the $200,000 investment), the decision should be made not to pursue the $25 offer.

In this example, the decision was split into two stages where the $290,000 investment was made but the additional $200,000 investment was not. There are also situations where the decision to proceed could come about much differently. Consider the same example with a slightly different projection of results.

In the next example, assume that the same direct-mail campaign without the offer eventually loses effectiveness due to the introduction of new competitive offers. The ROI on this campaign falls below the minimum ROI threshold, however, the projections remain the same for the direct mail with the $25 offer. The following results are being projected for the two campaigns:

	Direct Mail	Direct Mail +$25 Offer
Number targeted	500,000	500,000
Sales conversion rate	0.9%	1.6%
Number of sales	4,500	8,000
Marketing investment	$290,000	$490,000
Cost per sale	$64	$61
Incremental customer value (ICV) per sale	$75	$75
Net profit	$375,000	$600,000
Net ROI	16.4%	22.4%

The first conclusion is that an investment into the standard direct-mail campaign should not be made, since it does not meet the 20 percent ROI threshold. The next decision comes as a result of looking at the projections for the direct mail with the offer.

With the company ROI threshold at 20 percent, this same exact promotion achieving a 22.4 percent ROI is now a good choice. This decision is made based on the total ROI for the campaign, without the need for an incremental view. How can this be so different from the first scenario?

The decision to select the direct mail with the $25 offer must be based on the combined ROI, because in this scenario, the investment in the direct mail with no offer is ruled out as an option based on not reaching the ROI threshold, so there is no incremental investment to consider. At the root of this conclusion is how customers respond to the marketing strategy in each example. In the first example, the success of the campaign was being driven largely by the direct-mail campaign and, while the offer had some additional impact, it came at a significant cost. The payout of the $25 offer was going to many customers who would have responded anyway. In the second example, the direct-mail campaign was not generating strong results, so the addition of an offer was a necessary component in the strategy to bring in profitable new business.

The examples here are kept quite simple to show how this approach can be used at a basic campaign level. The bottom line is that breaking the marketing decisions down to align with investment opportunities gives you a clearer picture on optimizing your marketing campaigns.

The same principles of incremental value applied at the campaign level can be applied at the division level. In place of one campaign with and without an offer, the same process can be used to look at an acquisition campaign with and without a follow-up retention campaign. The ROI of a single campaign may not meet financial expectations yet the combination of multiple campaigns may show significant profit potential. Assessing the ROI of all campaigns within the division, both independently and in combination, will bring entirely new insights.

The ROI concepts have been presented, the benefits are clear and the implementation is on the horizon. Understanding the roles and responsibilities for adopting the marketing ROI process is essential to your success. The following three chapters provide the detail behind the responsibilities outlined earlier in this chapter.

CHAPTER 10

MANAGING CORPORATE-LEVEL PROFITABILITY

Like a scientist, I collect data, I look at it, and then I change my activities to reflect what I've learned. This is a crucial point: you've got to constantly collect information, and you have to be willing to change your mind. If you know what your goal is, and you are willing to admit to yourself what the data is really saying, you have to change your mind sometimes, maybe even often.[1]

SERGIO ZYMAN

Company executives are constantly working to maximize the profits of the company while keeping the business on course for overall success and viability. Each company has its process for allocating budgets to various divisions within the marketing organization. The intention of course is to place budgets where there is the greatest profit potential.

Company profits can be maximized by funding all marketing programs that can generate an acceptable return on investment as defined by the company's performance goals and ability to fund investments. In a corporate environment where the total marketing budget has a fixed dollar limit, profits can be maximized by prioritizing funds into the ROI rank-ordered list of marketing investments and selecting the top performers.

The budgeting process is not the only deterrent to making the right investments in marketing. There is no doubt that if you are in a midsize or larger corporation, you have gone through midyear budget cuts on more than a few occasions. This process is typically more chaotic than the initial budgeting process. Profit pressures usually drive budget cuts yet the cuts work against optimizing profits. The entire process of allocating and reallocating budgets unnecessarily burns up the time and energy of marketers that should be directed toward generating results.

The marketing ROI process is an opportunity to establish a more effective process for budgeting and adjusting marketing investments. It should not only optimize profits at a point in time, but also set off the triggers that indicate when an adjustment to the budget is needed. The process will require work to fully adopt but should ultimately simplify the ongoing process.

Executive Responsibilities

As a recap, here are the responsibilities at corporate level as presented in the previous chapter:

- Establish the standard measure of ROI to be used consistently across the organization.
- Set a minimum ROI threshold above which all marketing activities can be funded.
- Where applicable, conduct research to establish standard values to be used in ROI calculations to capture the full future impact on profits or expenses.
- Use the marketing ROI process to set and adjust division and program budgets.
- Align compensation and recognition with the corporate goal to maximize marketing ROI. Mobilization of the organization is just as important as building the tools and capabilities.
- Ensure that the company has access to financing to fund marketing activities that exceed the minimum ROI threshold.
- Monitor and modify the process as needed.

The core principle behind ROI is as simple as can be:

- *Investment* is the total of all expenses that are put at risk.
- *Net profit* is all of the financial gain (or loss) that comes as a result of that investment.

- *Return* is the difference between the two.
- *ROI* is the return as a percent of the investment.

The only real complexity that comes into the ROI measure is *what* gets counted within the investment and gross margin values and *how* those input variables are calculated. Establishing standards is necessary to simplify the use of ROI measurements.

Standardizing the ROI Formula

It is critical that clear standards be established for calculating ROI across an entire corporation. The return on investment calculation provides a numeric value that can be used as a measure or projection of performance. That value can have lots of meaning when put in the context of other ROI values. Measuring customer and campaign profitability may have unique nuances for some companies, which must be addressed at a high level in the corporation to maintain the consistency necessary for accurate comparisons. If a company is going to embark on profit optimization using the marketing ROI process, it must ensure strict adherence to a standard ROI formula set at the corporate level.

Standardization also minimizes the fudge factor that gets incorporated into the reporting of results to management. Employees, consultants, and agencies are motivated to make performance measures look as good as possible. The measurement of a marketing program's ROI is often enhanced by identifying additional value or using alternative assumptions. Completeness and consistency go a long way in providing valuable intelligence in measures and decision making.

There are many issues that will arise when setting the parameters of the ROI formula. Choices to include or exclude certain input variables will make the results and projections from some divisions and campaigns appear more favorable and others less favorable. This process will certainly be a catalyst for discussion and debate in those cases and should be handled carefully to ensure all management and employees buy into the process.

As mentioned previously, it is very important to differentiate the ROI formula for planning strategies and measuring performance. To maximize profits, you want to guide the marketing investment decisions, which typically happens at the planning stage. When goals and compensation are aligned with maximizing corporate profits, ROI measures of performance will also be very important. The key difference to keep in mind is that the ROI calculation for measuring performance should consider all related expenses past and present as the investment, while the ROI calculation for planning should consider only investments that have yet to be made relative to other investments that could be made with the same budget.

> The process to establish standards should be guided by the objective of empowering employees to make the best decisions for the company. It should influence and not deter the strategies and actions that are desired to maximize long-term profits.

Decisions that need to be made to establish the ROI formula for planning include:

- *Period of time.* The period of time determines which future profits and expenses get included in the calculations.
- *Incremental customer value.* Measuring the average expected incremental customer value must be done with consistency. The measurement process must establish guidelines for estimating revenue, Cost of Goods Sold (CGS), incremental savings, and ongoing customer maintenance. Determining if the cost of goods will incorporate fully loaded costs or purely incremental costs will be a very important decision that must come from the executive level.
- *Discount rate.* The discount rate(s) for adjusting future profits and expenses into net present value must be standardized at the corporate level. It is also important to designate whether the NPV applies on an annual basis, monthly basis, or some other period.
- *Referral value.* The value associated with customer referrals and the incidence of referrals coming from new customers and from influ-

encers both must have established procedures for being included in the ROI calculation.

- *Expense allocation.* For performance measurement using ROI, all expenses that contribute toward generating returns and are not included in the CGS should be allocated in such a way that aligns with decision making, does not overlap, and covers 100 percent of these shared-benefit expenses.
- *Investment.* The investment is defined as the total expenses "at risk." This includes any new expense that results from the decision to make the investment and that will be incurred independent of generating any sales. If the expense is directly related to the sale, it is considered a cost of goods and is deducted when calculating the gross margin.
- *Residual value view.* Guidelines must be established for capturing the residual value of a marketing investment on future marketing efforts, including impact on results from marketing, the value chain, and the use of market intelligence. This is not a component of the ROI equation but must be shown in a separate view and considered during the prioritization of marketing investments.

Here are some general guidelines for establishing standards for each of the above input variables included in the ROI equation.

Time Period

The time period in which the costs and profits should be captured will typically fall in the range of three to six years. The goal is to allow enough time to capture an accurate view of the stream of profits and expenses that flow from the investment included in the ROI equation. A period that is too short may eliminate marketing programs that have significant growth in value over time. A period that is too long may be difficult to measure and, even with adjustments, will be at risk for uncontrollable changes that impact future value.

The time period is partially influenced by the discount rate, which makes each successive period worth less in net present value. As this diminishes, there is less need to include the future value. The higher the discount rate used, the shorter the time period that needs to be used.

The considerations that can help determine the appropriate time period to use as the standard include:

- *What is a typical time period over which a marketing activity has impact?* The time period does not need to extend past the point where the majority of the value and costs are accurately captured.
- *What degree of uncertainty is there in future value?* Some degree of risk can be accounted for in the discount rate but the time period can also be used to focus the measurements on financials within a period where there is reasonable confidence.
- *How does the discount rate change over time?* If this increases significantly over time, it will accelerate the effect of diminishing returns.
- *How does customer value change over time?* If the customer value decreases quickly, the majority of value can be captured in a shorter period of time. If the value of the customer base generally increases at some point in the future, the time period should capture this.
- *What are the short-term priorities for profits?* Companies that place a greater importance on short-term profits can either standardize on a short time period or increase the discount rate each year, which will impact the effect of diminishing returns.

There is not only the length of time that must be standardized, but also the duration of a single period. It is easiest to discount the value of money on a yearly basis but for businesses that are highly dependent on cash flow in the near term, it may make sense to use quarterly or monthly increments. This would provide better comparisons of marketing investments that generate faster returns at a time when cash flow might make the difference in a company's ability to survive or thrive.

Time Periods and Discount Rates

Here are some examples of ROI calculations that show what goes into selecting the appropriate time period.

Example 1: Steady Discount Rate. The following chart shows the NPV of a customer that generates an ongoing profit of $1,000 per year.

The discount rate was held constant at 15 percent. The chart shows the value of the future $1,000 discounted to a present value ($1,000 in year two is valued at $870 today). Over 15 years, the customer will generate $15,000 and the company values that today at just $6,724. The cumulative percent of the total NPV shows that after 10 years, more than 85 percent of the value is captured. Using just the effect of diminishing returns, the decision could be to measure 100 percent of the value over 15 years or settle for 85 percent of the value over 10 years. Either time period is extremely long and would be dependent on high customer loyalty and a high confidence level that the predicted profits will come.

	Discount Rate	NPV of $1,000	Cumulative % of Total NPV
Year 1		$1,000	15%
Year 2	15%	$870	28%
Year 3	15%	$756	39%
Year 4	15%	$658	49%
Year 5	15%	$572	57%
Year 6	15%	$497	65%
Year 7	15%	$432	71%
Year 8	15%	$376	77%
Year 9	15%	$327	82%
Year 10	15%	$284	86%
Year 11	15%	$247	90%
Year 12	15%	$215	93%
Year 13	15%	$187	95%
Year 14	15%	$163	98%
Year 15	15%	$141	100%
TOTAL NPV		$6,724	

Example 2: Increasing Discount Rate. This chart uses the same assumption that a customer generates $1,000 in gross margin annually. The discount rate is increased over time to reflect the risk of uncertainty in future years and to put greater importance on the profits gen-

erated in the near term. Using these assumptions, the total NPV of a customer comes in just 12 years and is equal to just $4,626. Now 80 percent of the value is reflected in a five-year period.

	Discount Rate	NPV of $1,000	Cumulative % of Total NPV
Year 1		$1,000	22%
Year 2	15%	$870	40%
Year 3	15%	$756	57%
Year 4	25%	$605	70%
Year 5	25%	$484	**80%**
Year 6	50%	$323	87%
Year 7	50%	$215	92%
Year 8	50%	$143	95%
Year 9	50%	$96	97%
Year 10	50%	$64	98%
Year 11	50%	$42	99%
Year 12	50%	$28	100%
TOTAL NPV		**$4,626**	

The profit impact of a single investment will generally decrease over time. Factoring the decreasing value, the increasing discount rate and the accuracy of measuring value far into the future together would result in a general guideline that three to five years will be sufficient. It is best to run this analysis using your own values so that the information is clear for making a decision.

Incremental Customer Value

The challenge with incorporating customer value into the ROI calculation is collecting enough information to project future value with reasonable confidence. Incremental customer value is a critical component in the ROI measure, so assumptions must be made based on short-term data and then later validated.

There are two primary approaches to establishing an incremental customer value (ICV) figure that can be used in ROI calculations—assess historical purchase behaviors or estimate anticipated purchase behaviors. Viewing historical patterns of customer value should be done as a benchmark whenever possible. When using strictly historical values as the basis to establish ICV, it is important to measure this for different customer segments so those values can be associated with marketing targeted to those different customer segments.

Companies that are entering new markets and do not have a comparable customer segment to develop a historical view, or those that have solid reasoning that the future value will be much different than the past, will need to create estimated values based on anticipated behaviors. In many cases the historical view is the basis of the estimate and it is then adjusted to reflect a campaign designed to change specific behaviors.

Another method for establishing assumptions for ICV is to conduct research with customers of competitors or comparable companies to identify benchmark measurements. This needs to be done carefully to identify the specific factors that are driving the ultimate value so that the assumptions can be relied upon. For example, measuring the average value of a competitor's customer and estimating how much of that competitor's share your marketing efforts can capture is a sound process. However, your value from that same customer may be much different based on a difference such as customer service, which may be the primary driver of long-term value.

Each marketing campaign or program will generate sales from different types of customers. Using a general ICV, or even the average ICV for the segment of customers targeted, will neglect the impact of that specific marketing activity (at least until the actual ICV is tracked over a long period of time). To more accurately capture the ICV for each marketing activity, the company can determine which short-term behaviors of new customers predict long-term behaviors and lifetime value. Short-term behaviors such as lower customer satisfaction ratings with the initial transaction may indicate higher customer defection or lower future profits. Or the monetary value or type of product/service purchased in the initial transaction may be an initial indicator of future purchases. Monitoring these behaviors not only can establish the measure of ICV, but also be used as part of the Customer Pathing process to guide strategies for the next set of marketing efforts as described in the next chapter.

Technology that can track customer behaviors and modeling programs that can predict future value make it easier to establish standards for incremental customer value. It is important to remember that making decisions based on any quality information, in this or other areas, is generally better than making assumptions and decisions with no information.

In order to align measurements with decision making, there are several adjustments to ICV that can be factored in where appropriate. These include:

- *Price variations.* Frederick Reichheld indicates in his book *The Loyalty Effect* that loyal customers will often pay premium prices, which increases customer value. Typically the price premiums come from a reduced use of discounts and promotions. Adjustments should be made when the marketing strategy is geared toward increasing loyalty and there is the opportunity to realize price premiums.[2]
- *Cost of goods variations.* The marketing ROI process is based on comparing incremental marketing investments to incremental return. As sales volume increases, cost of goods or fulfillment costs will tend to decrease. If the decrease in costs is significant, it represents additional profit per sale, which should be reflected in the ICV. Determining which sales are the base volume and which are considered incremental may be complex; the key is to align the measure with the decision.
- *Overhead expenses.* Some costs such as customer service may be captured as an average spread across all customers equally. Expenses that can be tracked to a customer level should be captured in the ICV to better reflect the actual profits generated.

Factors to consider when establishing incremental customer values include:

- *How effective can historical measures be in determining value?* Historical measures are reliable if consistent behaviors are predicted.

- *Can internal benchmarks be established for specific customer segments?* The company may want to offer internal benchmarks for various customer segments so that all marketing managers can use the same assumptions prior to making adjustments for anticipated value.
- *Are external benchmarks necessary?* Research to establish external benchmarks for various customer segments may be necessary to ensure that all marketing managers can use the same assumptions prior to making adjustments for anticipated value.
- *What are the key behaviors that serve as indicators of ICV?* Identifying the key behaviors of customers that occur shortly after the marketing activity can help to assess the ICV of the converted customers.
- *Does the ICV represent the* **return on this investment?** Projections and measures must be monitored to ensure that only the portion of customer value that comes directly from the investment being measured is included in the ROI calculation.

This is an area where there will need to be corporate guidelines along with some latitude for marketers to change anticipated values. A validation process will help to refine the quality of anticipated values.

Discount Rate

The general concept of the discount rate was presented in Part II. Marketers should not be too concerned with how the discount rate is set, just leave this to the finance department. It is important to understand the fundamentals of the discount rate and how it can be used strategically to establish the corporate standards for ROI calculations. From a financial standpoint, the discount rate is intended to reflect the rate at which additional capital can be raised for investment into the company—in this case into marketing programs. The discount rate can be used as a tool to establish the priority of short-term profits relative to long-term profits.

The discount rate converts the future value of money into a value that would be considered comparable today. If you were indifferent to a dollar received today or next year, $1,000 next year would be valued at $1,000 and the discount rate would be zero. If you set your discount rate at 15 percent, you would be willing to trade off $1,000 of next year's profit for $870 of this year's profit. As the discount rate increases, the value of $1,000 of next year's profit will continually decrease until it becomes negligible.

Figure 10.1 represents the present value of $1,000 in each year (this is not cumulative value). The present value of $1,000 in future years decreases in each year. Higher discount rates decrease the present value of future profits at a much faster pace.

Figure 10.2 shows the sum of the NPV for a customer that generates a steady flow of $1,000 in profit per year for a full 10 years. For a company that sets its discount rate at 15 percent, the value of that profit stream is equivalent to $5,772 in today's profits. The company that sets the discount rate at 30 percent would trade off the future value for $4,019 in immediate profits.

Some company decision makers completely disregard future value and instead measure results based only on the initial or short-term sales. Concerns have been raised about investments that generate high future profits but have very low current profits. For some companies, the impact of low current profits would have too great an impact on cash

Figure 10.1 Net Present Value of $1,000 in Each Future Year Based on Discount Rate

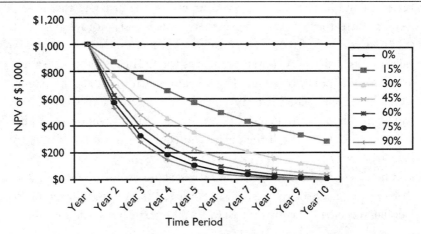

Figure 10.2 Total NPV of $1,000 Over 10 Years Based on Discount Rate

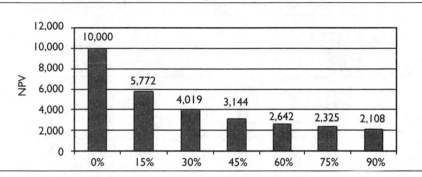

flow and could threaten the business. Current profits are very impor-tant to the survival of some companies, especially start-up, high-debt, or struggling companies. Adjusting the discount rate makes it possible for each company to set its own balance between short-term and long-term profits.

Figure 10.3 presents a modified version of the net present value fig-ures shown in Figure 10.2 where the profit stream increases from $1,000 to $2,000 but no profit returns begin until year three. Any com-pany having to choose between this profit stream and the previous would give this careful consideration. For companies with reasonable borrowing power who set their discount rate at 15 percent or even 30 percent, this latter opportunity provides greater value. Companies that set their discount rates at 45 percent or higher, place greater importance on short-term profits, which leads them to select the first opportunity.

Companies with a higher dependency on profits today, will increase the discount rate to a point that makes financial sense. That point will be dependent on the company's ability to borrow money and the cost of borrowing, or the potential ROI that could be achieved with cash today.

As demonstrated earlier in the chapter in the segment on time peri-ods, the discount rate does not have to be a constant number. It can be increased in each future year to better account for the value that may come in within the initial years. The discount rate can also vary for each

Figure 10.3 Total NPV of $2,000 in Years 3 Through 10 Based on Discount Rate

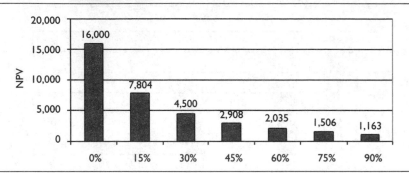

marketing investment opportunity so that campaigns with proven results are prioritized over campaigns that could be high risk (it is easier to maintain a constant discount rate and manage risk by setting different ROI thresholds).

Factors that can be used to determine the discount rate:

- *At what rate of return could money received this year be invested?* The discount rate of 15 percent has become the de facto rate in calculating ROI since that is fairly close to an average long-term return within the stock market.
- *At what rate could money be borrowed?* If a company could make marketing investments today that generate phenomenal profits in future years but not enough in the immediate years, the company should consider borrowing capital to cover the cash flow gap.
- *How does risk increase over time?* Different discount rates can be used for each future time period based on the risk of uncertainty.

Referral Value

Referrals are a great source of new business and the ROI calculation should capture any additional net value generated from referrals that can be traced back to the initial marketing investment. It's long been proven that highly satisfied customers tend to make referrals and highly dissatisfied customers make even more negative referrals. Marketing investments that bring in new customers or change customer opinions will have a ripple effect on profits.

Referral profits can result from customers and from influencers. Influencers are intermediaries such as experts, the media, or highly regarded individuals or entities that can help generate business by expressing their views and opinions. Marketing investments can have an impact on the influencers, leading to positive (or negative) growth in ROI. Influencers are defined here as unpaid individuals and entities to ensure that there is no confusion with paid endorsements, which is a more traditional marketing tactic.

Referrals can sometimes be difficult to track and measure. The company should either set up tracking procedures, commission a study on actual customer behavior, or establish some benchmark values that can be used throughout the corporation. The referral value comes from a combination of the rate of referrals (the ratio of customers to referrals) and the average ICV that can be associated with each referral. If five in every 100 customers refers $1,000 in new gross margin (adjusted to NPV), then the average new customer has a referral value of $50 (5 percent times $1,000).

Key considerations for referral value:

- *What is the ratio of referrals per customer?* Tracking procedures are necessary to capture or estimate this value.
- *What is the average ICV associated with each referral?* This could be based on an average or tracked specifically for referrals. It is necessary that the value from referred customers is not also counted in the *return* from other marketing investments.
- *How does a specific campaign increase or decrease the likelihood of receiving referrals?* Programs that are designed to have a viral effect or to reward referrals should reflect a higher referral value and not work off of an average. Programs that target referral-oriented customers or influencers should also reflect a higher referral value.

Expense Allocations

To get an accurate and complete picture of the total investment responsible for generating the measured returns, it may be appropriate to allocate certain expenses across multiple marketing initiatives. Investments into marketing technology, staff, and even some forms of brand advertising are done with the intention to generate their own ROI but in many cases will be dependent on additional future investments to capture that incremental value. It is critical that expense allocations be structured to lead to optimal decisions since the process does have the potential to backfire. The first step is to make sure that only pending investments be allocated into the ROI projections of individual campaigns. This allocation is part of the process to assess the value of this investment.

The next step is to make sure all allocated expenses are not duplicated in the Cost of Goods Sold or anywhere else in the ROI equation. Expenses such as staff or technology are sometimes treated as fixed overhead costs and not viewed on an incremental basis.

Finally, the trick to effectively managing an allocation process is that it may take a series of iterations. Once an allocation process is established and costs are spread among a number of marketing campaigns, the change in ROI may lead to the decision that some campaigns are no longer profitable. When one campaign is dropped, it will change the allocation amounts for all other programs. This is where caution is necessary to avoid cancellation of marketing campaigns that may be incrementally profitable if the expense can be covered by other marketing initiatives.

Corporate-level decisions are necessary to establish standard allocation procedures.

- **Which expenses get allocated and which belong in general overhead expenses?** The general overhead expenses get captured in the cost of goods.
- **What method of allocating expenses will be used?** Expense allocations should be made very carefully to guide decisions toward the greatest profitability. Allocations should not unnecessarily burden marketing programs that will result in a loss of profits if rejected.

Investment at Risk

The marketing expense for a specific campaign or marketing activity is usually known or is easy to estimate prior to making the decision to move forward. It should be clear that all committed expenses must be included, and all expenses associated directly with each sale should not be included. Committed expenses that are packaged as part of the planned marketing activity might include technology, training, incremental staff, or brand support. A good example of this would be a loyalty program where investments in many areas throughout the company would need to be committed before extending the offer to customers through marketing communications. The entire investment is at risk and should be compared to the total return that is expected.

Residual Value

The issues around capturing residual value in the ROI equation were presented in detail in Part II. Residual value can result from marketing impacts such as increasing the customer base, changing perceptions of prospects, and collecting market intelligence to improve future targeting.

Typically, a greater investment is required to sell something to a new prospect than to sell the same thing to an existing customer. Based on this fact, there is clearly value to having more customers so the company is in a better position to generate more sales. This value would not be captured in the typical ROI measure of an acquisition campaign since, as defined, only the gross margin that comes as a direct result of only the corresponding investment is considered. The future investment in the marketing campaign to the new customer is a separate decision with a separate ROI measure.

A similar gap is encountered when you consider that marketing campaigns not only generate sales but also influence the impact of future marketing campaigns to acquire the nonresponders. The campaign may increase awareness and understanding of the offer, change perceptions, and create interest that makes it easy to motivate purchase behavior in a future campaign. Conversely, the contact from the campaign may also have a negative impact if the prospect is being bombarded, which may deter any future purchases. Either way, this marketing campaign is changing the potential return on future investments and that needs to be captured in the decision-making process.

Collecting market intelligence on prospects or customers can also have a tremendous value in terms of future marketing. Like the other forms of residual value, this has no direct value until an additional investment is made.

No one wants to miss the opportunity to get credit for value that has been created through his or her marketing campaigns. There have been many executives, marketing managers, agencies, and consultants who have recognized this gap and have devised ways to establish values that can be added into the ROI measurement. It would be great if it were that easy but to maintain the integrity of your ROI measures, the complexity around residual value must be considered.

The funding process at the corporate level should be based on prioritizing campaigns based on the independent ROI with consideration being given to the residual value.

Key points in considering residual value:

- *How can interdependencies between separate marketing initiatives be identified?* A residual value exists when one investment influences the results of another investment.
- *Can residual value be replaced with measures of combined campaigns (i.e., by implementing Customer Pathing strategies)?* Aggregating investment decisions for multiple campaigns that show positive results when integrated is the ideal approach for maximizing profits.

Setting the ROI Threshold

The ROI threshold is used to guide marketing managers in their decision making for which campaigns and which incremental marketing investments should be pursued. This is the minimum ROI that the corporate executives expect from any marketing investment. It is not the average ROI that should be returned from all investments but clearly a cutoff point where marketing programs below the threshold are rejected, with the exception of emerging marketing programs that are being tested and improved as discussed in Chapter 14.

Ideally, a financially derived ROI threshold will be used to set the entire marketing budget for the corporation, but in many cases, the reverse occurs. Companies establish arbitrary marketing budgets, which override the ROI threshold. The marketing initiatives that fall below the fixed budget (and are not funded) but are above an ROI threshold level that would be financially acceptable to the company, represent lost profit opportunities (see Figure 10.4). In addition to setting the initial budget, the ROI threshold should be used by marketing managers on an ongoing basis to request additional funding, serving as the point where proven marketing initiatives are funded under a *blank check* policy. The company may have their own way of calculating their minimum ROI expectations. It can be determined by company goals for profits or profitability.

Figure 10.4 Marketing Investments Ranked by ROI

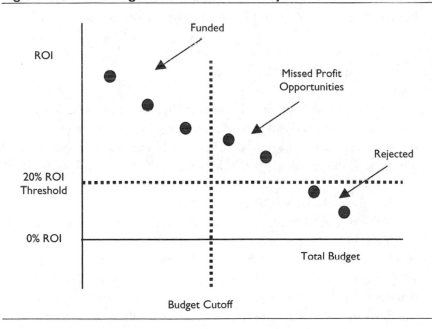

The company must establish and maintain a minimum
ROI (or hurdle rate) in order to empower marketers to
make decisions that maximize profitability.

When the marketing budget is established as a fixed amount without
consideration of a financially driven ROI threshold, the budgeting process to maximize profits is completed by ranking all possible marketing
investments from best to worst ROI and allocating the budget until
either all profitable marketing programs are funded or until the budget
is depleted. Remember that the company should expect a reasonable
return on its investment, so a positive ROI (such as 1 percent) is not
necessarily the decision point since better returns are available in a low-
risk mutual fund. The finance organization should help determine the
minimum cutoff point when the budget exceeds the availability of profitable marketing opportunities. When the budget does not cover all programs above the ROI threshold, the lowest ROI of the programs funded
becomes the ROI threshold for the organization. As new marketing
opportunities arise that can exceed that ROI threshold, the marketing
budget should be revised to fund the higher performing activities.

Setting Marketing Budgets

The process for setting marketing budgets begins at the corporate level
and generally filters down so that marketing divisions then prioritize
investments on a campaign level. The corporate executives deliver the
budget with the expectations of achieving revenue and profit goals for
the company.

Very often, the budgeting process is based on benchmarks such as
the previous year's budget or a standard percentage of sales as a starting point. Financial projections are then run to determine how funds
should be adjusted from previous benchmarks. At AT&T in the early
1990s, the process began with a starting budget and the assumption that
budgets would be similar to the previous year. The process then involved
running views of how much profit and revenue could be generated with

that budget amount. Those views were then revised over and over again at many different funding amounts during a three-month period, and then the numbers were set. In the next quarter, the process was repeated in a series of fire drills intended to cut that very same budget.

Most companies manage to stay in business and achieve their financial goals, so this inefficient budgeting process is not entirely ineffective. However, the budgeting process at AT&T and most other companies is not structured to maximize profits so there are significant profits to be found through improvements in the process. The following steps should be taken to create a budgeting process designed to maximize profits.

- Establish standards for ROI measurement as outlined above so that projections are prepared consistently.
- Either select each incremental marketing investment that exceeds the ROI threshold or rank all incremental marketing investment opportunities and fund the top opportunities until the budget is depleted.
- Structure the company's investment portfolio to manage marketing programs in four categories of reliable investments, high-potential investments, emerging investments, and innovation investments as explained in Chapter 14. ROI thresholds and specific criteria for each category must be established.

Monitoring and Modifying Marketing Budgets

The responsibility for managing the marketing budget is ongoing. There must be a process established at the corporate level to streamline budget revisions throughout the year. To deliver on the goal of maximizing profits, adjustments must be made as the projections for marketing programs are replaced with actual measured results or improved assumptions. Those investments funding underperforming programs must be shifted to fund higher performing programs.

Campaign management technology can play a significant part in both the initial and ongoing budget allocation processes. Through campaign management applications, executives can have access to marketing program results and projections. A custom designed application can be developed to automatically rank programs based on projected ROI, track performance relative to projections, and alert management when a reallocation is necessary.

Just as budgets between marketing divisions may need adjustments based on actual performance, the ROI threshold may need to be adjusted throughout the year. Keep in mind that the ROI threshold is the point where marketing investments that exceed the threshold are to be made. If the marketing performance overall is running below projections and there are no higher performing marketing programs into which investment can be shifted, it may be necessary to temporarily lower the ROI threshold. This must be done very carefully and with a strategic plan in mind. Lowering the threshold will allow additional profits to come in while not fully meeting the company's financial requirements (especially if the ROI threshold was properly set based on the cost of borrowing capital). Funding this increased marketing activity allows a period of time to improve the profitability of those programs.

Changes to the ROI threshold should not be confused with changes to goals for marketing. Marketing personnel should be motivated to achieve the highest level of ROI possible, however, the ROI threshold should be set as low as possible so that every marketing investment that can generate an acceptable return is funded.

Aligning Performance Rewards

New procedures for maximizing profits can have tremendous value to the corporation—but only if there is the proper motivation and mobilization of management and staff at every level within the marketing and sales organization.

The reality is that adopting the recommendations presented here must be supported by a shift in mind-set from everyone from the marketers to the executives. Marketers are not motivated to openly admit when their ROI performance falls below a corporate threshold or to sacrifice their own program results to help another marketer's results under a Customer Pathing strategy.

The marketing ROI process is designed to empower marketers to pursue all marketing programs that can achieve the minimum ROI threshold (eliminating much of the subjectivity and politics of budget allocations), provide tools and training to show them great insights during the planning and measuring process that will help them create stronger strategies and results, and receive credit for future value that they generate.

The key to motivation is to align rewards, in the form of compensation and recognition, with the desired behaviors and appropriate goals. With a goal of maximizing company profits, there must be a portion of the rewards that get measured at the corporate profit level. A strong motivator for the first year of implementing the marketing ROI process is to establish a bonus based on the incremental profits generated. Then once Customer Pathing is implemented, rewards can be made for each team that collectively manages and maximizes the profitability throughout a customer path process.

There is plenty of room for individual rewards as well. The profit growth is still dependent on improvements in marketing strategy and implementation. Rewards can be based on improvements that contribute to ROI instead of the actual ROI. For example, a marketer that creates a program for increasing customer-acquisition rates for a specific segment should be rewarded even if his or her program provides a lower immediate return, but other marketing programs can tap into this new customer base very profitably (i.e., the value when measured in the Customer Pathing view increases).

Funds should be reallocated to other more profitable programs as part of the profit maximization process without penalizing the team responsible for the programs losing the funds. When programs are being mismanaged and losing effectiveness, that would certainly be reflected in the performance assessment of an individual.

CHAPTER 11

MANAGING CUSTOMER PROFITABILITY

C ustomer profitability can be effectively managed by tracking, planning, and implementing a series of campaigns that contribute more profits when integrated than when implemented independently. Viewing ROI over the lifetime of customer relationships is at the heart of this. Customer Relationship Management (CRM) initiatives have grown steadily in recent years and continue to be at the forefront of marketing. While major corporations have tended to establish multiple, independent relationships with customers based on their different products and services from different organizations, customers tend to perceive a single relationship. Therefore, each contact with the customer has the potential to impact future sales efforts, either positively or negatively.

Consider the following scenarios:

- An interactive marketing promotion generates high involvement from the prospect base but only converts a marginal number into sales. When timed just prior to a separate direct-marketing campaign, the high awareness and positive interaction result in a significant lift on the response rate to the subsequent campaign.
- Three outbound telemarketing campaigns that generally perform well independently happen to reach a set of customers all within a two-week period. The campaign performance of the third campaign drops dramatically based on the first two calls. In addition, the set of three calls irritates customers to the point where they are unlikely to be responsive to any future sales contacts.

- A market test proves that one customer-acquisition campaign performs at a much higher level than an alternative campaign. The profile of new customers from the stronger acquisition campaign, however, proves to be disloyal relative to the profile from the alternative acquisition campaign. The higher ROI of one campaign leads to lower ROI on future cross-sale marketing campaigns.

CRM strategies for campaign management are designed to establish stronger integration and manage the customer relationship toward stronger loyalty. Marketing ROI measurements are perfect for transitioning toward better integration and guiding CRM strategies. While CRM offers many benefits, managing customer profitability can be beneficial even for companies that do not want to invest in building relationships.

Division Manager Responsibilities

The term *division* is intended to represent a decision-making group within the marketing organization that ideally manages a customer segment and reports to the chief marketing officer. As a recap, here are the responsibilities of the marketing division, which were presented at the beginning of this section:

- Measure multiple levels of ROI performance to capture the value of the independent campaigns, incremental options, and aggregated campaigns.
- Establish a methodology to measure mass marketing and investments contributing to a broad number of campaigns.
- Establish a Customer Pathing process for strategically managing marketing efforts at a higher level for maximum profits.
- Manage budgets dynamically to maximize ROI at the corporate level.
- Support marketing ROI measures with research, development, and benchmarking.
- Evaluate and implement systems to track and manage customer profitability.

Managing marketing ROI at the customer level will work best when basic ROI practices are in place at the campaign level and at least some support is provided at the corporate level.

Multilevel ROI Measurements

A key principle of marketing ROI is to align the measurement with the investment decision. Even if one investment has a residual value that changes the return on a future investment, incorporating that impact into the ROI measure on the first investment has too many complexities and a risk of guiding incorrect decisions. However, decisions can be brought up to a higher level where interdependent campaigns are measured and managed at an aggregated level.

The steps necessary to establish multilevel ROI measures are as follows:

* Identify where interdependencies exist.
* Measure the independent and aggregated ROI.
* Determine the appropriate use of independent, incremental, and aggregated ROI measures.

Identifying Interdependencies

There will be some interdependencies between campaigns to the same customer segment that exist by intentional design and some that occur unintentionally. Campaigns that are intended to support one another or to reach the same target audience are easily identified. To explore where unintentional interdependencies exist, start by looking at the stream of customer touch points that exist for segments of customers. Are there marketing activities that would logically support or interfere with the performance of subsequent marketing activities? Did any unusual results occur that could be traced back to previous marketing activities?

Once interdependent campaigns can be identified, the impact can be measured and decisions can be made for how to manage those campaigns. Companies with customer-centric organizational structures will be able to coordinate synergistic campaigns easier than companies with product-centric organizational structures.

Measuring Independent and Aggregated ROI

The next step is to measure the ROI for both the independent campaigns and the aggregated multicampaign investments. These represent the different investment decisions that can be made. The example presented below includes two different acquisition campaigns (A and B), of which only one can be selected, and a cross-sell campaign (C) that will follow whichever acquisition campaign is selected. The results for the cross-sell campaign have been measured for the different customers brought in by each acquisition campaign. Also included is an alternative campaign (D), which will be introduced to compete with the initial campaign combination that is selected. Campaign D can only be implemented in place of the acquisition and cross-sell campaigns.

The ROI measurements for several independent marketing campaigns are as follows:

	Investment	Net Return	ROI
Acquisition Campaign A	$1,000,000	$450,000	45%
Acquisition Campaign B	$1,000,000	$150,000	15%
Cross-Sell C to Customers A	$ 500,000	$ 50,000	10%
Cross-Sell C to Customers B	$ 500,000	$475,000	95%
Alternative Campaign D	$1,500,000	$615,000	41%

It is apparent from the results shown for Cross-Sell Campaign C that Acquisition Campaign A generates customers with high initial value but low cross-sell potential, while Campaign B generates low-value customers that have higher cross-sell potential (a trait likely to provide greater long-term value as well). An organization that allows marketing investment decisions to be made at the campaign level will have its acquisition marketing team choose Campaign A over Campaign B, since the return is so much higher. Then, assuming the company requires a minimum of 20 percent as its ROI threshold, the cross-sell marketing team will reject Campaign C which can only generate 10 percent ROI. The marketing team introducing Alternative Campaign D would compare the ROI to Campaign A only. Based on the incremental profit that can be generated, Campaign D would replace Campaign A (the additional $500,000 investment for D generates incremental $165,000 which has a 33 percent ROI, a process explained earlier).

Adding an aggregated view of ROI for Campaigns A and B in combination with Cross-Sell C changes this decision process. The results are aggregated between the acquisition and cross-sell campaigns, to show the following:

	Investment	Net Return	ROI
Acquisition Campaign A	$1,000,000	$450,000	45%
Cross-Sell C to Customers A	$ 500,000	$ 50,000	10%
Aggregated A + C	$1,500,000	$500,000	33%
Acquisition Campaign B	$1,000,000	$150,000	15%
Cross-Sell C to Customers B	$ 500,000	$475,000	95%
Aggregated A + B	$1,500,000	$625,000	42%
Alternative Campaign D	$1,500,000	$615,000	41%

The greatest profit potential comes from the combination of Acquisition Campaign B with Cross-Sell Campaign C. This demonstrates the benefits of using aggregated ROI in combination with independent campaign ROI.

For marketing campaigns that coexist in the marketplace, aggregated ROI can also be used to assess the positive or negative contribution one campaign has on another. In this case, the aggregated ROI would be compared to the independent ROI of a campaign. The earlier reference to a set of three outbound telemarketing (OTM) campaigns that reach a set of customers within a two-week period can be expanded to serve as an example.

Since these are existing campaigns that have a history of results, the company knows that independently, the following ROI performance can be achieved:

CAMPAIGN RESULTS (SEPARATE CUSTOMER SEGMENTS)

	Investment	Net Return	ROI
OTM A	$ 500,000	$170,000	34%
OTM B	$ 500,000	$105,000	21%
OTM C	$ 500,000	$425,000	85%
Total Profit	$1,500,000	$700,000	47%

When directed to a common segment of customers, the independent ROI changes to:

CAMPAIGN RESULTS (SERIES OF CONTACTS TO SAME CUSTOMERS)

	Investment	Net Return	ROI
OTM A	$ 500,000	$170,000	34%
OTM B	$ 500,000	$140,000	28%
OTM C	$ 500,000	−$ 50,000	−10%
Total Profit	$1,500,000	$260,000	17%

The impact of the OTM A campaign on the OTM B campaign was positive, providing a lift in results. The results of the OTM C campaign were severely hurt by the first two contacts. The aggregated ROI for OTM A and OTM B combined nets to 31 percent and the combination of all three campaigns nets to 17 percent. Running the independent and aggregated ROI ranking through the marketing ROI selection process would lead to the selection of OTM A and B integrated with OTM C clearly separated in timing.

CAMPAIGN RESULTS (SEPARATE CUSTOMER SEGMENTS)

	Investment	Net Return	ROI
OTM A + B	$1,000,000	$310,000	31%
OTM C	$ 500,000	$425,000	85%
Total Profit	$1,500,000	$735,000	49%

These simplified examples demonstrate the advantages of viewing aggregated ROI along with independent campaign ROI. There are also situations where it is necessary to include a view with incremental ROI at the customer level.

Understanding Incremental vs. Aggregated Views

Using marketing ROI to rank and select marketing investments includes a technique that breaks down previously aggregated decisions to show the incremental ROI. It is important to understand the distinction for when to aggregate measurements and when to break them down incrementally. As long as the measures align with the decisions, the process works.

The previous example with the acquisition campaign, followed by the cross-sell campaign can help demonstrate this point. If the Acquisition Campaign A and the Cross-Sell Campaign C were designed in the initial strategy as a single, two-step campaign, the ROI would have been measured as 33 percent. Because it is possible to choose the acquisition campaign separately from the cross-sell promotion, the marketing team would go through the steps to break down the ROI measurement, uncovering the fact that the acquisition investment was generating 45 percent ROI and the cross-sell was achieving only 10 percent ROI. The investment decisions to choose from based on just these two campaigns include:

- Make no investment at all if both the ROI for Campaign A and the ROI for the combination of A and C do not exceed the ROI threshold of 20 percent.
- Invest in Campaign A but not Campaign C if only Campaign A exceeds the ROI threshold of 20 percent.
- Invest in Campaign A and Campaign C if both the ROI of Campaign C and the ROI of A and C combined do exceed the ROI threshold of 20 percent.

Campaign A	Campaign C	Campaign A + C	Decision
<20%	<20%	Any value	Invest in A only
<20%	Any value	<20%	No investment
<20%	Any value	>20%	Invest in A & C

Notice that the first option is based on the independent campaign measures to choose A and the incremental value to reject C, while the other two options are dependent on the aggregated measures.

Mass-Marketing Measures

Measuring mass-marketing activities such as brand advertising or event sponsorships very often can be challenging or impossible. Investments into these channels reach a broad audience with the objectives of increasing awareness, building positive perceptions, and establishing competitive advantages. These investments are not necessarily intended to drive sales without the support of additional campaigns.

Managing marketing ROI at the customer level gives greater flexibility to establish measures that guide more informed decisions for strategies and investments. The use of mass marketing is ultimately intended to increase sales, and companies work hard to determine the right mix of marketing and advertising channels. Establishing a value for increased awareness and positive image on its own is much like establishing the value of half of a $100 bill. Unless you can get the matching half, it has no value. The goal for both strategic and measurement purposes is to establish a stronger connection between mass-marketing and sales-oriented marketing channels.

Ideally, the value of mass marketing is measured on its own. Running ads in test markets can be effective for determining the incremental impact on sales. Comparing sales activities prior to and during advertising periods gives insight into incremental sales as well, as long as other marketing activity remains consistent and no significant shifts in the general marketplace exist. Some ads that drive direct response incorporate tracking mechanisms such as unique phone numbers or website addresses.

Many marketers and researchers are searching for a secret formula that will convert advertising measures such as exposure, awareness, image, and likelihood to purchase into financial value. They are chasing the Holy Grail and spending lots of money where no solution is likely to exist. Individual companies that use advertising consistently in a standard sales process should be able to identify the relationship between a shift in these metrics and the increase in sales. However, a standard formula across the industry and even within most companies cannot be established when so many variables can vary significantly.

Marketing executives have three options with respect to the investments into mass marketing—aggregate, allocate, or ignore. Where a mass-marketing investment can be matched with the marketing campaigns that generate sales through its support, the aggregated ROI is a strong measure. For mass marketing that supports a number of customer segments, products, or markets, the total expense can be allocated into the ROI calculations for the associated marketing campaigns and sales channels. There will be some mass advertising, especially very general brand advertising, that may have such a broad impact and long-term benefits, that it is best to ignore these expenses for ROI measurements and let the expenses be assessed using brand equity measures.

Situations where aggregated measures can be used to capture a complete campaign inclusive of the mass advertising are very straightforward. Allocating mass-marketing expense across multiple marketing campaigns is likely to be a challenge based on a level of subjectivity that is inherent in the process. Campaigns will each align with the message and target audience of the mass marketing differently and realize different levels of impact. It may not be possible to develop a perfect allocation formula but the allocation process is likely to provide valuable insight to guide better investment decisions.

Project, Allocate, and Assess

A three-step process can be used for allocating mass-marketing investments in such a way that better aligns marketing strategies and investments toward the greatest profit potential. It begins by projecting a return needed from the investment and this amount will be allocated to the various campaigns supported by the advertising. The revised results will be assessed and additional iterations will need to be run before settling on the final allocation.

Project the Minimum Return. The mass-marketing investment is typically a known value. Using the ROI threshold, or an ROI target, the minimum return that must be reached can be calculated and converted into a sales target. The following example shows this calculation:

Mass-marketing expense: $800,000
ROI target: 20%

Calculating the return target using the ROI equation is done by using the following formula that factors the investment ($800,000) up to account for the ROI target (1 + 20%).

Investment × (1 + ROI target) = Return Target

$800,000 × (1 + .20) = $960,000

An investment of $800,000 must generate $960,000 of incremental gross margin (this must represent the net present value if the customer value is generated over multiple periods). This sales target can be allocated to marketing campaigns in its current form or converted into customers or product sales. If only one product is being sold and it generates $96 in gross margin per sale, 100,000 incremental sales are needed. If each customer has a net present value of $1,000, then 960 more customers are needed.

Without this analysis, sales targets may be set too low and investments can easily be made that do not recover the fully loaded investment. The team responsible for creating the mass-market ads should recognize that they are expected to generate incremental sales—motivating stronger integration, greater results focus, and tighter budget controls among the advertising, sales, and marketing organizations.

Allocate the Return Targets Across Campaigns. Quite honestly, allocating expenses is not easy and not fun. Marketing managers do not want to increase their sales objective and change their results analysis, especially if they've had the benefit of the mass marketing without the expense. Any allocation process is going to seem unfair from someone's perspective. Attitudes of the sales and marketing team may change if the process leads to greater collaboration with the advertising team to help drive additional sales.

The goal is to allocate the investment in such a way that will drive the best decisions. The process will provide insight into how marketing campaign managers perceive the value of the mass-marketing support. If the general consensus is that mass marketing is not providing a lift in sales, additional testing or analysis may be justified. If the target audience is not effectively aligned, or the timing of the mass-marketing support is not beneficial, strategies can be adjusted to improve the value of the support.

Factors to consider when determining the allocation process across multiple campaigns include:

- To what degree does the mass marketing reach the target audience of each campaign? The mass marketing must reach the same audience as the campaigns to have an impact.
- To what degree does the mass marketing promote the same products and services as each campaign?
- Is the mass-marketing activity reasonably timed to support the marketing campaign? Increased awareness and perceptions will fade over time and have a limited time period where incremental impact can be expected.
- How does the mass marketing integrate with each campaign in terms of message and positioning?
- Does the mass-marketing direct-sales activity to specific marketing channels match with each marketing campaign?

This example can be continued using simplified assumptions. The mass-marketing investment is determined to support only two campaigns. Two campaigns match 100 percent with the target audience and product promoted. The mass marketing reaches only 60 percent of the third campaign's audience and promotes just one of four products sold in that campaign. All campaigns are identical in size. The team comes to agreement that 40 percent of the sales target should be allocated to each of the first and second campaigns and 20 percent of the sales target to the third. They also agree that the results will be closely monitored and that testing will be conducted to help confirm assumptions. The allocation process is as follows:

	Allocation %	Investment	Gross Margin Target
Total		$800,000	$960,000
First campaign	40%	$320,000	$384,000
Second campaign	40%	$320,000	$384,000
Third campaign	20%	$160,000	$192,000

Each campaign will add this amount to the investment portion of their ROI analysis and anticipate that they are receiving an incremental gross margin in excess of the target.

Assess the Revised Results. The assessment can be completed at several levels. The most important assessment is whether the total return can be generated across the campaigns. If the allocation process does not show a combined positive return, the company should determine if a different allocation process is justified. Some campaigns may show a positive return while the incremental investment will make other campaigns fall below ROI thresholds.

The assessment process will require a number of iterations to determine the ideal allocation formula:

- For campaigns that become unprofitable with the addition of the mass-marketing investment, an assessment is necessary to determine if that campaign investment is justified. Can that campaign achieve positive results with less or no support from the mass marketing? Perhaps the allocation needs to be adjusted.
- Mass marketing cannot always be scaled back but a first step could be to determine how an overall reduction in this investment would impact the total return and individual campaign ROI measures. Shifting the target audience or intensity of the campaigns may also be an option.

- Cancellation of unprofitable campaigns may be necessary, which will change the allocation equation. Once campaigns are eliminated, do the remaining campaigns still prove profitable when absorbing the additional expense?
- Several iterations may be necessary to determine which campaigns are generating acceptable returns and how the return targets should be allocated.

Identifying campaigns that fall below the ROI threshold may drive changes in the campaign and mass-marketing strategies along with increased integration. As a checkpoint, if the aggregated investment that includes mass marketing along with the campaigns achieves an acceptable ROI, then it is possible to establish an allocation process that nets results at or above that ROI level. If the aggregated investment is not achieving an acceptable ROI, it is possible that the process will identify a combination of campaigns that is acceptable.

In some situations, this allocation process will be completed and it will suggest that the mass marketing is not generating the necessary return. It's possible that intuition will lead you to believe the analysis must be wrong and that the advertising or sponsorship in question is absolutely beneficial to the company. Congratulations to you. That type of thinking is essential for marketing ROI to continually improve in guiding the right decisions. Now you need to figure out where the formula could be wrong. Is the customer value or profit margin neglecting some future value that should be considered? Does the mass marketing have value in other areas of the business that should be included in the allocation process? The ROI formula is straightforward, so you should create a projection that truly shows the potential and then seek buy-in from those that can implement the change.

Strategic Alignment

Hopefully it is apparent that greater measurements around mass marketing not only help calculate the value of investments, but also help drive better strategies. By establishing that mass-marketing investments must generate acceptable returns, certain marketing managers will not be able to justify expenses as "strategic" or "a value impossible to measure."

Increased strategic alignment between the mass-marketing team and the campaign managers should come in the form of:

- Tighter integration over the entire sales cycle, linking those activities focused on generating awareness and nurturing prospects with those activities that close sales
- Better alignment of the target audience through media selection
- Stronger integration of the positioning and message, including customization to support individual campaigns where possible
- Improved timing for stronger synergies
- Increased attention to the budget, making decisions that are designed to increase sales impact
- Greater insight into the scale of mass-marketing investments to align with other channels that close sales

It may sound idealistic, but undoubtedly, room for improvement exists over the current level of integration in most corporate environments. Measurements linked to objectives and performance reviews can go a long way in motivating the right behaviors.

A primary strategic planning technique that improves customer profitability is Customer Pathing. The following chapter goes into further detail on Customer Pathing before moving into managing campaign profitability.

CHAPTER 12

CUSTOMER PATHING™ STRATEGIES

The secret to success is find out where the people are going and get there first.

MARK TWAIN

R eferences to Customer Pathing strategies have been made through-out this book. Now enough of a framework has been presented to cover the full concept. The need to monitor and identify interdependencies between distinct campaigns was presented in Chapter 11. Moving beyond this level of monitoring, division managers can engage in the technique of Customer Pathing, which involves proactively managing these interdependencies.

Managing customer relationships requires moving customers through different stages in the relationship, monitoring their needs to extend the right offer at the right time, and maximizing the long-term profit potential. Customer Pathing contributes toward CRM objectives by taking into consideration the ROI potential of marketing investments. It identifies the synergies, overlaps, and interferences that occur between independent marketing activities and establishes the total investment limits per customer. Marketing strategies and investments can be prioritized and coordinated to place customers on the optimal path to maximize company profits.

Using measures and projections based on independent, aggregated, and incremental ROI for various investments makes it possible to create Customer Pathing strategies. As with any major customer-relationship initiative, it will require controlled testing and constant monitoring.

The focus is on maximizing the aggregated ROI for marketing to customer segments, as close to the individual customer level as possible. In a sense, this is using marketing ROI projections to manage customer lifetime value by optimizing the stream of marketing investments to generate the highest possible return. The balance of customer profitability that is outside the marketing department comes from increasing the margins on sales, introducing new products, and increasing advantages that support customer loyalty.

Looking at the stages of customer relationships will help demonstrate the potential for Customer Pathing. There are many ways to divide and describe the stages of a relationship. This view breaks the relationship into five stages that each requires unique forms of marketing.

1. Cultivating: building awareness and positive perceptions among prospects
2. Acquisition: closing sales with new customers
3. Development: generating repeat sales and building share of customer
4. Retention: maximizing current share of customer spend and building loyalty
5. Growth: increasing the total spend per customer

In Chapter 11, an earlier example was presented to show how a lower-performing acquisition campaign in combination with a high-performing cross-sale campaign can provide the highest total profits. Customer Pathing is designed to leverage this same concept at a broader level. In a simple sense, a portion of a customer path can be presented as shown in Figure 12.1.

This represents the most profitable combination of marketing campaigns for a specific customer segment (or individual customer if possible). The Customer Pathing process overrides the fact that certain mass-marketing campaigns may score very high in awareness and perceptions and that other acquisition campaigns generate a higher response rate. This takes into consideration the support that mass marketing has for an acquisition campaign, the long-term value of the customers, the incremental value one campaign can have on future results, and increasing customer loyalty.

Figure 12.1 Customer Pathing Established by Selection of Optimal Campaign Combination Throughout Sales Cycle

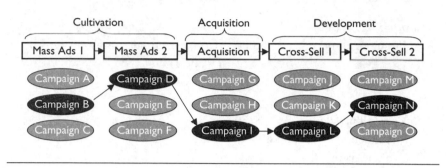

Marketing ROI also supports Customer Pathing by showing marketing strategists where performance changes can have the greatest impact. For each customer segment and possible path, there will be a flow of metrics that relate to one another. Once again, a simplified example based on the customer path outlined previously can be used to convey the concept. The first example shows key results, including the investment and return for the optimal combination of campaigns.

Campaigns B, D, and I: Mass Marketing + Acquisition

Target	100,000
Sales rate	3%
Closed sales	3,000
Margin per sale	$75
Investment	$300,000
Gross margin	$225,000
Return	−$75,000

Campaign L: Cross-Sell

Target customers	3,000	(from closed sales in Campaigns B, D, and I)
Sales rate	26%	
Sales	780	
Margin per sale	$500	
Investment	$105,000	

Gross margin	$390,000
Return	$285,000

Campaign N: Cross-Sell

Target customers	3,000	(from closed sales in Campaigns B, D, and I)
Sales rate	37%	
Sales	1,110	
Margin per sale	$250	
Investment	$60,000	
Gross margin	$277,500	
Return	$217,500	

Aggregated Results

Investment	$465,000
Gross margin	$892,000
Return	$427,500

The customer path shows that the number of customers generated from Acquisition Campaign I feeds into the target and results of Cross-Sell Campaigns L and N. Working under the assumption that results projections are fairly stable and the customer path is set in place, the value of improving acquisition performance can be viewed across the set of upcoming campaigns. Knowing this value can translate into an investment limit that is useful in planning new marketing strategies.

The numbers can be rerun to determine the value of an incremental closed sale in Campaign I. To make the numbers easier to understand, 100 new sales will be added (the equivalent of improving the close rate to 3.1 percent) and then the value will be divided by 100 to result in the value of a single new customer.

Campaigns B, D, and I: Mass Marketing + Acquisition

Target	100,000
Sales rate	3.1%
Closed sales	3,100
Margin per sale	$75

Investment	$300,000
Gross margin	$232,500
Return	−$67,500

Campaign L: Cross-Sell

Target customers	3,100	(from closed sales in Campaigns B, D, and I)

Sales rate	26%
Sales	806
Margin per sale	$500
Investment	$108,500
Gross margin	$403,000
Return	$294,500

Campaign N: Cross-Sell

Target customers	3,100	(from closed sales in Campaigns B, D, and I)

Sales rate	37%
Sales	1,147
Margin per sale	$250
Investment	$62,000
Gross margin	$286,750
Return	$224,750

Aggregated Results

Investment	$470,500
Gross margin	$922,250
Return	$451,750

Incremental Analysis

Additional new customers	100
Incremental return	$24,250
Incremental return per new customer	$242.50
Maximum investment to achieve	
20% ROI	$242.50 ÷ 1.2 = $202.08

All of the incremental expenses for Campaigns L and N are incorporated into the analysis. The conclusion of the analysis is that if an additional expense of $202.08 were added to Campaign B, D, and I investment to generate one incremental new customer, that investment would generate incremental return of $40.42 (the incremental return of $242.50 minus the incremental investment of $202.08). The current cost of a new customer is $100 ($300,000 investment divided by 3,000 new customers). It is highly likely that additional customers can be acquired for less than $202.08, and in this simplified scenario, investment into acquisitions should continue until that investment limit is reached.

Analysis such as this is made easy in a tightly integrated view of the customer path. This analysis goes beyond managing customer lifetime value by incorporating marketing expenses and performance projections into the process.

Here are additional examples of how Customer Pathing can be applied strategically:

- Each customer segment can be assessed and managed toward optimal profitability.

    Customers can be segmented to structure marketing offers, channels, and contacts to the optimal balance between customer needs and company profits.

    High-value customers that typically get plenty of attention can be managed toward high loyalty while closely monitoring the total level of investment.

    Middle-value customers can have investments scaled to the appropriate level when viewed over the long term. Using a view of incremental expenses, some marketing activities targeted to high-value customers may not require significant additional investment to expand into midlevel customers.

    Low-value customers may be increased in profitability or restricted in total investment.

- Incremental investments into acquisitions can be compared to incremental investments in customer retention, and campaigns for customer acquisition or even mass marketing can be planned through subsequent cross-sale, retention, and growth campaigns.
- Understanding the impact of multiple campaigns to the same customer factored into the optimal customer path will help set priorities when multiple campaigns or divisions are targeting the same customer. Synergies can be managed, access to the customer can be prioritized, and unnecessary overlap can be eliminated. Some customers may be designated exclusively for a single customer path, others can exist on multiple paths, and in some cases, multiple paths can be merged to form a new path for a segment of customers.
- The investment required to increase retention rates can be projected. If a 5 percent increase in retention can generate up to 100 percent in profits, the question that needs to be answered is how much is it worth to accomplish this, since it is not likely to happen for free? Where marketing investments are necessary to improve retention, an ROI analysis in the context of Customer Pathing can be very insightful. The key to making marketing investments for retention profitable is identifying those customers that are most vulnerable.

Customer Pathing fits right into CRM initiatives. Multiple customer paths will be developed for specific customer segments. Individual customers can be mapped to the appropriate path based on their profile. This information can be accessible to all customer contact representatives. Knowing that the ideal next marketing activity is, for example, to diversify sales into a new product line and generate a purchase within a specific time period can guide the actions of that representative. The intelligence can flow both ways and information the representative receives directly from the customer may be valuable in shifting the sales strategy from one customer path to another.

Customer Pathing is a sophisticated approach that can become quite extensive and require modeling applications to effectively determine the optimal path for many customer segments across a wide range of marketing programs. It is also a concept that can be manually implemented on a very limited scale for a set of customers or marketing programs.

Managing Budgets

Division leaders have a responsibility for managing budgets to achieve the results expected at the corporate level. In an organization committed to maximizing profits from marketing investments, division managers must manage the budget dynamically and move away from the rigidity of annual budget process and high-pressured budget cuts. This requires constant monitoring of new opportunities and threats to the projected ROI performance of marketing activities. It's not that each downturn in ROI performance should lead to the elimination of that marketing initiative, but with quality ROI tracking, the marketer can assess the financial impact of the performance change and determine if it is worth taking time to adjust the strategy or if temporarily reallocating the budget is justified. The role of the marketing division leader becomes similar to the manager of a financial portfolio. Some situations justify riding out a downturn as long as there is an expectation of improved performance, some situations require terminating the investment to cut losses and others justify increased investment as part of the recovery process.

Each division should establish a process for effectively managing its portfolio of marketing investments. Some considerations for this planning process are as follows:

- How frequently will investments be assessed and reallocated?
- How will adjustments be made when results vary from projections (both for positive and negative variations)?
- What are the less obvious costs of making adjustments, such as personnel, that must be factored into the decision to make changes?

- How can campaign managers be rewarded for giving back funds proactively and working toward total company profits over individual program performance?

Research, Development, and Benchmarking

Just as benchmark measures and research studies can be conducted cost effectively at the corporate level, similar actions can be beneficial at the division level. Under the assumption that a division can manage specific customer segments, some benchmark values should be established at this level. Unique customer behaviors or channels within the division can be benchmarked for use in guiding the Customer Pathing strategies.

Customer Pathing is highly dependent on making short-term decisions to guide long-term treatment that can achieve financial goals. This requires a combination of quality measurements, research into historical and current marketing activities, and modeling to predict future behavior. It is likely that new customers will need to be segmented to match up with the appropriate customer path. Analysis must be conducted to determine which early indicators, such as purchase behaviors, previous contacts, or customer demographics, can be used to prioritize the Customer Pathing strategy.

The division should assess the value of maintaining a set of customers as a global control group to track the performance of the many different combinations of marketing activity relative to a group with no marketing activity. Campaign managers typically can only set up their own control groups.

A portion of the marketing division budget should be allocated specifically for development of new marketing programs. This budget would not be held to the same ROI thresholds. New Customer Pathing strategies can be tested as part of this budget.

CHAPTER 13

MANAGING CAMPAIGN PROFITABILITY

Marketing managers are at the front line of the company, running campaigns and programs that drive sales opportunities and generate profits. These marketers develop strategies and implement campaigns, constantly trying to improve upon results. As companies move toward more effective management of their marketing investments and better profit optimization, marketers will need to understand and leverage ROI tools. All of the success for improving profits at the corporate and division levels depends on the implementation of solid practices with which to measure and improve individual campaign profitability.

At all stages of the marketing campaign development cycle, actions can be taken to integrate the benefits of ROI analysis as outlined in Table 13.1.

Marketers can improve campaign profitability by either increasing returns or decreasing investment costs. The following list details the primary ways to increase ROI if all other variables remain constant.

To increase return:

- Increase the total customer value through a greater share of current spending.
- Increase the total customer value through growth in total spending.
- Increase the sales-conversion rate for profitable customers.
- Increase the average purchase size.
- Increase the margin per sale.

Table 13.1 ROI Actions and ROI Tools That Align with Each Stage of a Marketing Campaign

Stage of Marketing Campaign	ROI Actions	ROI Tools
Preplanning research and intelligence	• What is a new customer, saved customer, or new sale worth? • How much can be spent per targeted prospect?	• Investment limit calculations • Marketing allowable charts
Campaign innovation and assessment	• What campaigns can be developed within the investment limits? • What are the cost projections for each new campaign concept? • How do the strategies alter the assumptions for ROI projections? • Which concepts should be tested based on the likelihood of exceeding the ROI threshold?	• ROI projections • Offer comparison analysis
Market testing	• How can market tests be designed to maximize the learning of strategies? • How will results be measured? What limitations exist on measurements and how can assumptions or benchmark measures be applied? • What indicators can be used to project customer value and campaign results?	• ROI projections
Results analysis	• How does the ROI compare for different campaigns? • How are ROI measures adjusted for different levels of investment? • What campaign strengths and weaknesses are identified through campaign metrics? • What are the ROI measures for independent, incremental, and aggregated results within the campaign?	• ROI analysis
Strategy decisions	• What is the optimal targeting for the campaign rollout? • What is the optimal mix of marketing channels? • As a checkpoint—how do the campaigns impact Customer Pathing strategies?	• Enhancements to marketing mix models • Enhancements to targeting models

- Decrease the Cost of Goods Sold through volume.
- Accelerate the timing of sales.
- Decrease customer defection.
- Increase the referral rate.
- Increase the average incremental customer value of each referral.
- Increase the savings from better customer management and lower cost servicing.
- Maximize Customer Pathing to benefit from the residual value of other campaigns.

To decrease investment:

- Decrease the cost per sale.
- Reduce marketing to nonresponders.
- Reduce marketing to unprofitable prospects.

Effective tracking, reliable testing, and access to quality data will determine how well marketing ROI can be implemented. With an ROI threshold set by executives and the core marketing ROI measures in place, campaign strategies can be optimized through every stage of development.

Marketing Manager Responsibilities

The responsibilities presented at the beginning of Part III for marketing campaign managers are as follows:

- Develop marketing ROI tools such as investment limits and marketing allowable charts for easy reference as a checkpoint in the initial planning stage.
- Streamline campaign innovation by applying ROI projections to compare potential campaigns against performance requirements.
- Design market tests to effectively maximize learning and effectively project profitability of large-scale rollouts.

- Strategically identify the most profitable campaign marketing mix by applying marketing ROI principles within marketing channel optimization modeling.
- Apply marketing ROI principles for results measurements to maximize campaign profitability.
- Strategically set the most profitable target-market profile by applying marketing ROI principles within targeting and marketing mix optimization modeling.
- Coordinate Customer Pathing based on division-level strategies.

Preplanning Research and Intelligence

Prior to developing new marketing strategies and campaigns, marketers will seek intelligence to serve as a foundation for planning. This may include researching customer needs, market trends, and competitive activities. Intelligence from historical marketing activity is valuable in terms of understanding what has worked, what has not, and what actions customers took as a result of previous contacts.

Financial intelligence is necessary in the planning stage as well. Marketing ROI tools can convert basic customer value information into investment limits and marketing allowable charts that serve as parameters for planning. Investment limits define the maximum amount that can be invested per estimated change in customer value and the marketing allowable is used to guide the spending limit per targeted prospect. The use of these values does not substitute for running complete ROI projections but does provide information in a format that is easily referenced.

Investment Limits

All company employees empowered to make customer-investment decisions, from the initial marketing campaign development through to customer service touch points, can benefit from knowing how much a company is willing to invest to achieve certain business objectives. The investment will be based on the expected return. New prospects can be assigned an expected value for customer acquisition that is linked to certain market intelligence. For example, a sales rep interacting with a prospect can identify a specific need or piece of demographic information, which is then translated into an estimated customer value and an associated investment limit.

Existing customers may have a number of investment limits—a *save* value based on the expected future value for retained customers, and other values based on specific sales opportunities or even an improvement in loyalty. These values can then be converted into investment limits using a modified version of the ROI formula.

Investment limits are basically the maximum cost per sale, adjusted to achieve the minimum ROI threshold. The investment limit is based on the projected value at, ideally, an individual customer or at least a customer segment level. Some companies calculate a break-even analysis based strictly on the actual value of a customer or sale, but if an investment generates only enough profit to recover the expense without meeting the minimum ROI threshold, the company loses profits from the underlying cost of using capital resources inefficiently. The investment limit presented here is a more accurate break-even point. The goal is to choose marketing investments that are expected to exceed the investment limit and reject those that are not.

Limits can be set for such sales activities as:

- Investment limit per customer acquisition
- Investment limit per Customer Pathing strategy
- Investment limit per specific sale
- Investment limit per customer save (retained customer)
- Investment limit per customer loyalty improvement

Marketers have most likely set limits for the maximum cost-per-sale or cost-per-customer acquisition in the past; however these may not be tied to a corporate ROI threshold and can either lead to unprofitable decisions or missed profit opportunities. As companies empower customer service representatives to make on-the-spot decisions, such as saving a customer from defecting or extending a special offer, reps can make better decisions by knowing the investment limit per customer.

The investment limits for key activities should be easily accessible by sales and service staff interacting with customers.

Calculating the investment limit is quite simple. It requires the projected net present value of the customer for the specific action (acquisition, sale, save, etc.) and the ROI threshold. Collecting the data to estimate future value is not so simple. Future value projections can be based on customer spending trends, the total customer spending levels (with the company and with competitors), models that identify customer needs, RFM models (based on recency, frequency, and monetary data), product and service profitability, and customer life cycle analysis. It is important to keep in mind that the projected customer value must be all incremental value that comes directly from the marketing investment under consideration.

$$\textbf{Investment Limit} = \frac{\textbf{Projected Incremental Value}}{\textbf{(1 + ROI Threshold)}}$$

The next example is based on a projected value of $1,000 and an ROI threshold of 25 percent.

$$\textbf{Investment Limit} = \frac{\textbf{\$1,000}}{\textbf{(1 + .25)}} = \textbf{\$800}$$

Marketing programs targeted to a customer base that generates an average incremental value of $1,000 must maintain total spending under $800 per sale to achieve the targeted ROI. The investment limits are based on projected values so it is important to confirm that the same assumptions apply to the specific marketing campaign. If a company invests $800 to save a defecting customer, the expectations must be that the retention period will be similar to that used in the initial estimate. For example, a retention program based on an immediate cash payout that saves the customer temporarily should not have the same estimated value as a retention program based on rewarding the customer for long-term loyalty.

Since higher-value customers or transactions will result in higher investment limits, marketing investments should be tiered to align spending with value. An effective campaign with a high cost may not be appropriate for a general population but can be profitable for select customer segments. Campaign strategies can be based on tiered levels of spending so that lower-cost channels (such as direct mail) can be used for customers with lower investment limits, while those same channels are supplemented with additional channels (such as outbound telemarketing) that can be implemented within the higher-level investment limits.

For example, in place of using the average value of $1,000 and investment limit of $800, the customer base can be broken down into quintiles based on value. The investment limit calculations for each customer segment makes it clear that additional spending can go toward generating new business or saving defectors from the higher-value segments.

Customer Segments	Value	Investment Limit
Top 20%	$3,000	$2,400
2nd 20%	$1,200	$ 960
3rd 20%	$ 500	$ 400
4th 20%	$ 250	$ 200
5th 20%	$ 50	$ 40

Strategically, marketers must look closely at how future value is projected. A low-value customer today may either be a high-value customer of tomorrow or be giving the company only a small portion of their total business. These customers may be worth greater investments if the company can factor in their potential value and implement strategies that convert this potential value into actual value.

Investment limits can be a good parameter for general planning purposes; however, marketing managers can get more use from the next level of analysis which establishes a *marketing allowable* per prospect.

Marketing Allowables

A marketing allowable establishes the maximum cost per targeted prospect for a specific campaign objective and market segment. Since the marketing allowable will vary based on the sales conversion rate, this is most useful in the form of charts showing a range of allowables. This planning tool can be more useful than the investment limit when marketers are creating a number of new strategies based on different channels and offers to different segments of the target audience, each with different costs and expected results.

Marketing ROI tools are intended to serve as a quick reference during the planning stage so that many different forms of campaigns can be developed. Take for example two very different campaigns that can meet the investment limit set in the previous example. Assume the prospect base that has a value of $1,000 per customer and an investment limit of $800 per new customer. Marketing to that prospect base can be profitable by spending $160,000 to achieve a 2 percent response (200 new customers) or $320,000 to achieve a 4 percent response (400 new customers). This translates to a marketing allowable of $16 per prospect and $320 per prospect, respectively. Higher investments are expected to achieve higher results. Marketers can build and test strategies at different spending levels.

A shortcut equation can be used to determine the marketing allowable based on the investment limit. It is calculated by multiplying the expected sales-conversion rate by the investment limit. The 2 percent conversion rate would be multiplied by the investment limit of $800 to result in a marketing allowable of $16 per prospect.

Maximum Marketing Allowable = Investment Limit × Expected Conversion Rate

The marketing allowable can be charted relative to the sales-conversion rate to show the possible combinations that meet the minimum ROI. Proving this out with complete formulas would show:

$16 per Prospect × 10,000 Prospects = $160,000 Investment

10,000 Prospects × 2% Sales Conversion rate = 200 Sales

200 Sales × $1,000 Value per Sale = $200,000 NPV Gross Margin

$200,000 Gross Margin − $160,000 Investment = $40,000 Return

$40,000 Return ÷ $160,000 Investment = 25% ROI

For a customer net present value of $1,000 and an ROI threshold of 25 percent, Table 13.2 shows possible combinations between sales conversion rates and marketing allowable amounts.

Marketers can draw upon previous experience and comparable marketing campaigns to determine the feasibility of various combinations of sales-conversion rates and marketing allowables. It may be clear that the range of marketing allowable can be narrowed for this example if the marketing team determines that spending less than $10 per prospect has no chance of generating any significant sales and that generating greater than 4 percent response rate has never been achieved, regardless of marketing investment.

Table 13.2 Marketing Allowable Chart Showing Possible Associated Sales Conversion Rate Values

Sales Conversion Rate	Maximum Marketing Allowable
0.50%	$ 4.00
1.00%	$ 8.00
1.50%	$12.00
2.00%	**$16.00**
2.50%	$20.00
3.00%	$24.00
3.50%	$28.00
4.00%	$32.00
4.50%	$36.00
5.00%	$40.00

Reversing the equation is beneficial when marketers know the cost per prospect for the various campaign strategies developed and need to know the expected sales-conversion rates for each. A minimum sales-conversion rate can be calculated by dividing the cost per prospect (i.e., marketing allowable) by the investment limit.

$$\textbf{Minimum Sales-Conversion Rate} = \frac{\textbf{Cost per Prospect}}{\textbf{Investment Limit}}$$

Table 13.3 shows the minimum conversion rates for three different campaigns developed to meet an $800 investment limit.

The original marketing allowable chart, shown in Table 13.2, can be used to compare the three new campaigns relative to sales conversion rates required at other spending levels (see Table 13.4).

Once again, the marketer applies experience and existing intelligence to eliminate any campaign strategies that are not likely to achieve the minimum sales-conversion rate. Marketing allowable charts can be created to show quick comparisons of the relationship between any two variables within the marketing ROI formula. The previous examples assume customer value will remain constant for the different campaigns

Table 13.3 Example Showing Three Levels of Campaigns, Along with the Associated Cost per Prospect and the Minimum Sales-Conversion Rate

Campaign	Channel/Offer	Cost per Prospect	Minimum Sales-Conversion Rate
Campaign A	Targeted advertising, direct-mail series, low-value premium	$12	$12 ÷ $800 = 1.5%
Campaign B	Targeted advertising, direct-mail series, trade show, high-value premium	$20	$20 ÷ $800 = 2.5%
Campaign C	Mass advertising, direct-mail series, trade show, telemarketing call, high-value premium	$36	$36 ÷ $800 = 4.5%

Table 13.4 Marketing Allowable Chart Showing Conversion Rates Necessary for Each Example Campaign

Marketing Allowable	Minimum Sales-Conversion Rate	
$ 4.00	0.50%	
$ 8.00	1.00%	
$12.00	1.50%	**Campaign A**
$16.00	2.00%	
$20.00	2.50%	**Campaign B**
$24.00	3.00%	
$28.00	3.50%	
$32.00	4.00%	
$36.00	4.50%	**Campaign C**
$40.00	5.00%	

under consideration. A different version of the marketing allowable chart can be created to show a marketing allowable per customer value. An expected sales-conversion rate and the ROI threshold are necessary to establish this chart.

$$\text{Max. Marketing Allowable} = \frac{\text{Customer Value} \times \text{Expected Sales Rate}}{(1 + \text{ROI Threshold})}$$

Based on a targeted sales conversion rate of 2 percent and an ROI threshold of 25 percent, Table 13.5 presents the correlation between customer value and marketing allowable.

Table 13.5 Marketing Allowable Chart Showing Correlation with Customer Value Levels

Value of Customer	Maximum Marketing Allowable
$ 250	$ 4.00
$ 500	$ 8.00
$ 750	$12.00
$1,000	$16.00
$1,250	$20.00
$1,500	$24.00
$1,750	$28.00
$2,000	$32.00

This very simple chart can be used as a quick guide for campaign planning in several different ways. First, campaigns that can generate a 2 percent sales conversion rate but do not meet the ROI threshold may be modified to be more profitable by either increasing the average customer value or decreasing the marketing allowable (while still achieving the same response rate). Next, campaigns can be designed with scaled investments so that customers worth $500 have a campaign based on an $8 marketing allowable and customers worth $1,500 get either additional channels or offers that fall within their $24 marketing allowable.

Multivariable Charts

Taking the marketing allowable concept one step further, the ROI formula can be charted to show the relationship between three variables. Table 13.6 is an example of a marketing allowable chart that identifies the marketing allowable at various sales conversion rates for the entire customer base ranked into 10 segments.

Table 13.6 Marketing Allowable Chart with Three Dimensions: Customer Value, Projected Sales-Conversion Rate, and Marketing Allowable

NPV Customer Value Per Segmented Decile	Marketing Allowable per Prospect Based on Sales Conversion Rate (ROI = 25%)			
	1%	5%	10%	100%
$1,000	$8	$40	$80	$800
$ 850	$7	$34	$68	$680
$ 650	$5	$26	$52	$520
$ 500	$4	$20	$40	$400
$ 375	$3	$15	$30	$300
$ 250	$2	$10	$20	$200
$ 150	$1	$ 6	$12	$120
$ 50	0	$ 2	$ 4	$ 40
$ 5	0	0	0	$ 4
$ −50	n/a	n/a	n/a	n/a

Marketing allowable at 100% sales conversion represents the investment limit.

A marketer would use a chart such as the one shown in Table 13.7 when planning a marketing campaign limited to a budget of $200,000. This chart shows the budget amounts necessary to meet projected combinations of target size and sales conversion rates (also showing the matching marketing allowable). The worksheet is created using an assumption of average customer value and an ROI threshold ($1,000 and 25 percent, respectively, for this example). The total budget spent against the target population size and achieving the appropriate sales conversion rate will exactly achieve the ROI threshold.

This is a simple chart showing that decreasing the campaign size from 10,000 to 8,000 prospects increases the marketing allowable from $20 to $24 but also requires a sales-conversion rate to increase from 2.5 percent to 3.0 percent. If the decrease in the quantity targeted can be done by dropping the least responsive 20 percent of the prospect base, it may be very possible to achieve the increased sales-conversion rate; plus additional spending is possible based on a higher marketing allowable per prospect.

Table 13.7 Chart Showing the Relationship Between Budget, Target Size, Sales Conversion Rate, and Marketing Allowable

Sales Conversion Rate	1.00%	1.50%	2.00%	2.50%	3.00%	3.50%
Marketing Allowable	**$8.00**	**$12.00**	**$16.00**	**$20.00**	**$24.00**	**$28.00**
Target Size 4,000	$32,000	$48,000	$64,000	$80,000	$96,000	$112,000
6,000	$48,000	$72,000	$96,000	$120,000	$144,000	$168,000
8,000	$64,000	$96,000	$128,000	$160,000	$192,000	$224,000
10,000	$80,000	$120,000	$160,000	$200,000	$240,000	$280,000
12,000	$96,000	$144,000	$192,000	$240,000	$288,000	$336,000
14,000	$112,000	$168,000	$224,000	$280,000	$336,000	$392,000
16,000	$128,000	$192,000	$256,000	$320,000	$384,000	$448,000

Modifying the ROI Threshold

The ROI threshold sets the minimum ROI to justify an investment. Where market testing is being done to identify new campaigns that can exceed the performance of a successful campaign already in place, the ROI threshold that must be achieved is that of the existing campaign. The investment limits and marketing allowable charts can be developed by substituting the ROI of the existing campaign in place of the corporate ROI threshold. This sets a minimum level that is required for new campaigns to be considered successful.

Campaign Innovation and Screening

Marketing allowables, investment limits, and planning charts provide quick reference during the development of new campaign strategies. They can also help marketers that are less comfortable with ROI calculations understand the correlation between different variables that go into marketing strategies and tactical plans. These tools are no substitute for using actual ROI projections, especially since the tools are based on the "break-even" levels to achieve minimum ROI while the goal is to optimize ROI for maximum profits.

New marketing strategies and campaign concepts are an essential part of remaining competitive and improving marketing profitability. ROI projections based on available assumptions are the first checkpoint to determine the viability of an investment. The next step is a market test to confirm assumptions with limited expenditures. Market tests are not always possible based on either a limitation of measurement capabilities or the need to take the chance on an immediate full-scale roll-out. Standards should be set for how development and start-up costs should be allocated using the direction provided in Chapter 8. New campaigns do not always achieve full potential in the first attempt so a portion of the marketing budget should be set aside for emerging marketing investments that continue through the testing stage until achieving performance beyond the ROI threshold level.

The assumptions used in ROI projections for each campaign concept should reflect the customer behaviors that are likely for each specific campaign and not based on averages for variables such as customer value or sales conversion rates. For example, a campaign that incorporates strong viral marketing activity may be expected to generate above average value from customer referrals. Or a campaign based on short-term price promotions may be expected to generate less long-term customer value than the average value per customer. Even if all campaigns target the same prospect base with the same product, adjusting the values to reflect the nature of the campaign will result in more accurate projections and better investment decisions.

ROI Projections

The basic ROI equation is used to calculate projections for each campaign concept. Assumptions will need to be based on the intelligence available. Each campaign concept will then have an estimated ROI to allow categorization ranging from high potential to small incremental potential. For campaigns where the assumptions are weak, consider running best-case and worst-case projections in addition to the most likely view.

In the planning phase, decisions are not based on ROI alone. Each company will use its own method for prioritizing the campaigns to be tested. Here are some factors to consider in assessing which concepts to test:

- *Which campaigns have the highest likelihood of exceeding the minimum ROI for rollout?* Even if these do not have the highest ROI potential, those with a better chance for achieving incremental profits should be strongly considered.
- *Which campaigns can potentially generate the highest ROI?* If the concept is valid and the chance for success is reasonable, a big gain can be very valuable to the company.
- *How much budget is available for testing?* The budget limit may require a choice between testing several small concepts and testing very few high-cost concepts.
- *How valid is the testing?* Some marketing concepts will be more difficult to evaluate through a market test. Consider if other forms of research can help confirm or establish assumptions for a rollout.

- *How much can be learned within the market test?* A well-designed market test can lead to results that provide insight across multiple concepts.
- *What is the relative scale to which the campaigns can be launched?* Campaigns that are expected to generate lower ROI (still above the threshold) but can scale to a larger size and generate more profits than other campaigns should be given strong consideration.

Offer Comparison Analysis

Marketing expenses that are directed to prospects are part of the "investment" side of the ROI equation while special offers paid out as part of the sale shows up as a deduction on the "return" side. This creates an interesting dynamic that is worth presenting as part of campaign strategy development.

In the following chart, the special offer pay-out value of $125 in Campaign B was calculated to match the ROI projection of the $2 up-front marketing cost in Campaign A:

	Campaign A	Campaign B
Number of prospects	10,000	10,000
Base marketing expense	$60,000	$60,000
Additional $2 per prospect marketing cost	$20,000	
(Campaign A) $125 discount offer to responders		$0
(Campaign B—no up-front costs)		
Total marketing investment	**$80,000**	**$60,000**
Sales conversion rate	2%	2%
Number of sales	200	200
Customer value ($500 each)		
Sales × Value	$100,000	$100,000
Less discounts		($25,000)
Total gross profit	$100,000	$75,000
Net return (GP − I)	**$20,000**	**$15,000**
ROI	25%	25%

A comparison like this may make it easier to identify how the cost of an additional marketing communication or a small gift (valued at $2 per prospect in this example) can be equivalent in terms of ROI to making a large offer (valued at $125 per responder in this example) if key assumptions are kept constant. Marketers must determine which type of campaign strategy is likely to have a greater impact on the sales conversion rate and incremental customer value. In some cases, a small investment per prospect may be appropriate to build the right level of awareness and understanding necessary to convert better long-term customers. In other situations, the larger offer may be more appealing and generate a greater response. One of the benefits of making the large offer where the cost is limited to purchasers is that there is less investment at risk if the campaign fails to generate any return.

Calculating an offer on the investment side that will generate the same ROI as an offer that is to be deducted on the return side is relatively simple. It can be done by running an ROI projection for one scenario and then using that ROI value to back into the appropriate offer value. Another ROI projection that can be very valuable in the planning process can be developed by defining the two offer amounts and calculating relative sales-conversion rates. If the offer options for the preceding example had been a $2 per prospect up-front investment and a $200 discount offer for buying customers, the campaign with the discount offer would need to generate a 2.5 percent sales conversion rate to match the 25 percent ROI of the up-front offer.

Market Testing

Conducting actual in-market testing of new campaign concepts to a limited segment of the prospect population where incremental profit is measured relative to incremental investment improves the reliability of ROI projections for large-scale campaign rollouts. Qualitative research or opinion surveys can provide insight into campaign potential and can eliminate campaigns likely to flop but very rarely provide the data necessary to choose new campaigns without a market test.

Capturing market test results and estimating the ROI must be done quickly and effectively. The standard marketing ROI calculations to show independent, incremental, and aggregated measurements should be used. The sooner market testing can be completed and more effective campaigns can be implemented, the better for the company. Planning for the market test should identify how customer value will be estimated and how long results will be measured before making decisions. Additional analysis may be required on the results to determine the ROI on the incremental value of certain channels, offers, or target segments. The rollout decision may depend on a full analysis or proceed quickly with an understanding that adjustments will be made later if the analysis leads to a different conclusion than the initial decision.

The different forms of measurement are covered in detail in Chapter 14. Some key practices are relevant to market testing, which will be first mentioned here. The goal is to develop good market test designs that will capture learning to be applied across several campaign concepts without requiring an in-market test for each. For example, learning the incremental value of adding an offer in one creative concept can serve as a benchmark assumption for that same offer in another creative concept. This concept can become quite complex, in which case experimental design known as fractional factorial design can be applied (see "Boosting Your Marketing ROI with Experimental Design" in the October 2001 issue of the *Harvard Business Review* for an excellent overview). The assumptions learned from the market test can be applied to campaign concepts that were not actually market tested as part of the analysis process.

Case Study Brief

The most important aspect of a market test may be how little gets tested. A new company launching a portfolio tracking software product was interested in testing several positioning strategies, several price points, and E-mail marketing channels. Per the customer's request, consulting firm Lenskold Group devised a cost-efficient test structure that would identify the incremental value of each test element without testing every possible combination.

Prior to implementing the full market test, Lenskold Group suggested testing the minimum quantity possible to first determine how well the product could sell. The test included just the high and low price points to 10,000 prospects from a very good E-mail marketing list, randomly split into two groups of 5,000. The test showed that the E-mail marketing could drive traffic to the website, but the website could not effectively convert sales and also had problems with the E-commerce functionality. The comparisons between each test cell did not matter and a large-scale test would have been a waste of money at that time.

The lesson learned: campaigns that have no comparable history based on reaching new markets, offering new products, or being highly innovative in nature can benefit from a multistep testing process that collects basic intelligence that can be applied to subsequent tests.

Results Analysis

Marketers must assess ongoing marketing investments as well as market test results to determine if future campaigns should be added, replaced, modified, or cancelled. In many cases the campaigns are very different in nature. Campaigns developed toward the same objective can be very different in costs required, profit generated, timing of cash flow, and future value to the company. ROI analyses can be run to guide these decisions.

The first segment on the choice between ROI and profits explains how to handle comparisons between campaigns that require different levels of investment, and the second segment breaks down the results analysis process to demonstrate the key principles underlying even the most complex ROI optimization models.

Choosing Between ROI and Profits

Maximizing profits does not always mean choosing the marketing campaign that generates the most profits when different investment levels are involved. It also does not mean that choosing the higher ROI figure will lead to the most profits for the company. As long as an ROI thresh-

old has been set as the criteria for funding additional marketing investments, any two campaigns can be effectively compared.

Campaigns that begin with the same level of investment do not run
into this problem since a higher ROI will also mean a higher profit generated. The issue at hand is how to compare two competing marketing
campaigns when the investment level is different. The following example demonstrates the potential confusion. The marketer must choose
between two campaigns that can reach the same target audience. Both
campaigns exceed the ROI threshold of 25 percent. One campaign generates a higher ROI and the other generates greater profit.

	Campaign A	Campaign B
Marketing investment	$3,000,000	$4,500,000
Prospects	250,000	250,000
Sales-conversion rate	2%	3%
Total sales	$5,000	$7,500
NPV customer value	$900	$825
Gross margin	$4,500,000	**$6,187,500**
Return	$1,500,000	$1,687,500
ROI	**50%**	38%

The easiest way to determine which campaign should receive future
investments is to measure the ROI of the incremental investment
required for Campaign B because one of the decisions available is to
fund Campaign A and place the incremental $1.5 million into another
investment above the ROI threshold.

The following chart shows the incremental investment, return, and
ROI. The ROI of the incremental measure does not represent an investment decision on its own but is used strictly as part of the decision process between these two campaigns. If the ROI in the incremental view
exceeds the ROI threshold, the decision should be to select Campaign
B. If it does not exceed the ROI threshold, the decision should be to
select Campaign A.

	Campaign A	Campaign B	Incremental
Marketing investment	$3,000,000	$4,500,000	$1,500,000
Prospects	250,000	250,000	
Sales-conversion rate	2%	3%	
Total sales	$5,000	$7,500	
NPV customer value	$900	$825	
Gross margin	$4,500,000	$6,187,500	
Return	$1,500,000	$1,687,500	$187,500
ROI	50%	38%	13%

The incremental view shows that the best investment decision is to select Campaign A and place the balance of the $1.5 million budget into another campaign above the ROI threshold. It seems as if the company will forgo the incremental profit of $187,500; however, the $1.5 million invested into alternative campaigns that exceed the 25 percent threshold will net the company at least $375,000, a substantially higher gain. For those companies that do not have alternative investment options, the ROI threshold will still be the benchmark as to which investments should or should not be made.

ROI Analysis for Campaign Comparisons

Standard ROI formulas can be used in market test analysis to determine which promotions and channels can make the campaign most profitable. ROI measurements must be broken down to the smallest incremental investment decisions that can be made. Optimal campaigns are then selected based on ROI measures for the independent (base-level) campaign, each incremental investment (for channels, offers, target, segments, etc.), and the aggregated level (total campaign combined). Multilevel measurements were explained in detail for multicampaign analysis in the previous chapter. The same comparison between campaigns also applies to campaign components.

A marketing campaign is optimized for profitability when each measurable component of the campaign is ranked by the ROI for the incremental investment and selections are made down the list until the last available investment above the threshold is chosen. Some investment decisions will be incremental, others will be mutually exclusive, and others will be dependent on prior decisions.

Campaign Measurement Principles in Step-by-Step Examples

To understand how more advanced ROI comparisons can be made to generate increased profits, the following examples show the key principles in their most basic form. These examples exclude the option to scale the target population level, which will be covered later in this chapter.

Level 1: Basic Comparison. An E-mail campaign is tested with three different promotions. The promotions are mutually exclusive so the decision is to select one of the three to roll out to the target audience. The minimum ROI threshold is 20 percent. At this first level, each has the same cost and the results are as follows:

	Budget (I)	NPV Profit	Net Return	ROI
E-Mail Promotion A	$10,000	$11,500	$1,500	15%
E-Mail Promotion B	$10,000	$13,500	$3,500	35%
E-Mail Promotion C	$10,000	$13,000	$3,000	30%

The clear decision is to choose Promotion B, which exceeds the ROI threshold, achieves the highest ROI, and nets the highest total profit.

Level 2a: Incremental ROI. Promotion B is then tested with and without a bonus offer. The promotion with the bonus offer can only be made in addition to Promotion B and not without it. Based on this dependency, the decision is to choose or reject the addition of the offer.

	Budget (I)	NPV Profit	Net Return	ROI
E-Mail Promotion B	$10,000	$13,500	$3,500	35%
E-Mail Promotion B plus bonus offer	$12,500	$16,250	$3,750	30%

The total ROI of the promotion with the bonus offer does exceed the ROI threshold; however, the decision must be made based strictly on the *incremental* value. The incremental ROI is based on the incremental return relative to the incremental investment.

	Budget (I)	NPV Profit	Net Return	ROI
Incremental ROI	$2,500	$2,750	$250	10%

The incremental investment does not generate enough return to exceed the ROI threshold and is therefore rejected.

Level 2b: Incremental ROI. Promotion C, which was not selected because it achieved a lower ROI than Promotion B, is then tested with and without a bonus offer. For this view only, Promotion B is excluded from the decision and Promotion C is considered to be viable since it exceeds the ROI threshold. The test is to determine the best investment opportunity available using Promotion C. The results will be compared independent of other promotions so the decision is to choose or reject the addition of the offer to the base promotion.

	Budget (I)	NPV Profit	Net Return	ROI
E-Mail Promotion C	$10,000	$13,000	$3,000	30%
E-Mail Promotion C plus bonus offer	$12,500	$16,100	$3,600	29%

Both versions of the promotion exceed the ROI threshold; however, once again the decision must be based on the incremental ROI.

	Budget (I)	NPV Profit	Net Return	ROI
Incremental ROI	$2,500	$3,100	$600	24%

This time the incremental investment generates a return above the ROI threshold so Promotion C plus the bonus offer is accepted and would be selected over the base promotion.

Level 3: Aggregated ROI. E-mail Promotion A, which originally did not meet the ROI threshold, is tested with and without an option to use an 800 number for response in addition to the standard online response. The base investment would not be made on its own so the decision is to choose or reject the aggregated promotion. For this view only, it is assumed that this promotion stands on its own and is not to be compared with results for Promotion B.

	Budget (I)	NPV Profit	Net Return	ROI
E-Mail Promotion A	$10,000	$11,500	$1,500	15%
E-Mail Promotion A plus an 800-number response option	$19,000	$25,000	$6,000	32%

No incremental view is necessary here because that is not part of the decision. The promotion with the 800-number response channel does exceed the ROI threshold, so in this isolated decision without comparison to other promotions, the version of the promotion with the 800 number would be accepted.

Level 4: ROI Comparison of Unbalanced Investments. The new results for Promotions A, B and C must be compared to select the best option between the three. The original Promotion B, which had been the highest performing version of the campaign, must be compared to Promotion A with the 800-number response option and Promotion C with the bonus option. The challenge here is that each promotion requires a different investment than the others so the ROI of each is not enough to make decisions that will maximize profits. Looking at the results, Promotion B still has the highest ROI while Promotion A has the highest net return along with the highest investment requirement.

	Budget (I)	NPV Profit	Net Return	ROI
E-Mail Promotion A plus an 800-number response option	$19,000	$25,000	$6,000	32%
E-Mail Promotion B	$10,000	$13,500	$3,500	35%
E-Mail Promotion C plus bonus offer	$12,500	$16,100	$3,600	29%

As shown in the previous segments, investment decisions can be based on the ROI of the incremental investment required. The decision is between Promotion A and Promotion B. An incremental analysis between the two would show the following:

	Budget (I)	NPV Profit	Net Return	ROI
Incremental Investment to Promotion B	$9,000	$12,500	$2,500	28%

This exceeds the ROI threshold and indicates that Promotion A is the best investment. Incremental analysis can become complex when comparing more than two campaigns. An alternative approach uses the ROI threshold to simplify the analysis that is shown in the next examples.

Profits can only be maximized by comparing the total ROI at equivalent investments levels. Given that incremental investments must exceed the ROI threshold to be accepted, the investment levels can become equal by investing the difference between two options at the ROI threshold level.

This is shown in the following chart for each of the three promotion options. The highest investment level is $19,000 so all promotions are brought up to that level. Once the new comparison is made using equal investments, the highest ROI will also show the highest profit potential.

	Budget (I)	NPV Profit	Net Return	ROI
E-Mail Promotion A plus an 800-number response option	$19,000	$25,000	$6,000	32%
Balance into 20% ROI promotion	$0	$0	$0	20%
Total ROI Potential	**$19,000**	**$25,000**	**$6,000**	**32%**

	Budget (I)	NPV Profit	Net Return	ROI
E-Mail Promotion B	$10,000	$13,500	$3,500	35%
Balance into 20% ROI promotion	$9,000	$10,800	$1,800	20%
Total ROI Potential	**$19,000**	**$24,300**	**$5,300**	**28%**

	Budget (I)	NPV Profit	Net Return	ROI
E-Mail Promotion C plus bonus offer	$12,500	$16,100	$3,600	29%
Balance into 20% ROI promotion	$6,500	$7,800	$1,300	20%
Total ROI Potential	**$19,000**	**$23,900**	**$4,900**	**26%**

This version of Promotion A offers the greatest profit potential in this scenario. On its own, it does not offer the highest ROI but it is clearly the best investment since the additional investment beyond the level of Promotion B is attractive to the company.

Strategic Decisions

The simple scenarios presented in the preceding examples are fine for explaining general concepts, but these do not come close to representing the existing complexity in developing campaign strategies. An incredible number of possible combinations between the multiple marketing channels, offers, target markets, timing, and frequency can make up a campaign. Sophisticated models are one source for managing more complex analyses. For example, Colgate-Palmolive has a promotion optimizer tool and AT&T Consumer Marketing has used marketing mix modeling to simulate combinations of marketing channels and budget levels.[1] The AT&T model was developed through an analysis of historical data on advertising, marketing, and sales results. The optimization process provided direction on the right combination of channels, key messages, and call scripts.[2]

Applying marketing ROI analysis in the modeling process can further add to profitability improvements. The process is fairly straightforward for factoring marketing ROI into the marketing channel selection but a little more complex for modeling the target audience.

Optimizing the Campaign Marketing Mix

Strong marketing campaigns involve multiple contacts through multiple channels and customer touch points. The integration of these various channels creates a synergistic approach to delivering a consistent and cohesive message motivating customers to take a desired action.

Creating an optimal marketing mix for a campaign requires more sophisticated modeling to analyze and project the profit potential for the many different combinations of outbound communications channels, inbound response channels, offers, advertising channel support, and frequency of communications. Many models exist today, but not all will take into consideration the key principles of marketing ROI that have been presented and demonstrated in this chapter. The principles highly relevant to optimization modeling are as follows:

- Capture the independent measure of each channel where there is an option for that channel to stand alone.
- Measure the ROI impact of each incremental investment at the smallest level possible.
- Ensure that additional incremental investments are made until the ROI threshold is reached.
- Scale the audience targeted to the level where investments into each additional customer are expected to exceed the ROI threshold.

The Optimal Point in Targeting

Targeting marketing efforts toward the population that has higher value and a higher likelihood to purchase is considered to have the greatest impact on the success of marketing campaigns. Over and over again companies conducting analysis of their customer base find that the majority of their profits come from a relatively small percentage of their customers. Whether the statistics follow the Pareto Rule of 80 percent of the profits coming from 20 percent of the customers, or some variation of that trend, every company would prefer to spend their marketing where the greatest profit potential exists. As Clancy and Shulman eloquently stated in *The Marketing Revolution*, "the only target that makes sense to go after is one on which the company can make money."[3]

Efforts to improve targeting can range from subjectively choosing certain customer segments over others, to highly sophisticated modeling analysis. In either case, having some intelligence on the profile of more profitable customers is typically used as the basis for targeting new customers.

Many reliable techniques can be used for modeling a customer or prospect database to prioritize the target audience. Where marketing ROI analysis offers the opportunity for significant improvement in this process is in determining the optimal cutoff point for achieving the greatest profits. Companies that are not using ROI in the targeting process are missing profit opportunities by establishing arbitrary cutoff points. Profits are impacted by targeting too few prospects, overspending on a larger target than necessary, or rejecting marketing campaigns that could become more profitable if targeting was applied effectively.

The financial value of targeting comes from both increasing the value generated and decreasing the marketing investment. The increase in value comes as a result of reaching those prospects that will be profitable for the company and cutting out those that will be unprofitable. The marketing investment is decreased by eliminating prospects profiled as unprofitable and also eliminating prospects that are not likely to respond to the marketing, even if they are profiled as high value. The marketer begins with a large potential prospect population and narrows it down to a smaller target population. The result of the targeting process is a smaller marketing investment, which is expected to generate a higher sales response from higher-value customers.

The key question for any targeting or modeling effort is how far should the target be narrowed? Modeling analysis can create a ranked list from best prospects to worst. Marketers use a variety of approaches to establish the cutoff point. A fixed budget means a fixed number of prospects can be reached for a specific campaign, so those will be selected from the top of the list. Some companies determine arbitrarily that the top 20 percent of the prospects is the best selection, others want to match the profile of the most valuable existing customers and will take as many prospects that can match that profile. A recent trend has been to maximize customer lifetime value. There are certainly companies applying a basic ROI analysis or a break-even analysis within the modeling process, both of which can come close to the optimal point of profitability.

The ideal targeting model uses the process of *incremental ROI* measures to identify the targeting level that reaches the ROI threshold. Starting at the top of the prospect list, each additional set of prospects will have an expected value and expected sales conversion rate, which can be used with the incremental marketing expense to calculate an ROI projection. The incremental view must be used for marketing because of the scalability and the fact that variable costs become less as the target size increases. If additional sales can be generated profitably at a fraction of the cost, that is an opportunity to increase profits.

The following is an example of how modeling can be better optimized by setting the cutoff criteria to a corporate ROI threshold. To establish the appropriate corporate environment, assume the company has set a minimum ROI threshold of 25 percent. To demonstrate how profits are impacted by different modeling approaches, the assumption is that the company has only two marketing campaigns—the campaign presented below and one other, call it the generic marketing campaign, which generates exactly 25 percent ROI. The marketing budget of $6.8 million must be placed entirely into some combination of the two campaigns.

The example will be based on a direct marketing acquisition campaign. A market test is done with a random sample drawn from the total population of one million potential customers. The budget to reach one million prospects is estimated and the results of the market test are projected out to the entire population to determine the ROI potential for a campaign rollout.

Prospect base	1,000,000
Marketing budget (investment)	$6,800,000
Sales-conversion rate	3.35%
Customer value (NPV of GM)	$207
Return[4]	$108,000
ROI	1.7%

The untargeted market test is barely profitable and would not be funded without modeling to improve profitability. The cost per prospect increases as the quantity is reduced but the sales conversion rate and the customer value will clearly increase by prioritizing the best prospects.

For purposes of simplifying the example, the modeling output is shown for 10 customer segments. A sophisticated modeling analysis will conduct the analysis at the individual customer level. Taking the approach of modeling customer segments can still result in a precise selection of the targeting cutoff point through a drilling-down process of conducting additional analysis on just the next possible segment. For example, if an analysis results in selecting the top five deciles, the sixth decile can be further analyzed to determine what percent of that decile can also meet the selection criteria.

Table 13.8 shows the results of the modeling process including the expected sales conversion rate, the expected customer value, and the total ROI as each segment is added into the campaign. Incremental ROI is not yet shown.

The first conclusion that can be drawn from the analysis and projections is that the campaign can meet the ROI threshold and be funded once targeting is applied. The incremental analysis can now be conducted to determine the optimal level of targeting (see Table 13.9). Similar to information presented on the incremental value of multichannel campaigns in the previous chapter, the incremental analysis is not relevant until the total ROI exceeds the ROI threshold, so the first two deciles where the high development costs decrease the ROI are not investment options.

As shown in Table 13.9 (see page 204), the incremental ROI exceeds the threshold up through the fifth decile. The sixth decile does not achieve the ROI threshold and would either be excluded from the campaign in total, or further analyzed to determine the exact point within that segment where the ROI approaches the 25 percent threshold. The marketer sets up the rollout campaign targeted to the best 500,000 prospects and requires a budget of $4,480,000 to generate a gross margin of $5,787,000 and a net return of $1,307,000.

Table 13.8 Example ROI Projections Based on Value and Responsiveness Modeling

Segments of 100,000 Prospects Each	MODELING PROJECTIONS		CAMPAIGN PROJECTIONS			
	Expected Sales Conversion Rate	Expected Customer Value (NPV)	Cumulative # of Prospects	Total Gross Margin	Total Investment	Total ROI
Top 10%	5.00%	$300	100,000	$1,500,000	$1,300,000	15%
2nd 10%	4.70%	$280	200,000	$2,816,000	$2,270,000	24%
3rd 10%	4.40%	$260	300,000	$3,960,000	$3,140,000	26%
4th 10%	4.20%	$240	400,000	$4,968,000	$3,830,000	30%
5th 10%	3.90%	$210	500,000	$5,787,000	$4,480,000	29%
6th 10%	3.60%	$170	600,000	$6,399,000	$5,070,000	26%
7th 10%	3.00%	$100	700,000	$6,699,000	$5,600,000	20%
8th 10%	2.20%	$ 70	800,000	$6,853,000	$6,050,000	13%
9th 10%	1.50%	$ 50	900,000	$6,928,000	$6,450,000	7%
Bottom 10%	1.00%	$−10	1,000,000	$6,918,000	$6,800,000	1.7%

Table 13.9 Revised Example of ROI Projections Based on Incremental Investments for Each Decile

MODELING PROJECTIONS

Segments of 100,000 Prospects Each	Expected Sales Conversion Rate	Expected Customer Value (NPV)
Top 10%	5.00%	$300
Top 10%	5.00%	$300
2nd 10%	4.70%	$280
3rd 10%	4.40%	$260
4th 10%	4.20%	$240
5th 10%	3.90%	$210
6th 10%	3.60%	$170
7th 10%	3.00%	$100
8th 10%	2.20%	$ 70
9th 10%	1.50%	$ 50
Bottom 10%	1.00%	$ −10

INCREMENTAL ANALYSIS

Cumulative # of Prospects	Incremental Gross Margin	Incremental Investment	Incr. ROI
100,000	$1,500,000	$1,300,000	15%
100,000	$1,500,000	$1,300,000	N/A
100,000	$1,316,000	$ 970,000	N/A
100,000	$1,144,000	$ 870,000	31%
100,000	$1,008,000	$ 690,000	46%
100,000	$ 819,000	$ 650,000	26%
100,000	$ 612,000	$ 590,000	4%
100,000	$ 300,000	$ 530,000	−43%
100,000	$ 154,000	$ 450,000	−66%
100,000	$ 75,000	$ 400,000	−81%
100,000	$ −10,000	$ 350,000	−103%

In this example, the marketer only has this marketing program and the generic marketing program to choose from. The marketer must optimize the investment available for this campaign that was originally projected to be $6,800,000 prior to the modeling analysis. In addition to presenting the profit impact of using the incremental ROI approach, the profit potential is shown had the model been prioritized to maximize the ROI of the total campaign or to maximize the customer value, which is the equivalent of choosing the top decile.

The investment options (as shown in Table 13.10) are as follows:

- *Maximize profits.* Use the incremental ROI analysis in Table 13.9 to fund each decile above the ROI threshold showed the highest profit potential.
- *Maximize total ROI.* A decision based on the total ROI as shown in Table 13.8 does not fully optimize profits. The cutoff point is at the fourth decile instead of the fifth, which misses a profit opportunity.
- *Assess based on aggregated ROI.* Those companies that do no modeling at all and use only the total ROI for the entire campaign will reject it completely, missing out on profits.
- *Maximize customer value.* Companies that do not use ROI analysis and instead develop models based on customer value alone are taking chances on profitability. The investment into just the top decile was actually below the ROI threshold and should not have been selected.
- *Fully fund without ROI analysis.* Those companies that do not use ROI analysis at all but rely on other metrics such as cost-per-sale, response rates, or break-even analysis are ineffectively using company resources.

The goal is to use incremental ROI measurement across the entire corporate marketing department where the overall net increase in profits can be quite significant.

Customer Pathing Checkpoint

The goal for Customer Pathing is to manage customer profitability by linking together independent campaigns into a single decision wherever

Table 13.10 Investment Options for the Targeting Example Are Shown Along with the Financial Impact of Each

Investment Decision for New Campaign	$ Invested in New Campaign	ROI for New Campaign	$ Invested in Generic Campaign	ROI for Generic Campaign	Total $ Return	Net ROI
Fund incremental ROI above threshold (first 5 deciles)	$4,480,000	29%	$2,320,000	25%	$1,887,000	27.7%
Maximize total campaign ROI (first 4 deciles)	$3,830,000	30%	$2,970,000	25%	$1,880,500	27.6%
Reject based on aggregated ROI (no deciles)	0	0%	$6,800,000	25%	$1,700,000	25.0%
Maximize customer value (first decile only)	$1,300,000	15%	$5,500,000	25%	$1,575,000	23.1%
Fully fund without ROI analysis (all deciles)	$6,800,000	1.6%	0	25%	$108,800	1.6%

the results of one campaign are discovered to be dependent upon other marketing campaigns. Marketing managers must seek a deeper understanding of their results and market test analysis by looking beyond their own campaign. It begins with the question, "what previous activities could have influenced these results?" In addition to other marketing campaigns, previous activities can include external factors related to the customer or the marketplace. For the development of Customer Pathing strategies, the search should be focused on those activities that can be integrated into a larger, multicampaign strategy. Previous activities should be examined for both positive and negative impacts on the campaign's results.

The process for identifying connections between other marketing campaigns and external factors can be done through analysis of the campaign results. The analysis should focus on the differences between segments of the target market based on their behaviors related to the campaign. The analysis may show that prospects making a purchase have recently been in contact from previous campaigns. It's possible that prospects making inquiries, but not purchasing, were less clear about the offer based on receiving fewer previous communications than other prospects.

Looking back at previous contacts to analyze possible impacts on the existing campaign should then be followed by analysis of the existing campaign on future contacts. It is not practical to complete a detailed analysis on every campaign, so this should be done selectively where there is reason to believe an impact might exist. Campaigns that strengthen the relationship with customers or capture valuable intelligence on customer needs, may demonstrate incremental value by comparing the results of future campaigns with a control group.

Identifying these underlying connections can help marketers increase profitability by controlling these campaign dependencies proactively. Synergistic campaigns can be targeted and timed to generate a lift in results. Conflicting campaigns can be avoided by prioritizing and managing communications on a customer or market segment level.

CHAPTER 14

THE MEASUREMENT PROCESS

When you develop respect for the data, when you start getting more organized, when you start really looking at exactly how much things cost and how much profit you are getting as a result of incurring those costs, you become a much better marketer.[1]

SERGIO ZYMAN

There's a saying in business that "you can't manage what you can't measure." Well, the reality is that not everything is measurable and some measurements are either inaccurate or misinterpreted. Even so, measurements are critical to providing business intelligence and, when used in conjunction with the marketing ROI process presented here, have the potential to deliver more profits to the bottom line. Measurements that feed the ROI projections upon which marketing investments will be based are rarely perfect. Measurements need only have a reasonably high degree of accuracy and provide valid insight to have value to the decision-making process. A statement that best fits with the value of digging deeper through measurements and analysis is: *"You can better manage what you can better understand."*

Marketing measures are part of the insight and intelligence that can connect marketing actions and customer behaviors to understanding and decision making. To support *better management* and draw conclusions that support *better understanding*, measurements must have an acceptable level of accuracy, be complete, and be aligned with business goals. Poor quality data, flaws in the measurement formulas, or errors in calculations can make otherwise good decisions into costly ones. Highly accurate measurements that are incorrectly assumed to be complete, or that do not effectively align with business goals, can also lead to poor decisions. For example, companies that evaluate and choose marketing campaigns based totally on comparative cost-per-sale measures lack the ability to capture differences in long-term customer value that is likely to exist. Ignoring long-term customer value leads to decisions that do not maximize profitability. Similarly, decision making is sometimes based on measures that are assumed to correlate with profits, such as increased customer satisfaction or awareness. Most of the time, existing marketing measurements will be directionally in line with an ROI measure and lead to the correct decision—but is *most of the time* good enough when the potential exists to generate more profits from the same marketing budget?

The measurement process of data collection, assumptions, calculations, analysis, and interpretation requires continuous refinement and improvement. It is always important to understand which information can be fully trusted and which information has room for error or subjective interpretation. Where measurements are less reliable or possibly based on outdated data, the marketing team must determine whether gut instinct should override the projections or if further investments are justified to clarify the assumptions. Keep in mind that gut instinct typically is based on a person's history with previous measures, analysis, and logic that is often beneficial in the decision process. Also keep in mind that gut instinct incorporates personal preferences, background, and irrelevant history that may not be appropriate for the decision to be made.

Insight for Smarter Decisions

Measures are focused on past performance, which may be important to determine employee evaluations and compensation, but, for the most part, will benefit the company most when used as insight into future decision making. As access to data is improved and marketing becomes more real time through the use of technology and automated processes, measurements can be used to monitor performance and lead to faster decisions. Instead of waiting for results to be calculated several weeks later, the results-in-progress for a marketing campaign can be used to make strategy and tactical modifications during the campaign instead of just applying postcampaign analysis on future campaigns.

Not all marketing is measurable and not all measurements are complete or precisely accurate. The challenge is to improve accuracy and make the best assumptions possible to enable better decision making. Improvements can come from better measurement practices, increased access to data, more powerful processing power and automated analysis capabilities, and market research studies and predictive models that link known data points to future financial contributions. As marketing strategies evolve, especially with respect to the recent migration toward CRM, the measurements will need to evolve as well.

Some basic principles to follow when planning out measurements:

- *Design measurements for optimal learning.* How will the information provide greater understanding of the actions and behaviors generated by the marketing activity?
- *Invest in measurements intelligently.* How much value can be generated from the insight gained through the measurement research and analysis relative to the cost? If the measurement is strictly for an evaluation of past performance, how much value does that really have to the company?
- *Understand correlations between metrics that can be measured and the actual business goals behind the investment.* How can you link metrics that are indicators with the goals through experimentation, validation research, or benchmark measures?
- *Avoid double counting results.* If a measurement analysis uncovers that a marketing investment has contributed to a financial return through some other sales channel, can you confirm that this return was not counted elsewhere? Is there a need to establish an offsetting deduction from another marketing investment that was originally assumed to generate that return?
- *Design the measurement to optimize future predictability.* Is the analysis objective enough that results are replicable and not over-

stated? Are there any hidden costs that must be factored into the next projection? Is there any value that should be attributed to a different marketing investment?

Using measures of existing campaigns to predict future performance is effective when setting up a small-scale test market prior to launching the full marketing initiative on a large scale, or for ongoing marketing programs that are repeated based on trigger events such as customers moving households or first-time buyers. The ROI measured on this completed marketing test then becomes the basis for the ROI projection for identical marketing investments. Even a clear-cut direct measure of actual results is subject to error when used as a projection. The accuracy of the ROI projection is dependent on reaching a similar target market with the same offer, through the same channels. If the marketing initiative is not identical, adjustments must be made.

The effects of time on a repeated marketing effort can be difficult to predict. Seasonality and economic trends may be known or easily assumed and should require adjustments to the assumptions. Other time-oriented factors such as shifts in market needs, changes in competitive activity, unusual market conditions, or a company PR crisis can interfere with a market test or cause a marketing initiative underway to miss its target. Projections should always be based on the best estimate of the conditions expected for the time period in which the income stream will occur.

Marketing ROI measures are dependent on the ability to track actual behaviors and to predict future behaviors. Companies that have a direct relationship with each customer have the advantage of connecting the prospects from the campaign with first-time buyers. Those without direct relationships, such as companies that rely on cash sales driven through retail outlets or intermediary companies that hold the customer relationship, are much more difficult to track. Controlled test markets can be used to compare the change in sales for markets with marketing treatment relative to those without the same marketing treatment. Market research of customer attitudes or intentions may be justified in some situations; however, the ability to rely on customer perceptions to link actual actions with marketing campaigns must be based on proven methodologies. Other marketing activities that can assist in tracking include rebates direct to the company, product registrations, or service inquiries. These activities do not provide a complete picture but, with the appropriate analysis, can be used as a factor to estimate sales levels.

Predictive capabilities are necessary whenever customer value is partially based on a future stream of sales activities. Marketing ROI has the added benefit of guiding investments toward marketing campaigns that are more effective at generating high-value customers instead of assuming all new customers are of an equal value. Marketers cannot wait for the actual customer value to be measured, so understanding how initial behaviors and intelligence can be used to predict future value will make the ROI measures more accurate. Information such as initial purchase amount, purchase type, demographic profiles, or key questions asked during the sales process can be used in modeling and analysis to serve as indicators of future value.

Types of Measurement Processes

There are a number of techniques that are used to measure marketing efforts and analyze data for the purpose of developing more accurate ROI projections to compare and select the best marketing investment opportunities. Each technique has its advantages and limitations. The ability to apply certain techniques will vary based on the industry, nature of the business model, and access to customer data.

Measurements for ROI projections will primarily be necessary to predict the gross margin component of the return since the investment will be known or estimated with reasonable reliability. Gross margin is driven by incremental customer value so the measurement analysis typically must focus on capturing changes in customer behaviors and predicting future behaviors. The following techniques can be used to capture the customer value data points that feed into ROI projections. (See also Figure 14.1.):

- Direct measurement
- Controlled testing
    Test vs. control
    Pre/post analysis
    Experimental design
- Benchmarking assumptions
    Data mining and modeling
    Performance indicators as profit drivers
    Market research
- Assumed impact
    Inferred response
    Break-even analysis

Many books and articles have been written describing research and measurement methodologies. Only the highlights of some key measurement techniques will be presented here.

Figure 14.1 Reliability Levels of Measurement Approaches

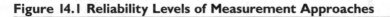

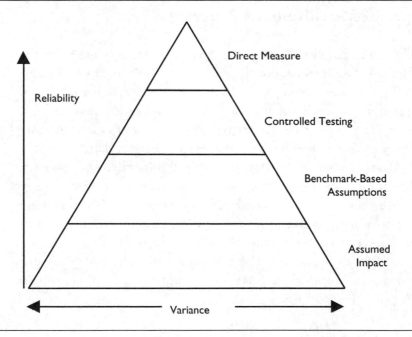

Direct Measure

A direct measure is the simplest and generally the most accurate because it captures results that are clearly generated by the marketing activity being measured. The purest example would be a new product from a new company that is offered exclusively through a single-channel promotion since absolutely all of the profit generated for that product can be attributed to the one investment. Other internal measures such as marketing expenses, cost of goods, and cost savings are also possible to measure directly.

Controlled Testing

Marketers often rely on controlled test environments that can isolate the incremental impact of a marketing campaign or variables within the campaign. Three types of controlled testing are used quite often—test vs. control, pre/post analysis, and experimental design.

The classic testing technique based on comparing the results of a test group to those of a control group has long been used for marketing measures. When designed appropriately, the test versus control experiment is one of the most accurate measures to capture the impact of a marketing activity relative to what would have occurred without the marketing activity. The test group receives the marketing treatment and the control group receives either no treatment or a treatment considered to be a base level for comparison. This measurement approach can be used to determine the value of a particular variable within a marketing initiative, such as an offer, an incremental marketing channel, or even an envelope teaser on a direct mail package.

The test design is set up by providing a portion of an audience group with the marketing treatments to be measured (test groups) and selecting another portion of the group to receive standard treatment strictly for tracking purposes (control group).

Following is an example of a basic test design that would capture the incremental value of the direct mail program (test group A compared to the control group), the incremental value of telemarketing support (test group B compared to test group A), and the incremental value of an incentive offer (test group C compared to test group B).

Group	Quantity	Treatment
Test group A	500	Direct mail
Test group B	500	Direct mail with telemarketing support
Test group C	500	Direct mail with telemarketing plus incentive offer
Control group	500	No offer (no exposure to print ad)

It is important to note that the control group must be valid and reliable. This group must be identical to the test groups with the expectation that there would be no difference in results if the test and control groups were switched. The test must be controlled to be predictive. Trying to establish a control group after a marketing campaign using "natural" control groups, such as those that recall an advertisement compared to those that do recall an advertisement is not valid since the groups cannot be considered identical.

Using pre/post analysis is not as accurate as the test versus control design. In this analysis, measurements are made, the marketing activity is completed, and then measurements are made again. The assumption is that the difference in customer behaviors and financial value are attributed to the marketing activity. This may work in environments where sales are steady or can be predicted with a high degree of accuracy. The lack of a control group means it is very possible that external factors can influence the change in results, decreasing the reliability of the test.

Experimental design is much more sophisticated than either of the other two controlled test measurements presented here. Eric Almquist and Gordon Wyner of Mercer Management Consulting present one form of experimental design referred to as fractional factorial design in a *Harvard Business Review* article. They eloquently describe the advantages this technique has for measuring the impact of many possible combinations of marketing variables in a cost-effective design that does not require each combination to be tested.[2] An experimental design that measures variables such as price, channel mix, offers, and different investment levels can be used to provide the data necessary to complete very sophisticated ROI analysis, helping companies to optimize the profit potential within a customer segment.

Benchmark-Based Assumptions

The cost of measuring or researching every change in customer behavior can be reduced where it is reasonable to assume common outcomes will result from common marketing activities. Companies can measure these outcomes and establish benchmark values to be used as assumptions in the ROI measurements and projections. The incremental value of an online response option, a follow-up customer service call, or personalization of all communications are examples of the types of marketing initiatives that can be measured periodically and used as benchmarks. Customer value can be measured and tracked back to profile information to serve as benchmarks for future ROI analysis. Benchmark values can also be based on external measures such as the behaviors of competitors' customers or measurements made in other industries that can be assumed to be comparable. Gupta and Lehmann published an article in which they used a benchmark value, referred to as the "margin multiplier," to calculate customer lifetime value based on the annual profit margin of a customer. They claim this multiplier typically ranges between one and five.[3]

The danger with any benchmark is the possibility of missing a sudden change in actual behavior, which results in a miscalculation of ROI that goes unnoticed until further analysis is conducted. Benchmarking is a more accurate "rule of thumb" that must be constantly updated. The potential impact of an inaccurate benchmark value should be known to determine the risk involved. In some cases, additional validation of the results will be justified prior to making significant investments based on the results in question.

Some methods used to establish benchmark values include data mining, market research, predictive modeling, and performance indicators. Data mining is regularly used to establish benchmark values. With data mining, the analysis is completed using historical data to identify where correlations exist between the data points. This is different from controlled tests where the variables being tested are known in advance.

Modeling involves analyzing historical data to identify which variables were responsible for driving certain results. Sophisticated models are used to predict outcomes based on changing the values used in the key variables. Relying on historical data to guide decisions on future actions can be risky. Martha Rogers of the Peppers & Rogers Group suggests that modeling based on historical data can lack relevance to the future needs of customers. She suggests taking the predictive analysis that the model produces and sharing that information with employees that have frontline access to customers. Sales staff and customer service representatives are in a position to provide valuable insight based on their firsthand experience and understanding of customer needs. This input can be used to modify the model and the decisions that are made.[4] The same process can be applied to modeling that projects future customer value for use in ROI analyses. The insight that experts can share into how future behaviors will differ from past behaviors should be applied to adjust benchmark values derived through modeling. It is valuable to continually validate assumptions from the modeling and the adjustments made by individuals. This validation process will not only correct inaccurate assumptions, but also guide the future use of subjective insight to adjust modeling output.

Quantitative market research with existing and prospective customers can be used in the process of establishing benchmark values. Research can be used to collect attitudes and self-reported actions or intentions. Correlating this information with actual behaviors is difficult but not entirely impossible. The challenge is identifying a calculation that can consistently convert self-reported actions or intentions into actual behavior. Once a reliable conversion is established, market research can be used as an early predictor of future behavior and value.

Performance-based metrics can also be used to feed assumptions in the ROI calculation. Certain performance metrics will act as profit drivers when a direct correlation is established between the metric and actual profits. These measures, such as increase in online registrations or enrollment in a customer loyalty program, can be used to calculate an interim measure of customer value.

Assumed Impact

For situations where tracking may not be possible there are several alternative methods for estimating the value used in ROI calculations. Take for example measurement of a marketing campaign that has multiple response channels and is placed in the market along with a number of other campaigns promoting the same products. Tracking mechanisms, such as including a promotion code in a mailing, do not always get captured during the sales process and this impacts the results measures. According to Tom Hannigan, a senior consultant at the CRM firm Chatham Systems Group (chathamsystems.com), "inferred response" can be used to capture lost sales. Using inferred responses involves matching customer sales information to either an original marketing list or a recent action, such as a website visit (when tracked to the specific customer level) or phone call. The process to connect an action in the sales process with the actual sale is based on carefully defined rules and is automated in certain campaign management software applications.[5] Of course, identifying a sale that belongs with a specific campaign ROI measure means that the same sale cannot be counted in the ROI of a separate campaign or channel measure.

For some marketing investments, not enough information will be available to calculate an exact ROI measurement. In this situation, a break-even analysis can be completed using the information available to determine what results are needed to achieve the minimum ROI threshold. While it is not always possible, and certainly risky, in some cases there is enough rationale, based on experience and intuition, to assume with confidence that the marketing investment resulted in more than enough impact to exceed the minimum ROI. This provides the marketing organization with a decision to proceed but does not give a relative ROI value that may be necessary when investments must be prioritized.

Data Integrity

Quality, reliability, and accessibility to the right data are essential to make marketing ROI possible. Companies often underestimate the data quality issues that exist in their company. Many customer data problems were uncovered when implementing CRM systems. As Tom Hannigan and Christina Palendrano describe in their article, "How Reliable is Your Enterprise Data," "Companies have invested millions of dollars

The Need for Key Metrics at Dendrite International

Companies with long sales cycles and low-volume or high-value sales must contend with additional measurement challenges. To manage marketing investments, performance metrics other than closed sales and profits are necessary. Dendrite International, a provider of CRM technology serving the pharmaceutical industry, began a significant marketing and advertising campaign in 2001. The financial impact of the ongoing campaign would not be known for at least six to twelve months, yet marketing investments had to continue. David Bonthrone, vice president of marketing for the company, established comprehensive tracking mechanisms to monitor key performance metrics. This included tracking inbound calls and faxes, website visits, website registrations, and customer perceptions pre- and post-campaign. The impact of the campaign was significant enough to show measurable improvements in not only awareness and perceptions, but also lead generation. The sales pipeline was being filled with qualified leads that had high potential to generate a very healthy ROI. This information based on multiple performance metrics was enough to extend the campaign with additional marketing investments while continued tracking would either demonstrate the actual ROI, or identify the barriers between lead generation and closed sales.[6]

into CRM solutions only to find that the systems could not deliver on the strategy due to issues with data." They go on to discuss how corporate data typically comes from multiple sources and that the quality will be perceived differently by different people based on their intended use.[7]

Sales results, customer value, and gross margin information will be faced with the same data reliability challenges as the CRM initiatives. Technologies such as the CMX product, offered by Delos Technologies (delostechnologies.com), are now very sophisticated resources to help companies manage data reliability on an ongoing basis. A centralized repository of quality data offers consistency in measurements across the organization plus access to customer and profitability information for planning, modeling, targeting, and measuring.

CHAPTER 15

STRATEGIC PROFIT MANAGEMENT

Corporate budgeting is a joke, and everyone knows it. It consumes a huge amount of executives' time, forcing them into endless rounds of dull meetings and tense negotiations. It encourages managers to lie and cheat, lowballing targets and inflating results, and it penalizes them for telling the truth.[1]

MICHAEL C. JENSEN

P ut marketing ROI fully into place across the marketing organization and you'll create a whole new process for strategically managing profits. It all comes down to better information driving better decisions. Clarity in understanding ROI potential at the campaign level flows up to customer profitability and spreads across the organization to allow executive-level control.

Take a utopian view of the marketing organization for a moment to picture the possibilities that exist when the right ROI information is captured, analyzed, projected, and rolled up into a powerful management application. Your marketing budget can now be managed like an investment portfolio and executives can be equipped with a powerful control panel. It does not take a utopian environment to make marketing ROI practices worthwhile—each improvement can lead to immediate and incremental profits. This chapter covers some investment strategies that can be applied to specific customer segments, key strategies for maximizing customer profitability, guidance for managing the marketing investment portfolio, and a vision for the executive control panel.

Customer Segment Investment Strategies

Marketing profits are driven by the effectiveness of the marketing effort on changing purchase behaviors and the value generated from the customer. When information on propensity to respond to marketing initiatives or incremental value can be reasonably predicted, investment strategies can be applied to improve profitability. Propensity to respond to marketing offers will depend on understanding customer needs and the customer's current level of loyalty.

The Experience Mindset

Customers' likelihood to purchase will be based on their mind-set established through their experience with both your brand and competitive brands, which can be shown on a loyalty scale (see Figure 15.1). Loyalty levels have significant impact on retention and acquisition marketing. Table 15.1 shows a profile and investment strategy for each seg-

Figure 15.1 Loyalty Segments

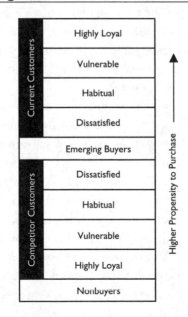

Table 15.1 Investment Strategies Shown for Customer Segments Based on Loyalty Scale

Current Customers (Retention Targets)	Investment Strategy
Highly loyal: This segment does not consider competitors as viable alternatives and will continue as a customer until a significant event causes them to shift to another segment.	**Minimally invest in retention marketing;** ensure product, service, and experience sustain loyalty; continuously learn of customer needs to strengthen competitive barriers; cross-sell to meet needs.
Vulnerables: This segment has a clear preference to continue as a customer but is susceptible to competitive offers.	**Highest priority for retention investments;** build greater loyalty; create barriers to exit by demonstrating strength of existing relationships.
Habitual: This segment of customers do not place high importance on the product/service category and make low involvement decisions. Brand preference is out of convenience as much as preference and their purchases are subject to impulse and offers.	**Limit marketing investments to short-term profit gains or long-term purchase commitments** since lifetime value will be limited and price/offers will restrict profit potential; create relevant differentiators to shift perceptions; create purchases that lock out competitors (bulk purchases, contracts).
Dissatisfied: This segment will defect with minimal effort based on a preference against the brand.	**Minimize further marketing investment;** minimize migration of other customers into this category.

Noncustomers (Acquisition Targets)	Investment Strategy
Emerging buyers: This segment is currently not purchasing within the product/service category.	**Highest priority for acquisition marketing;** learn needs and preferences to migrate toward loyalty.

Competitor Customers (Acquisition Targets)	Investment Strategy
Dissatisfied: This segment can easily be won away from competitors and may have the potential to become loyal.	**Limited investment should be required** since the prospect is ready to defect from the competitor; understanding defection reasons will indicate customer preferences.
Habitual: This segment of customers is very similar to habitual current customers and may in fact overlap, as purchase behavior shows constant switching between competing offers.	**Limit marketing investments to short-term profit gains or long-term purchase commitments** to minimize competitive purchases.

(continued)

Table 15.1 Investment Strategies Shown for Customer Segments Based on Loyalty Scale (continued)

Vulnerable: This segment will continue to purchase with competitors until won over through marketing.	**High priority for investments into acquisition marketing** based on the likelihood of long lifetime value; a positive experience is needed to reinforce the initial decision to switch; learning customer needs and preferences is essential to matching the knowledge of their previous relationship, and acting on that knowledge is necessary to retain the customer and establish new competitive barriers.
Highly Loyal: This segment is not likely to alter purchase decisions without a very disruptive event.	**Minimally invest in acquisition marketing investments;** use research to identify potential weak areas of the existing relationship.
Noncustomers (Nontargets)	**Investment Strategy**
Nonbuyers: This segment does not purchase within the product/service category.	**Avoid any marketing investments.**

ment, assuming customers have already been modeled into equal value segments.

In some situations, it will be possible to target these segments based on intelligence on customer behaviors and preferences through data collection or predictive modeling. In other situations, behaviors that indicate which segments are responding to certain marketing investments will not be known until after the marketing campaigns are completed. This is still important information to track because it can identify the types of offers that appeal to each segment. It has long been believed that short-term, price-oriented offers cannot deliver a positive ROI based on attracting customers that would be categorized as "habitual" in this segmentation.

Customer Value

In a very informative interview, Martha Rogers shared her insights on the topic of strategic value, a term introduced in the book *Enterprise*

One to One. Strategic value does not show up in ROI measurements since it represents the potential value of a customer instead of the actual value. It should, however, be a key factor guiding marketing investments, especially for retention marketing initiatives. Marketing designed to tap into the strategic value of customers has the potential to generate incremental profits by changing the actual lifetime value of a customer.

Figure 15.2 is a visual representation of strategic and actual value developed by Peppers & Rogers Group. A company that relies strictly on its own internal data to create customer value segments can easily be misguiding marketing investments by pushing out customers with low actual value but high strategic value right at the time when the company may be well poised to further extend a very positive relationship. Strategic value can consist of competitive business, behavior changes that would change customer profitability, and customer growth. Predicting strategic value through the collection of customer intelligence or modeling provides additional insight into better knowing your cus-

Figure 15.2 Customer Strategic and Actual Value Paths

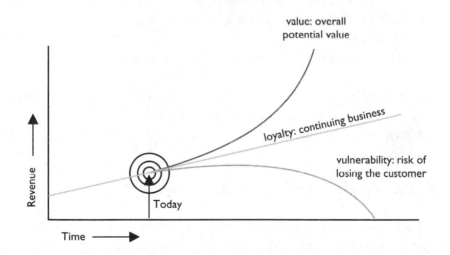

tomers.[2] The ROI analysis will be influenced by the increased customer value potential that results from targeting based on strategic value in place of actual value, allowing for higher investment limits.

The use of strategic value fits well with Customer Pathing strategies, just as it does with CRM initiatives. The steps necessary to maximize customer profitability through Customer Pathing are as follows:

- Collect customer intelligence to understand and model future needs.
- Assess the effectiveness and interdependencies of existing marketing campaigns for customer acquisition, retention, and cross-selling that can boost aggregated ROI.
- Identify optimal strategic customer paths consisting of offers, relationship building, and marketing contacts that can be presented to customers over their lifetime.
- Using predicted customer needs and strategic value, map each customer to a number of possible paths.
- Set a priority list of possible next sales or interaction steps for each customer.
- Identify additional intelligence that can be used to continuously refine the Customer Pathing strategies.
- Establish investment limits for each possible next sale or interaction.
- Monitor and adjust assumptions and strategies as needed.

Customer Pathing represents the profit perspective of managing customer relationships. It is a new concept that will evolve as it is applied to marketing or CRM initiatives.

Managing the Marketing Investment Portfolio

Treating marketing campaigns as investments with expectations for generating positive returns makes it possible to manage the entire marketing budget as an investment portfolio. Maximizing long-term profits requires more than just funding marketing investments above the ROI threshold. In the mix of possible marketing investments, there will be some campaigns that are based on solid historical performance that are highly likely to succeed and others with high ROI potential based on risky assumptions. Investments must also be made into developing and testing innovative campaigns that will eventually achieve ROI thresholds.

Figure 15.3 shows the investment portfolio categories based on the profitability (projected ROI) and the confidence in achieving the profit projections. Further definition of each category shown in the figure is presented here.

- **Reliable investments.** Marketing investments into ongoing campaigns that achieve fairly consistent results, or those based on highly reliable data, fit into this category. A strong investment portfolio must have a good portion of the investments allocated into this category.
- **Emerging investments.** Those marketing campaigns that have not achieved the ROI threshold in the past but are believed to have high potential if results can be improved with further development belong in this category. Campaigns that just miss the ROI threshold should be carefully assessed to determine if further investment on a limited scale should be made.
- **High-potential investments.** Unproven marketing campaigns that are projected to achieve high ROI are also an important part of the investment mix. It can be expected that a portion of these campaigns will miss their projected ROI. As these campaigns are implemented, those that can be repeated will either move to the *reliable investments* category if they prove to exceed the ROI threshold, move to the *emerging investments* category if additional development is needed, or be dropped if unable to achieve the ROI threshold. Some high-potential investments will be one-time opportunities that require significant investments, such as a high-level corporate sponsorship or a major website enhancement.
- **Innovation investments.** A portion of the marketing budget needs to be set aside strictly for innovating new campaigns. This may involve investments into research, market testing, and high development costs that cannot achieve a return on investment. Much like

Figure 15.3 Investment Portfolio Categories

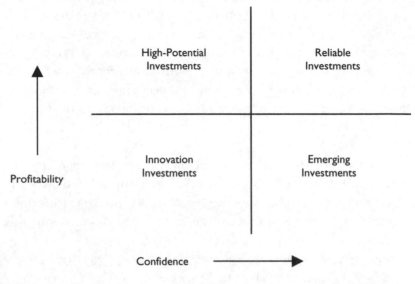

Note: The horizontal line represents the cutoff above which marketing investments are funded (ideally the ROI threshold). The vertical line is the split between campaigns with previously measured ROI vs. those with projected ROI.

R&D budgets, the investment into innovation must be set so that over the long term, a few new marketing initiatives prove to be highly successful in generating enough returns to exceed the total investments.

Two other categories can be overlaid into this view of the investment portfolio. Figure 15.4 shows the addition of *pending investments* just below the horizontal cutoff for funded investments and *long-term brand investments* just above that cutoff.

- *Long-term brand investments.* Marketing investments determined to have a long-term benefit to the brand that cannot be aggregated with other marketing campaigns or measured in terms of direct contribution to profits, will need to be managed as part of the marketing investment mix. In terms of profit management, the expense

Figure I5.4 Enhanced Investment Portfolio Categories

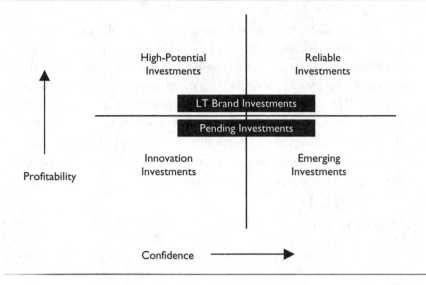

should be captured in other campaigns either as an allocated expense or a part of the cost of goods.

- **Pending investments.** This applies only to companies that cannot fund potentially profitable investments based on budget constraints. Between the cutoff point for funding and the ROI threshold that represents true profitability will be campaigns that should be considered as pending investments. In the event of a major shift in ROI assumptions, campaign performance, corporate strategy, or budget availability, these campaigns may be brought into the investment mix.

Clearly, managing the investment portfolio is necessary to ensure that the process of ranking ROI for setting budgets does not result in investments that are all in the *high-potential investments* category. The high risk of these types of investments must be balanced with campaigns that fall into the *reliable investments* category. Also, strict adherence to the ROI threshold does not allow for opportunities to develop through a learning process, justifying the need for an emerging investment category. *Innovation investments* are held out of the ROI process altogether, but managed as a portion of the overall marketing budget that must demonstrate a contribution to profits under similar expectations as an R&D department.

Just as individual investors each manage their portfolio mix very differently, so will marketing organizations. More aggressive, risk-taking companies will allocate a greater portion of their investments into the *high-potential investments* category than more conservative firms. Companies in stable market environments that operate in a fairly routine manner will have less of a need for innovation investments than companies in highly dynamic environments. Budget-restricted companies and low-margin companies will invest heavily in *reliable investments* until increased profits provide more flexibility.

Cash Flow Overlay

In addition to managing risk and long-term development within marketing investments, companies need to manage cash flow. The optimal profit point generated from marketing investments may not work if the profits are all received far in the future or very sporadically. The ability for the company to access additional funds to manage cash flow will have some limitations and reach a point where the cost of borrowing becomes excessive. Public companies must demonstrate a level of stability in revenues and profits along with consistent growth to maintain investor confidence.

In order to balance long-term profits with cash flow needs, the following actions should be considered:

- Determine the ability to shift the timing of marketing campaigns without impacting profit projections.
- Set parameters as overlays to the ROI process such as maximum budget available per time period or minimum profits generated per period. The reprioritization of marketing investments can be optimized through modeling.

When it is necessary to override decisions to maximize profits with other business priorities, the opportunity cost of lost profits should be calculated and assessed relative to the benefit. Information on profits sacrificed for other short-term objectives may motivate and guide alternative actions.

The Marketing ROI Control Panel

In an ideal world where marketing ROI can be fully implemented with quality information and highly automated processes, executive management will have access to key data points with the ability to manipulate alternative scenarios. Executives should be positioned to quickly assess new situations and make critical decisions related to the investment levels into, and profits out of, marketing communications. Even partially implemented marketing ROI systems can benefit from the control panel described here.

The information presented in the executive control panel would fall into the categories of projections, performance results, criteria and assumptions, external and internal metrics, strategic progress, and market intelligence. All high-level statistics would have drill-down capabilities to provide greater insight as needed. The values used in the ROI projections and the ROI formula, standardized across the organization at the corporate level, would be easily adjusted either for analysis purposes or to initiate global changes across the organization.

Projections
- Total budgeted marketing communications investment
- Total projected profits and ROI
     NPV view
     Cash flow view
- Drill down to campaign-level projections and ranking
- Drill down into customer segment projections
- Drill down into product segment projections

Performance Results
- Actual marketing communications investment relative to budget year-to-date (YTD)

- Actual profit, projected profits, and ROI relative to projections YTD
    - NPV view
    - Cash flow view
- Drill down to campaign-level actual vs. projections
- Drill down into customer segment actual vs. projections
- Drill down into product segment actual vs. projections

Criteria and Assumptions Driving ROI Calculations
- Base-level discount rate
- ROI threshold
- Customer value assumptions
- Corporatewide benchmark values
- Expense allocation procedures

External and Internal Metrics
- Loyalty measures
- Customer activity metrics
    - Sales inquiries
    - Website visits
    - Program registrations or participation
- Brand image trends
- Competitive performance metrics and trends
- Industrywide trends
- Financial market trends

Strategic Progress
- Progression on customer path
    - Shown by customer value segment
- Customer loyalty trends
- Share of customer spend
- Trends in total customer spend

Market Intelligence
- Improvements in customer-level data collection

Each company will develop its own version of a control panel and then offer customized views based on individual executive responsibilities. This improved access to financially and strategically focused sales and marketing information is a key component to better management of marketing profitability. The role of marketers in motivating customer behavior needs to be driven more toward the profit objectives of the company, which can be guided by executive input into the ROI calculations. The role of the CEO, CFO, and key executives in making decisions about budget allocations needs to be based on better insight into the profit impact, which can be guided by real-time marketer maintenance of campaign and customer profit projections.

Managing Profitability

Business and market conditions are in constant change, requiring senior executives to monitor and adjust the company's direction with precision and speed. In large corporations, making adjustments with precision and speed—especially in crisis situations—is no simple task.

Using consistent ROI formulas, calculating ROI at very small incremental investments, and providing access to current performance measures and projections will position executives to assess and implement strategic shifts in response to business threats or opportunities. Consider the following possibilities:

- *Change in priority of short-term profits.* When companies are under pressure to increase short-term profits, marketing investments can be reprioritized by increasing the discount rate for future profits. The discount rate does not need to be constant for each period and can be adjusted on an annual, quarterly, or even a monthly level depending upon how future profits need to be valued relative to immediate profits. The revised ROI projections for marketing investments will provide insight into where additional investment can be made or where budgets can be trimmed. Conversely, in the event the company is under less pressure for short-term profits, the discount rate can be set closer to the cost of capital to maximize long-term profits.

- **Change in the cost of capital.** As the company's cost of capital increases or decreases significantly, the ability to fund marketing investments may need to be changed. A change to the ROI threshold instantly establishes a new funding level for marketing investments.
- **Change in budget availability.** A cut in the marketing budget can be done with the least impact on profits by eliminating the lowest performing marketing campaigns. In a full view of the marketing investment portfolio, considerations can also be made in terms of cutting back on investments into emerging campaigns. Increases in budget availability will go to pending campaigns above the ROI threshold, which will only be possible if the company does not already use the ROI threshold to set funding levels. Increases in budget can also be used to fund an increase in additional strategic development.
- **Change in competitive threat.** A new competitive threat that is expected to decrease the performance for certain marketing activities can be quickly assessed to reprioritize investments. The threat may be limited to a product line or customer segment. Those marketing investments that no longer meet the ROI threshold can be suspended, scaled back, or considered as "emerging" investments while new strategies are tested to combat the competitive impact.
- **Change in customer value.** Large-scale changes in customer value that are not specific to individual investments can be applied at a corporate level to reprioritize marketing investments. The change in value may result from new pricing, adjusted cost of goods, or new methods of allocating expenses. Changes in value for specific customer segments will impact how investments are selected.
- **Changes in marketing effectiveness.** While this will primarily be adjusted at the campaign level, planning for overall changes in converting sales may be necessary when dictated by economic, regulatory, or general market conditions.
- **Change in channel profitability.** When select marketing channels change in either cost or effectiveness, this can be reflected across the organization to determine the necessity to reallocate the budget. For example, postage increases impact primarily the direct-mail channel and changes to regulations on outbound telemarketing may impact effectiveness of only that channel.

The shift to instill greater accountability for investments within the marketing organization is of benefit to executives, shareholders, employees, and even the marketing organization. There is no shame in managing a business toward greater profits. The financial resources available to a company must be put to good use and the budget provided to the marketing organization is intended to drive profitable sales. Increased brand image, awareness, satisfaction, and loyalty for both customers and employees, are all essential to achieve profit goals but mean little when a correlation to profits does not exist. Yes, there are gaps in measurement capabilities that must be understood and managed. Marketers must embrace financial measurements and accountability to establish a firm commitment to improvement in both the process and results. Growth in profits should lead to greater company value, higher returns to shareholders, increased cash for reinvestment into marketing, and higher employee compensation.

What are the benefits that can be expected from a successful implementation of the marketing ROI process? Here are a few.

- Decisions to secure additional budget are faster and better informed.
- The budget reallocation is clear and effective. As the total budget changes or needs to be reallocated to fund stronger opportunities, the lowest performing campaigns can be identified and suspended.
- Campaigns are planned and measured consistently. Once the process is learned, it applies regardless of the division or marketing function within the company.
- Greater insight is available in planning and designing profitable strategies.
- Investment limits and Customer Pathing direction are provided to customer contact channels to empower decisions, guide sales efforts, and prioritize information collection.
- Customer profitability can be increased by linking synergistic campaigns.
- CRM strategies can be used to form new Customer Pathing options at the customer level.

- The marketing investment control panel will allow for quick response to external conditions, changes to performance of existing campaigns, and changes to corporate-level parameters. Priorities for increased short-term profits, increased share, or decreased budget can easily be projected and implemented.

Strategically using the ROI process and the marketing investment control panel has tremendous capabilities to help maximize profits generated for the company. Building the processes and systems to make this possible can take significant time and commitment. It may be impossible for some companies to achieve an ideal environment where all marketing investments can be managed with the desired level of precision and speed. Profit improvements can also be achieved through smaller-scale implementations that follow the principles and practices presented here.

CHAPTER 16

THE IMPLEMENTATION PROCESS

You can either take action, or you can hang back and hope for a miracle. Miracles are great, but they are so unpredictable.

PETER DRUCKER

Increasing your awareness and understanding of marketing ROI and the new concepts presented here has little value on its own. The only way to generate a positive return on the time you've invested is to take actions that will achieve results. No marketing measurement and profit management process is perfect so there is certainly room for improvement. The question is where to start? Is the right profit focus in place? Are existing measurements consistent across the organization? What barriers must be addressed? How can simple tools, techniques, and training be used to gain momentum?

If the vision is to build an organization-wide or company-wide marketing ROI to take profit optimization to its fullest extent, the process should begin with careful planning. As with any large-scale, enterprise-wide implementation, the best approach is to implement and achieve success incrementally. The marketing ROI process requires change at the campaign, division, and executive level. It will take time to establish standard procedures, refine the accuracy, and shift the existing culture. It's clear from interviews with leading marketing gurus that a transition in managing marketing investments will meet some resistance from marketers.[1] The cultural barriers should be taken seriously to smooth the transition.

The key steps for implementing ROI measures within the marketing organization are as follows:

- *Form the cross-functional project team.* Many people cringe at the thought of another project that requires a cross-functional team, but it is the right path toward success. Many of the problems and failures with CRM implementations can be linked back to a lack of communication and commitment between organizations in a company.[2]
- *Review existing marketing measures at the campaign level.* The review process needs to address several key questions. How are the current measures aligned with maximizing profits? What is required to introduce ROI as the new primary measure for guiding investment decisions? If ROI measures are in place, are all of the key principles applied to guide decisions with accuracy? Are decisions based on the combination of independent, incremental, and aggregated measures?
- *Establish a commitment and equip the team.* Senior management must make a clear statement that aligning marketing decisions with company goals can be greatly improved through the use of ROI measurements. The commitment must be backed by equipping the marketing staff with training and tools. Make the measurement and projection process simple so marketers can apply their expertise in developing strategies and delivering results.
- *Assess the quality and accessibility of key data.* Quality measures depend on timely access to quality data. The Data Warehousing Institute conducted a study that indicated poor data quality is costing businesses more than $600 billion annually.[3] Data integrity issues primarily result from conflicting data that exists in multiple databases or data decay where good data eventually becomes outdated.[4] Customer value estimates will require quality historical data, accurate results reporting, and reliable modeling of expected future value.
- *Map out the full-scale marketing ROI process and set standards.* The process for using ROI to guide campaign, customer, and corporate profitability will need to be customized to the business model and specific needs of each organization. Having a clear vision for how the company can best apply ROI measurements in the long term will help define how the implementation is phased in. The entire project

team needs to have input and buy-in at this stage. The initial standardization of the ROI formula will need to consider the broad range of investments made and measurement issues in different areas in order to establish a single consistent formula.

- *Set up a pilot program.* The principles of marketing ROI can, for the most part, be initially applied to a subgroup of the marketing organization. Applying ROI tools in strategic development and campaign measurements, prioritizing marketing investments, and maximizing profitability can all work effectively for a small segment of the marketing organization. The company can understand the potential benefits and refine the process before implementing on a large scale. The pilot program should be completed with a group that is highly capable and motivated to take on a new initiative, manages highly measurable marketing activities, and ideally has some level of control over communications with a customer segment. This last point allows for some initial testing and development of Customer Pathing strategies.

- *Monitor and adjust the process.* Translating principles of ROI measurements into processes that guide better investment decisions will require ongoing assessment and adjustments. Success in the pilot project and in each incremental phase should be confirmed by the entire team to identify potential problem areas. Don't fall into the trap of accepting a process that delivers "good news" and rejecting a process if the outcome shows "bad news." Focus on the quality of the process itself to ensure the output is accurate.

- *Build an executive control panel.* Once the process is considered reliable, the executive control panel can be created. Use of this control panel should go through a testing period as well. Adjustments may be necessary to both the control panel and the core process.

- *Rollout the ROI processes in phases.* While the implementation of the marketing ROI process organization-wide should generate additional profits for the company, it should not be rushed. Each new marketing function brought under the marketing ROI process will require a unique transition. Training and tools need to be implemented with quality as well.

- *Build Customer Pathing strategies.* Viewing profitability at a customer level will vary for different companies based on their preexisting orientation towards customer management versus product management. Companies with CRM initiatives underway should be able to identify and develop Customer Pathing strategies with greater ease. Other companies may need to experiment over time. Two approaches to Customer Pathing can occur simultaneously. The first is identifying where existing campaigns to the same customers have synergy, and the second is developing and testing new strategies that maximize profitability across multiple campaigns.

- *Manage the marketing investment portfolio.* Managing the budget process as an investment portfolio will follow the successful implementation of the core marketing ROI processes across the organization. This function can happen at the division level just as easily as at the corporate level.
- *Validate projections and adjust assumptions.* Decisions will be made based on projected values that must constantly be validated to ensure the projection process is accurate. Benchmark values that are used in place of actual measures must also be kept fresh.
- *Constantly improve the process.* The ROI process requires using data that is available, assumptions, and projections of the future. It is expected to improve the decision-making process but is not expected to achieve 100 percent accuracy. Once the process is up and running, you will have plenty of opportunity to refine and improve the process. Profits and expenses can be brought closer and closer to an individual customer level. Expenses and cost of goods can be increasingly viewed on an incremental basis to identify greater profit opportunities that result as total volume increases, as additional sales are made to current customers, and as the cost of servicing customers decreases over time. The process will always have room for improvement. In addition, marketing practices are dynamic and will require changes to keep current with new innovations.

The Cross-Functional Team

Building on the team that Don E. Schultz outlined for the implementation of ROI measurements in his book *Measuring Brand Communications ROI*, the following roles[5] and responsibilities are outlined:

- *Marketing strategy and communications* will ensure the ROI measurements can effectively guide investment decisions toward the greatest profits. This group will implement the tools and techniques to maximize the value from more advanced strategic development and analysis processes.
- *Sales* will provide the connection between actual results and marketing activity, capture intelligence, and serve as the reality check on predictive model analysis.[6]
- *Product management* will monitor customer needs by value segment, provide pricing-related input, and provide insight into where profit improvements can be supported by marketing initiatives.
- *Finance* will manage the development and standardization of the ROI formula and process to align with corporate profit goals, set the ROI threshold, and monitor external market conditions.
- *Accounting* will monitor the process of capturing and applying financial data.
- *Research* will work to support the measurement process that is dependent on primary research, establish benchmark measurements where necessary, and collect research data that serves as predictors of future value. Tracking of marketing metrics on customer loyalty and understanding reasons for customer behavior will continue to be critical to the strategic planning process.
- *Information technology* will automate the ROI process, provide access to data, ensure data integrity, and facilitate timely reporting of results.
- *Business analytics* will handle predictive modeling requirements and more advanced results analysis.
- *Channel management*, including customer service and the website interface, will support the flow of results, provide reps with ROI data that empowers customer-oriented decisions, and implement Customer Pathing strategies to make offers and collect intelligence.
- *Operations and logistics* will provide direction on where profit improvements can be supported through marketing initiatives and stay current with shifts in marketing priorities.
- *Human resources* will align compensation and performance reviews to new measures of success, which must take into consideration contribution to corporate profit over individual campaign profits.

- *Senior executives* will need to establish the ROI process as the way the marketing organization will operate and use the control panel approach to guide the corporation toward improved profitability.

The initial planning team will need to define the desired benefits, map out the process, and identify potential and barriers to success. The team must be made up of individuals who are committed to the project success because failure in any one department can easily result in a breakdown of the entire process. Lessons can be learned from the implementation of CRM initiatives, which also required multidepartment support.

The Role of Technology

Processes such as marketing ROI measurements are certainly candidates for automation. Undoubtedly, technology can play a significant role in ROI calculations, data quality and access, results analysis, modeling, and results reporting. Automated processes provide speed, consistency, and processing power. Campaign management and modeling tools are often in place to manage a good portion of the marketing process. Both enterprise resource planning (ERP) and CRM initiatives are changing the way marketers interact with technology.

The marketing ROI process has many components that can either stand alone or be integrated into existing technologies. Many of the basic campaign management tools such as ROI projections, investment limits, and marketing allowable charts are simple enough to develop as spreadsheet applications. Comparisons of a small number of campaigns using independent, incremental, and aggregated views may be possible in a spreadsheet but can easily become complex enough to justify a more automated process. Many sophisticated marketing software applications and marketing profit optimization models already incorporate many aspects of ROI analysis, but may require enhancements to fully adopt the key principles outlined here.

In some ways, technology is already ahead of the marketing organization with respect to marketing ROI capabilities. Discussions with marketing automation companies indicate that most marketing organizations are underutilizing the ROI management and optimization capabilities that exist in the software they already own. Marketing organizations have adapted the technology to existing processes, which are less profit-oriented, instead of adapting their organizations' processes to the increased capabilities of the technology. Realistically, implementing marketing automation with existing processes is a necessary first step, but few companies have plotted their course to take full advantage of the automated capabilities.

Consider the following input from several technology companies that have shared their insight in this area. Marketswitch Corporation, a provider of real-time optimization software headquartered in Dulles, Virginia, offers a sophisticated, highly scalable, decisioning engine used in the planning stage of optimizing marketing campaigns. Market-switch's unique mathematical process to optimize profits and ROI at the customer level, selecting the ideal target customers, offers, channels, and timing is based on the company's specific business goals and constraints. The decisioning software is designed to allow companies to define their business goal (e.g., profit, customer lifetime value, revenue) and incorporate their unique operational constraints (e.g., limited budget, product-specific sales goals, call center capacity, and so forth) as criteria for optimization. The decisioning software identifies the most effective use of a company's resources given these very real operational constraints and corporate objectives. The technology has the capability to help optimize profitability, but it is in the hands of the marketers to determine the weight placed on other goals and constraints, which can result in missed profit opportunities. Marketers can use the software to evaluate and manage the financial impact of these operational constraints before executing their campaigns. The net result is that Marketswitch clients are able to achieve performance improvements of 10 percent to more than 200 percent over their previous methods without increased marketing activity. A top-ten credit card issuer was able to use Marketswitch optimization software to gain a 10 percent lift in the NPV of its cross-sell marketing campaigns, which translated into an additional $5 million in NPV during the first three months of using the software.[7]

Aprimo, Incorporated, a provider of enterprise marketing management systems headquartered in Indianapolis, has the capability to guide marketing investments based on objectives set by the client company. Their system is very sophisticated in the capture and identification of expenses that make up the marketing investment, including resource costs such as sales and marketing staff. Once again, decisions are greatly improved and profits increased through this process, however the full profit potential is restricted not by the technology but by the constraints set by the companies. Hewlett-Packard and Compaq effectively used Aprimo as the two entities were being merged. They realized significant savings in the marketing budget by tracking and eliminating campaigns that did not contribute to current business initiatives and created an environment of greater accountability for results.[8]

It's a case of good news–bad news. The companies that are implementing marketing optimization technologies—even if not used to their fullest potential—are clearly leading the effort to make better decisions on marketing investments. Profitability is at least getting factored into the campaign decisions in the planning stages and used in the prioritization process.

In a Forrester Research report, *Mastering Marketing Measurement*, analyst Jim Nail projects that "measurement will usurp CRM as the focus of marketing automation apps." The report details a research study conducted jointly with the Association of National Advertisers (ANA). In terms of seeking technology-based advancements, measurement was ranked as a top priority by marketers, 60 percent of whom expect to increase spending on marketing technology over the next year. "Marketers are in need of correlative measurements to capture meaningful results in today's complex environment of highly integrated marketing," indicates Nail. "Technology makes it easier for marketers to effectively incorporate marketing mix modeling and other sophisticated optimization models into their strategic and tactical planning process. To be successful, companies will need to align a change in their corporate culture with the implementation of automated marketing measurements."[9]

Low-Tech Solutions

Technology can simplify the marketing ROI process but there are profitable approaches that are low tech as well. One of the sales organizations at Bank One in Indianapolis has been maximizing customer profitability with minimal automation for several years. The sales staff uses a series of questions when they profile customers to fully understand their current and future needs (this is what Peppers & Rogers Group refers to as the "potential value" of a customer). The salesperson then has a clear picture of the share of the customer that they do not have and the potential growth in incremental customer value. This information helps to prioritize their sales activities and guide their time investment into each customer. Lloyd Lyons, vice president of this sales team, indicates, "the manual process has definitely helped us to refine the process and improve sales effectiveness while also benefiting the customer, as it helped us to anticipate needed solutions. We are currently implementing an automated version of the process which will help us to capture more data and better quantify the impact."[10]

Another example of a high-impact, low-tech approach comes from consultant and author Jim Novo who has been a strong advocate of better marketing measurements to improve profitability. He has developed a process called "Simple CRM" which is based on the essentials of CRM, including customer service improvements, combined with marketing measurements for customer retention and lifetime value. The process involves measuring customer retention, managing marketing programs to improve retention, and then maximizing profitability with marketing ROI analysis applied to actual results.

The ROI Champion

So, who is most likely to take the lead within your company to champion additional improvements in marketing ROI measurements? It will take someone who has the vision to look past existing barriers—and there certainly will be barriers. Bob Boehnlein of Aprimo has found that analytic-oriented or process-oriented marketers and CEOs, as well as those with a financial direct report, tend to be the typical champions.[11] Jim Novo has found that CIOs and IT managers are taking the lead for some companies, based on their role in managing online measurements.[12] CFOs also have a strong interest in bringing greater financial accountability into the marketing organizations. Regardless of where the ROI efforts are initiated, the success will certainly be dependent on gaining buy-in from a combination of marketing, finance, and senior management.

The trend will always be toward greater accountability, especially with the increased measurability, greater access to data and processing power, and better insights into how measurements can be applied strategically. The question marketers face is whether to embrace or resist the trend and whether to lead the effort or be lead by another department within the company. It's no longer acceptable that half of your advertising is wasted.

Marketing consultant and Columbia University Graduate School of Business instructor, Ruth P. Stevens, wrote an article addressing new measurement standards set for banner advertising by the Interactive Advertising Bureau (IAB). In this article, she appropriately pointed the finger at the advertising industry (not the IAB) for placing reach and frequency as the primary measures for banner advertising when the Internet had originally been hailed as a highly measurable sales and communications channel. This is cited as a similar move to that which shifted advertising from a sales medium to a "brand" medium three decades ago.[13] Marketers making investments into channels such as banner advertising must demand more than reach and frequency and not let the industry dictate how investments will be measured.

First Steps to Greater Profits

You've invested your time to go through this book and advance your knowledge in marketing ROI. As with most marketing investments, the big returns take more effort and more time. The list below is provided to give you short-term opportunities to generate additional profits from your current marketing investments.

- *Shift to ROI measures for your next set of campaigns.* If you are not using ROI to prioritize future investments and can gain access to the data, compare the decisions using an ROI analysis. Run the

ROI analysis concurrent with your previous measurement process. In many cases it will lead to the same decision, but finding the difference in a select set of decisions is your first chance to deliver incremental profits.

- *Make any necessary corrections to existing ROI measures.* Review the list of common errors in Chapter 6 and checkpoint against the key principles outlined throughout this book. The improvement in investment decisions that result from these corrections can have immediate value.

- *Measure incrementally.* Treat each incremental investment as a decision that must generate an acceptable return. Averaging results or using a total ROI value without viewing incremental value can easily lead to costly decisions.

- *Automate basic ROI tools.* Calculate investment limits and create marketing allowable charts to use in strategic planning. If you have not done a similar process in the past, this can open your mind to innovative strategies based on the combinations of investment levels and sales conversion rates that are possible.

- *Assess data quality for customer value.* If poor quality data is being used to calculate incremental customer value, especially for projections of future value, this could be a hidden drain on profits, turning good measurement practices into a source for bad decisions.

- *Develop select benchmark measures.* What is the information that can make a difference in your ROI calculations but is either too difficult or too expensive to research? This could include the incremental value of a marketing channel or capturing the typical ratio of tracked sales to untracked sales. If this information can lead to better decisions over a long period of time or across multiple organizations, the investment to measure and establish a benchmark value may be worthwhile.

These first steps will help establish a comfort level and generate some initial successes. The real profit gains will come from more advanced ROI processes such as Customer Pathing and managing the marketing investment portfolio.

Conclusion

Strategic development and marketing creativity can absolutely thrive in an environment based on a strong commitment to maximizing profits. The focus on customers and relationship management has always been about a better way to increase long-term profitability. Used in combination with more advanced ROI measurement and planning techniques, these strategies can be guided toward more effective integration, streamlined decision making, and effective investment management. Companies with superior processes for managing profitability can gain competitive advantages and provide better returns to employees, customers, and investors.

There are many paths to profitability. The traditional paths are well marked and familiar but include unnecessary detours that are costly. Big gains in profitability require taking some less familiar paths and forging some new paths. The marketing organization is responsible for motivating customers from the first impression through a lifetime of repeat purchases. In today's competitive environment, it's unacceptable that billions of dollars are being wasted each year on ineffective marketing initiatives. Without question, smarter marketing can generate more profitable returns, so it's time to manage the budget as an investment and not an expense. It will take champions at every level of the organization to establish the passion, processes, and practices necessary to deliver more profits.

NOTES

Introduction
1. Sergio Zyman, *The End of Marketing As We Know It* (New York: HarperBusiness, 1999) 11.

Chapter 1
1. Sergio Zyman, 11.
2. *Intellitracker* (intellitracker.com/datasheet.htm) and *Australian Financial Services Directory* (afsd.com.au/article/action/action2a .htm), accessed August 2002.
3. Research study by professors Elizabeth Demers of the University of Rochester and Baruch Lev of New York University as reported by Sunil Gupta and Donald R. Lehmann in "What Are Your Customers Worth," *Optimize Magazine*, May 2002 (optimizemag.com/issue/007/roi.htm), accessed May 2002.
4. Don E. Schultz, "Being an expense can sometimes be good," *Marketing News*, September 16, 2002, 12.
5. Based on the common perspectives identified in telephone interviews conducted with Don Schultz, Jim Novo, and Bob Boehnlein in July and August 2002.
6. Frederick F. Reichheld and W. Earl Sasser Jr., "Zero Defections: Quality Comes to Services," *Harvard Business Review*, September–October 1990, 105.

7. Frederick F. Reichheld with Thomas Teal, *The Loyalty Effect* (Boston: Harvard Business School Press, 1996).

8. "Insight Driven Marketing," research report (Accenture, 2001) 44–46.

9. James McQuivey of Forrester Research was interviewed by telephone on September 5, 2002.

10. APQC and ARF, *Maximizing Marketing ROI* (American Productivity & Quality Center and the Advertising Research Foundation, March 2001) 6–8. Supplemented by conversations in August 2002 with Bill Cook, Senior Vice President, Advertising Research Foundation and Rachele Williams, Project Manager, American Productivity & Quality Center.

11. Kevin J. Clancy and Robert Shulman, *The Marketing Revolution: A Radical Manifesto for Dominating the Marketplace* (New York: HarperBusiness, 1991).

12. *U.S. Ad Expenditures by Type of Media, 1997–2001*, Source: Universal McCann, New York (*Marketing News*, July 8, 2002) 15.

13. James D. Lenskold, "Marketing ROI: Playing To Win," *Marketing Management*, May/June 2002, 31–35.

Chapter 2

1. Frederick F. Reichheld, *Loyalty Rules* (Boston: Harvard Business School Press, 2001) 122.

2. Don Peppers and Martha Rogers, Ph.D., *Enterprise One to One* (New York: Doubleday, 1997) 99–100.

3. Jim Stanton was interviewed numerous times between March and September 2002 and provided input into the example presented.

4. George Michie of Crutchfield Corporation was interviewed on July 3, 2002 after presenting information at the DMD New York marketing conference on June 17. Subsequent E-mail and phone contacts were made to discuss the ROI analysis of his figures.

Chapter 4

1. Kevin J. Clancy and Robert Shulman, *Marketing Revolution: A Radical Manifesto for Dominating the Marketplace* (New York: HarperBusiness, 1991) 304.

2. Chip Hoyt, "The Software Side of Marketing" (reveries.com, April 22, 2002).

3. Tom Nicholson, "What Every CEO Wants to Hear from Communications: Objective Measures Essential to More Effective Communications Planning" (Evanston, Illinois: *Journal of Integrated Communications*, Northwestern University, 2001–2002) 7–10, supplemented with a telephone interview with Nicholson on September 4, 2002.

Chapter 5

1. This benefit was specifically mentioned by the benchmark companies in the best-practices research report, *Maximizing Marketing ROI* and in subsequent conversations with Bill Cook and Rachele Willams. (See also Chapter 1, note 10.)

2. See previous note.

Chapter 6

1. Sunil Gupta and Donald R. Lehmann in "What are Your Customers Worth" (*Optimize Magazine*, May 2002, optimizemag.com/issue/007/roi.htm).

2. James D. Lenskold published in *Web Metrics* by Jim Sterne (New York: John Wiley & Sons 2002) 260–262.

3. In the original publication customer lifetime value was not discounted over the five-year period, for the sake of simplicity.

Chapter 8

1. Peter Drucker, *The Practice of Management* (New York: Harper & Row, 1982) 37.

2. Jim Sterne and Matt Cutler, *E-Metrics: Business Metrics for the New Economy*, white paper (Cambridge, MA, NetGenesis Corp., 2000) and Jim Sterne, *Web Metrics: Proven Methods for Measuring Web Site Success* (New York: John Wiley & Sons, 2002) 216.

Chapter 9

1. Louise O'Brien and Charles Jones, "Do Rewards Really Create Loyalty?" *Harvard Business Review*, May/June 1995.

Chapter 10
1. Zyman, 43.
2. Frederick F. Reichheld, *The Loyalty Effect* (Boston: Harvard Business School Press, 1996) 49.

Chapter 13
1. APQC and ARF, *Maximizing Marketing ROI*, 43–52.
2. Randy Zeese of AT&T was interviewed by telephone on August 20, 2002.
3. Clancy and Shulman, 54.
4. Return = (prospects × conversion × customer value) − Total Investment.

Chapter 14
1. Zyman, 45.
2. Eric Almquist and Gordon Wyner, "Boost Your Marketing ROI with Experimental Design" (*Harvard Business Review*, October 2001) 135–141.
3. Gupta and Lehmann, (optimizemag.com/issue/07/roi.htm).
4. Dr. Martha Rogers of Peppers & Rogers Group was interviewed on August 7, 2002. She provided insight on the role sales and customer service should play in reviewing the output of predictive models. This reality check is essential to adjust models based on historical data with real-time trends that can be identified through direct contact with customers and prospects.
5. Tom Hannigan of Chatham Systems Group provided an overview of inferred responses in March 2002 and covered the topic in several subsequent conversations.
6. David Bonthrone of Dendrite International was interviewed in person on March 14, 2002.
7. Tom Hannigan and Christina Palendrano, "How Reliable is Your Enterprise Data?" (*DM Direct*, dmreview.com/master.cfm?navid=55&edid=5620, August 9, 2002).

Chapter 15
1. Michael C. Jensen, "Corporate Budgeting Is Broken—Let's Fix It," *Harvard Business Review*, November 2001.

2. Dr. Martha Rogers of Peppers & Rogers Group was interviewed on August 7, 2002. Additional information was drawn from Don Peppers and Martha Rogers, Ph.D., *Enterprise One to One* (New York: Doubleday, 1997) 99–100.

Chapter 16

1. Jim Novo and Bill Cook interviews, July and August 2002.
2. Tom Hannigan of Chatham Systems Group, personal interview, 2002.
3. Wayne Eckerson, *Data Quality and the Bottom Line*, white paper (The Data Warehousing Institute, 2001). Download available at dw-institute.com/dqreport.
4. Hannigan and Palendrano, (*DM Direct*, dmreview.com/editorial/dmdirect/dmdirect_article).
5. Don E. Schultz and Jeffrey S. Walters, *Measuring Brand Communication ROI* (New York: Association of National Advertisers, 1997) 71–72.
6. Dr. Martha Rogers, interview, August 7, 2002.
7. Peter Accorti and Donna DePasquale of Marketswitch Corporation were interviewed by telephone on February 1, 2002 and subsequently provided additional information.
8. Bob Boehnlein of Aprimo, Incorporated was interviewed by telephone on August 7, 2002. Rob McLaughlin provided case studies on September 30, 2002.
9. Jim Nail, *Mastering Marketing Measurement* (Cambridge, MA: Forrester Research, September 2002), supplemented with a telephone interview with Jim Nail on October 2, 2002.
10. Lloyd Lyons of Bank One was interviewed in person in May 2001 with follow-up communications by E-mail in October 2002.
11. Bob Boehnlein, August 2002.
12. Jim Novo, author and consultant, shared insights by E-mail and telephone between June and July 2002.
13. Ruth P. Stevens, "The Point Is To Sell Something" (*iMarketing News*, February 21, 2002, dmnews.com or ruthstevens.com).

INDEX

Accenture, 6, 11, 14
Accounting division, 243
Actual value, 23, 227–28. *See also*
    Customer lifetime value
Advertising filtering technology, 41
Advertising Research Foundation
    (ARF), 6, 18, 49
Aggregated return on investment
    (ROI), 85, 107–8, 152–56, 228,
    244
    campaign profitability and, 190,
        193, 196
    Customer Pathing™ and, 163, 164,
        166, 167
    incremental ROI vs., 155–56
    mass marketing and, 157
    modeling and, 205
Allocated investments, 61–62
Almquist, Eric, 216
American Productivity and Quality
    Center (APQC), 6, 18, 49
Aprimo, Incorporated, 42–43,
    245–46, 247
ARF. *See* Advertising Research
    Foundation
Association of National Advertisers
    (ANA), 246
Assumed impact, 214, 218–19

AT&T, xi–xii, 18, 25, 89, 144–45, 198
Audience profiles, 45
Awareness, 4–5, 7, 45, 55, 98, 100,
    141, 156, 164, 210

Bank One, 247
Benchmark values, 48, 58, 103, 133,
    242, 243
    assumptions based on, 214, 217–18
    Customer Pathing™ and, 171
    developing, 249
    external and internal, 135
Blank check policy, 143
Boehnlein, Bob, 247
Bonthrone, David, 220
Bonus offers, 119–23, 194–95, 196
Borrowing, 137, 138, 146
Brand advertising, 62, 63, 98, 156
Brand equity calculations, 63
Break-even analysis, 19, 54, 201, 205,
    214, 219
Bristol Technology, 43
Broadscale marketing support
    expenses, 62–63
Budgets. *See also* Expense allocation
    change in availability, 236, 237
    Customer Pathing™ and, 170–71
    for market testing, 187

in marketing ROI process, 47, 48
modeling and, 201, 202
monitoring and modifying, 145–46
point-of-decision perspective and,
    26
power of, 17
process for setting, 144–45
ROI threshold rate and, 143–44,
    145, 146
Business analytics division, 243

Cable television, 40
Campaign profitability, 115, 173–207,
    240. *See also* Marketing
    campaigns
    comparison analysis in, 188–89
    innovation and screening in,
        186–89
    marketing manager responsibilities,
        175–76
    research and intelligence in,
        176–86
    results analysis, 191–98
    ROI projections in, 187–88
    strategic decisions for, 198–205
Capital costs, change in, 235, 236
Capital investments, 33–34
Cash flow overlay, 232–33
Cell phones, interactive, 41
CGS. *See* Cost of Goods Sold
Change, fear of, 17
Channel management, 243
Chatham Systems Group, xii, 219
Chief executive officers (CEOs), 247
Chief financial officers (CFOs), 247
Chief information officers (CIOs), 5,
    247
Clancy, Kevin J., 7, 39, 200
CLV. *See* Customer lifetime value
CMX product, 220–21
Coca-Cola, 3
Colgate-Palmolive, 18, 198

Columbia University Graduate School
    of Business, 248
Compaq, 246
Comparison analysis, 188–89
Compensation, 15, 17. *See also*
    Performance rewards
Competitive advantage, 6, 7, 156
Competitive threat, change in, 236
Control groups, 15, 76
Controlled testing, 212, 214, 215–16
Corporate-level profitability, 47, 48,
    115, 125–47, 240
    discount rate in, 128, 135–38
    executive responsibilities, 126–27
    expense allocation in, 129, 140
    expenses at risk in, 129, 141
    incremental customer value in, 128,
        132–35
    performance rewards for, 146–47
    referral value in, 128–29, 138–39
    residual value in, 129, 141–42
    time period for, 128, 129–32
Corporate-level responsibilities,
    115–16
Corporate sponsorships, 98, 229
Cost(s). *See also* Expense(s)
    development, 61–62
    fixed, 25–26
    fulfillment, 65, 134
Cost of Goods Sold (CGS), 55, 56,
    60, 128, 129, 140, 175
Cost of goods variations, 134
Cost per new buyer (CPNB), 29–31
Cost per sale, 120, 175, 205, 210
    investment limit for, 177
    investment overstated with, 65
    shortfalls of, 10, 11
Cost savings, 57
CPNB. *See* Cost per new buyer
CRM. *See* Customer Relationship
    Management

Cross-functional project teams, 240, 242–44
Cross-sell marketing, 228
    Customer Pathing™ and, 165–66, 167, 169
    Customer Relationship Management and, 150
    multiple campaigns and, 152–53, 155–56
    patterns of, 83–86
Crutchfield Corporation, 29–32
Customer acquisition, 5, 77, 87, 88, 141, 224, 228
    Crutchfield analysis of, 29–32
    customer lifetime value and, 67–69
    Customer Pathing™ and, 164, 165, 166–67, 169
    Customer Relationship Management and, 13, 150
    customer retention differentiated from, 92–93
    customer value and, 93–95
    excessive costs for, 105
    investment limit for, 177
    marketing patterns for, 71–75
    multiple campaigns and, 152–53, 155–56
    profit drivers in, 90–92
Customer defection, 74–75, 78–80, 175. *See also* Customer vulnerability
    lasting impact on rate, 89–90
    rates of, 77, 83
Customer life cycle analysis, 178
Customer Life Cycle Funnel, 101, 102
Customer lifetime value (CLV), 14, 40, 42, 133, 201, 227
    Customer Pathing™ and, 164, 168
    defined, 23
    explained, 23–24
    incremental customer value vs., 56

incremental profits vs., 65
ROI vs., 66–69
shortfalls of, 10
Simple CRM and, 247
Customer loyalty, 13, 55, 76, 85, 89, 90, 218
    customer acquisition relation to, 91–92
    Customer Pathing™ and, 164
    discount rate and, 131
    economics of, 6
    investment limit for, 177
    marketing patterns and, 81–83
    price variations and, 134
    research on, 243
    segmentation by, 224–26
Customer needs, 91
Customer Pathing™, 4, 14, 72, 85, 104–5, 133–34, 144, 146, 162, 237, 249
    building strategies for, 241–42
    campaign-level responsibilities in, 118
    campaign profitability and, 175, 176, 205–7
    channel management for, 243
    customer profitability and, 150
    division-level responsibilities in, 117
    investment limit for, 177
    residual value and, 142
    strategic value and, 228
    strategies for, 163–71
Customer profitability, 33, 47, 48, 115, 149–62, 227–28, 237, 240
    building strategies for, 241–42
    division manager responsibilities, 150–51
    low-tech implementation, 247
    mass marketing for, 156–62
    multilevel measurements in, 151–56

Customer Relationship Management
(CRM), xii, xiii, 4, 5, 6, 33, 34,
40, 43, 211, 246
  Customer Pathing™ and, 169, 237,
    242
  data integrity in, 219–21
  expenses associated with, 62, 63
  implementation failures, 240
  multidepartment support for, 244
  profits associated with, 104
  scenarios, 149–50
  Simple, 247
  strategic value and, 228
  synergies between ROI and, 13–14,
    50
Customer retention, xii, 13, 33, 71,
    87, 99, 224, 228
  customer acquisition differentiated
    from, 92–93
  customer acquisition relation to,
    91–92
  Customer Pathing™ and, 164, 169
  customer value and, 93–95
  increase in, 81–83
  investment limit for, 177, 178–79
  lasting impact in, 89–90
  marketing patterns for, 75–80
  as performance indicator, 11
  profits and, 76–77, 88–90
  ROI with steady impact, 76, 77
  short-term, 78, 79, 80, 90
  Simple CRM and, 247
Customer sales cycle, 101–4
Customer satisfaction, 7, 114, 210
Customer segmentation, 42, 135, 168,
    171, 224–28
Customer-service improvements,
    98–99
Customer value, 54–55, 71, 77, 89,
    91, 173. *See also* Customer
    lifetime value; Incremental
    customer value

change in, 130, 236
data quality for, 240, 249
investment limit for, 177, 178
marketing allowables per, 183, 184,
    185
measurement of, 210
modeling, 202, 205
responding to differences in, 93–95
shortfalls of, 10
strategic profit management and,
    226–28
Customer vulnerability, 79–80, 89,
    90, 92
Cutler, Matt, 101

Data, 57
  assessment of, 240, 249
  getting access to, 14
  gross margin, 58
  integrity of, 219–21
  investment, 60
Data mining, 214, 217
Data Warehousing Institute, 240
Decisions
  for campaign profitability, 198–205
  measurement alignment with, 65,
    95–97, 108
  measurement for smarter, 210–13
Delos Technologies, 220–21
Dendrite International, 220
Development
  Customer Pathing™ and, 164, 171
  recovering costs of, 61–62
Diminishing returns, 130, 131
Direct-mail campaigns, 97, 119–23,
    179, 215, 236
Direct marketing, 39, 90
Direct measures, 214, 215
Direct sales expenses, 55, 56
Discount rate, 74, 75, 80, 129–32,
    235
  change over time, 130

corporate-level profitability and, 128, 135–38
explained, 22–23
factors used to determine, 138
increasing, 131–32
ROI threshold relation to, 24
steady, 130–31
Division-level responsibilities, 116–17, 150–51
DMD New York Marketing Conference, 29
Double counting, 100, 103, 211–12
Drucker, Peter, 87, 239

E-mail marketing, 7, 39, 101–4, 194, 196. *See also* Internet; Websites
Emerging investments, 229, 230, 231, 236
End of Marketing As We Know It, The (Zyman), 3
Enterprise marketing management systems, 245–46
Enterprise One to One (Rogers), 226–27
Enterprise resource planning (ERP), 40, 244
Executive control panels, 223, 233–38, 241, 244
Executives
importance of ROI involvement by, 9
in marketing ROI process, 49, 116
responsibilities of, 126–27
senior, 244
Expense(s), 58–60. *See also* Cost(s)
broadscale marketing support, 62–63
direct sales, 55, 56
incremental customer, 55, 56
long-term, 59, 60
overhead, 3, 134, 140

up-front, 58, 59–60, 61–62
variable, 25, 26, 58, 59–60
Expense allocation, 15, 63. *See also* Budgets
corporate-level profitability and, 129, 140
for mass marketing, 157–61
staff, 59–60, 64
Expense at risk, 58, 59, 65, 126, 129, 141
Experience mindset, 224–26
Experimental design, 214, 215, 216
External metrics, 233, 234

Finance division, 243
Financial Accounting Standards Board, 5
Financial concepts, key, 21–24
Financial measures, 97–99
Financial values, 55, 56
for all returns, 96
of performance metrics, 96, 101–4
Fixed costs, 25–26
Ford, Henry, 5
Forrester Research, 6, 246
Fractional factorial design, 190, 216
Fulfillment costs, 65, 134
Future value projections, 14. *See also* Discount rate
investment limit and, 178
uncertainty in, 130, 131, 138

Global Positioning Systems (GPS), 41
Goodwill donations, 98
Gross margin, 3, 54–55, 56, 67, 96, 98, 101
in Crutchfield analysis, 29, 31
customer retention and, 77, 82
data needed for, 58
discount rate and, 131
explained, 22
formula for, 55

incremental customer value and, 24,
25, 26, 120
incremental investments and, 36
mass marketing and, 158, 160
measurement of, 57, 213
NPV conversion formula, 22
point-of-decision perspective and,
27, 28
potential value and, 23–24
of referrals, 55, 139
residual value and, 141
revenues in place of, 64–65
in ROI formula, 19, 20
Gross rating points (GRPs), 45
Guiness/UDV, 43
Gupta, Sunil, 53, 217
Gut instinct, 210

Hannigan, Tom, 219–20
Harvard Business Review, 6, 190, 216
Hewlett-Packard, 246
High-potential investments, 229, 231,
232
High-value customers, 40, 89, 168,
179
Historical marketing activity patterns,
133, 134, 176, 217–18
Hoyt, Chip, 43
Human resources, 243
Hurdle rate. *See* Return on
investment threshold

ICV. *See* Incremental customer value
Implementation process, 239–50
low-tech solutions, 246–47
technology for, 244–46
Incremental customer expenses, 55,
56
Incremental customer value (ICV),
10, 55, 120, 189
corporate-level profitability and,
128, 132–35

customer lifetime value vs., 56
defining, 24–26
explained, 23–24
key indicators of, 135
measurement of, 42, 57
primary approaches to establishing,
132–33
referrals and, 139
Incremental investments
assessing, 61–62
campaign profitability and, 192–94,
195, 197
Customer Pathing™ and, 168,
169
customer retention and, 77
greater scope of, 35–37
ROI projections based on, 204
total investment vs., 66
Incremental measurement, 118–23,
249
Incremental profits, 65, 77
Incremental return on investment
(ROI), 244
aggregated ROI vs., 155–56
campaign profitability and, 190,
194–95
Customer Pathing™ and, 163, 167,
168
modeling and, 201, 202, 205
Incremental savings, 55
Incremental value, 195
Independent return on investment
(ROI), 152–55, 163, 190, 193,
244
Inferred response, 214, 219
Influencers. *See* Third-party
influencers
Information technology (IT), 5, 16,
243, 247
Innovation investments, 229–30,
231–32
Intelligence. *See* Market Intelligence

Interactive Advertising Bureau (IAB), 248

Interdependencies, identifying, 142, 151–52

Internal metrics, 233, 234

Internet, xiii, 11, 39–40, 41, 62. *See also* E-mail marketing; Websites

Investment(s)
  allocated, 61–62
  calculating, 58–64
  campaign profitability and, 176–79, 180, 186
  challenges associated with data, 60
  comparison of unbalanced, 196–98
  complete and accurate, 96
  by customer segmentation, 224–28
  decreasing, 175
  defined, 53, 126
  emerging, 229, 230, 231, 236
  high-potential, 229, 231, 232
  incremental (*see* Incremental investments)
  innovation, 229–30, 231–32
  limits of, 176–79, 180, 186
  long-term brand, 230–31
  overstatement with cost of sales, 65
  patterns of, 71–86
  pending, 231
  reliable, 229, 230, 231, 232
  return relation to, 72, 73
  in ROI formula, 19–20
  in ROI process, 48

Investment at risk. *See* Expense at risk

Investment portfolio, 228–33, 242

IT. *See* Information technology

Jensen, Michael C., 223

Jones, Charles, 113

Journal of Integrated Communications, 44

Kmart, 13

Kraft, 18

Launch.com, 41

Lehmann, Donald R., 53, 217

Lenskold Group, 190–91

Lever and Kitchen, 5

Leverhulme, Lord, 5

Long-term brand investments, 230–31

Long-term expense commitments, 59, 60

Low-value customers, 168, 179

Loyalty Effect, The (Reichheld), 6, 134

Lyons, Lloyd, 247

Margin multiplier, 217

Market intelligence
  executive control panel and, 233, 234
  preplanning, 176–86
  strategic value through, 227, 228

Market research. *See* Research

Market testing, 39, 61, 63, 117, 175
  budget availability for, 187
  campaign profitability and, 187, 188, 189–91
  case study, 190–91
  knowledge gained from, 188
  validity of, 187

Marketing allowable(s), 179, 180–85, 186

Marketing allowable charts, 175, 176, 181, 182–85, 244, 249

Marketing campaigns, 84. *See also* Campaign profitability
  multiple, 15, 151–56, 169, 242
  referrals and, 139
  residual value and, 141–42
  responsibilities at level of, 117–18
  reviewing measures at level of, 240
  ROI actions and tools in, 174

ROI analysis for comparison,
193–98
ROI process at level of, 47
technology for, 42, 43, 244
Marketing investments. *See*
Investment(s)
Marketing Management, 11
Marketing managers, 175–76
Marketing measurement. *See*
Measurement
Marketing return on investment
(ROI)
accurate and complete accounting
of, 99–100
aggregated (*see* Aggregated return
on investment)
calculating, 21
control panel (*see* Executive control
panels)
customer lifetime value vs., 66–69
defined, 127
formula (*see* Return on investment
formula)
incremental (*see* Incremental return
on investment)
incremental customer value as,
135
independent, 152–55, 163, 190,
193, 244
key principles for, 95–108
marketing flexibility in, 34–35
negative, 54
positive, 54, 65, 66
power of, 8–10
process, 47–49, 113–23
profit vs., 191–93
readiness for, 4–8
ROI differences from, 33–37
threshold (*see* Return on investment
threshold)
total, 66
zero, 54

Marketing Revolution, The (Clancy and
Shulman), 7, 200
Marketing strategy and
communications group, 243
Marketswitch Corporation, 43, 245
Mass marketing, 97, 99–100, 156–62
assessment of results, 160–61
cross-campaign allocation, 158–60
Customer Pathing™ and, 164, 165,
166–67, 169
measurment of, 39
projection of minimum return, 158
strategic alignment in, 161–62
Mass media advertising, 40–41, 42
Mastering Marketing Measurement
(report), 246
Maximizing Marketing ROI (report),
6–7, 49
MCI, xii
McQuivey, James, 6
Measurement, 7–8, 209–21
assumed impact, 214, 218–19
basic principles for, 211–12
benchmark-based assumptions, 214,
217–18
for campaign profitability, 194–98
controlled testing, 212, 214,
215–16
decision alignment with, 65, 95–97,
108
direct, 214, 215
errors in, 64–66
establishing cost-effective, 15
hierarchy of, 12
improvements in, 39–46
incremental, 118–23, 249
making corrections to, 249
multilevel, 151–56
reliability of approaches, 214
of retention and acquisition
marketing, 93
risk of hard, 17

of ROI, 53–69
ROI alternatives, shortfalls in,
    10–11
ROI as primary and ultimate, 9
for smarter decisions, 210–13
standardizing, 15
switching to ROI, 248–49
two-part, 108
types of processes, 213–19
Measuring Brand Communications ROI
    (Schultz), 242
Mercer Management Consulting, 216
Michie, George, 29, 32
Middle-value customers, 168
Minute Maid, 18
Mobile devices, advertising on, 41
Modeling, 34, 42, 48
for campaign profitability, 198–205
of customer behavior, 134
expense allocation, 60
optimization, 176, 198, 199
point-of-decision perspective and,
    27–28
predictive, 217–18, 226
strategic value through, 227, 228
technology for, 244
MSN Entertainment, 41
Multichannel marketing. *See*
    Marketing campaigns, multiple

Nail, Jim, 246
Natural control groups, 216
Negative return on investment (ROI),
    54
Net present value (NPV), 20, 33, 55,
    64, 67, 74, 99
customer retention and, 82–83
discount rate and, 129, 130–31,
    132, 136, 137
explained, 21–22
in gross margin conversion
    formula, 22

incremental customer value and,
    120
investment limit and, 178
marketing allowables and, 181
mass marketing and, 158
in potential value, 23–24
software for, 245
time period for, 128
Net profit, 126
NetGenesis, 101
New York Times, 44, 45
Nicholson, Tom, 44–45
Novo, Jim, 247
NPV. *See* Net present value

O'Brien, Louise, 113
Operations and logistics division, 243
"Oprah Winfrey Show, The," 44
Optimization modeling, 176, 198, 199
Organizational barriers, 15, 16–17
Outbound telemarketing (OTM), 149,
    153–54, 179, 236
Overhead expenses, 3, 134, 140

Palendrano, Christina, 219–20
Pareto Rule (80/20 rule), 199
Pending investments, 231
Peppers, Don, 23
Peppers & Rogers Group, 210, 227,
    247
Perceptions, 4–5, 55, 101, 141, 156,
    164, 213
Performance metrics, 11, 100–104,
    217
financial value of, 96, 101–4
as profit drivers, 214, 218
Performance results, 233–34
Performance rewards, 16, 17, 146–47
Pilot programs, 241
Point-of-decision perspective, 26–28,
    95
Point-of-sale data, 43

Positive return on investment (ROI), 54, 65, 66
Potential value, 23–24, 94, 247
Pre/post analysis, 214, 215, 216
Predictive modeling, 217–18, 226
Price variation, 134
Privacy issues, 40, 41, 43–44
Product management, 243
Product registration, 213
Profit(s), 87–108. *See also* Campaign profitability; Corporate-level profitability; Customer profitability; Strategic profit management
    addressing pressures, 11–13
    benefits of increasing, 114
    customer acquisition and, 90–92
    customer defection and, 74–75
    customer lifetime value vs., 65
    customer loyalty and, 6
    customer retention and, 76–77, 88–90
    discomfort with focus on, 113–14
    five steps to greater, 248–49
    immediate vs. future, 65
    importance of, 3–4
    incremental, 65, 77
    incremental investments and, 37
    key ROI principles in, 97–108
    long-term, 135, 136–37, 235
    net, 126
    performance metrics as drivers of, 214, 218
    return, investment, and, 73
    revenues in place of, 7
    ROI vs., 191–93
    short-term, 130, 135, 136–37, 235
    strategic initiative impact on, 98
Profit opportunity measures, 108
Projections, 233
    campaign profitability and, 187–88
    executive control panel and, 233
    validating, 242

Promotional offers, 55, 59, 90
Purchase intention, 4–5, 45

Radio advertising, 41
Rebates, 213
Referral(s), 55, 57, 139, 175
Referral value, 57, 128–29, 138–39
Reichheld, Frederick F., 6, 19, 134
Reliable investments, 229, 230, 231, 232
Replay TV, 41
Research, 5, 48, 63, 133, 214, 217, 218
    Customer Pathing™ and, 171
    preplanning, 176–86
    teams, 243
Residual value, 15, 56, 91
    basic concept behind, 106–7
    corporate-level profitability and, 129, 141–42
    defined, 104
    key points in considering, 142
    taking into consideration, 96, 104–8
Response rate, 11, 120. *See also* Sales conversion rate
Return(s)
    calculating, 54–58
    complete and accurate, 96
    defined, 53, 127
    gross margin and, 54, 64–65
    increasing, 173–75
    incremental, 195
    investment relation to, 72, 73
    in mass marketing, 158
    patterns of, 71–86
Return on investment (ROI). *See* Marketing return on investment
Return on investment (ROI) formula
    basics of, 19–21
    by different names, 28–29
    misunderstanding or misapplying, 53

standardizing, 100, 127–42,
    240–41
Return on investment (ROI) threshold
    (hurdle rate), 28, 33, 48, 98, 116,
    120, 121, 122, 145, 146, 147,
    194, 195, 197
    corporate-level profitability and,
        142–44
    explained, 24
    impact of change in, 236
    incremental investments and,
        35–36, 37
    investment limit and, 177, 178
    marketing allowables and, 181, 183,
        184, 185, 186
    in mass marketing, 158
    modeling and, 201, 202
    modifying, 186
    profits and, 191–93
Revenues, 3, 54, 55
    as performance indicator, 11
    in place of gross margin, 64–65
    in place of profits, 7
Reverse analysis, 98–99
Rewards. *See* Performance rewards
RFM models, 178
Rimm-Kauffman, Alan, 29, 32
Rogers, Martha, 23, 218, 226–27
"Rosie O'Donnell Show, The," 44

Sales conversion rate, 87, 120, 173,
    189
    marketing allowables and, 180, 181,
        182, 183, 184, 185
    modeling and, 201, 202
    shortfalls of, 10, 11
Sales division, 243
Sasser, Earl, Jr., 6
Satellite subscription radio, 41
Save value, 177
Saved customers, 90, 92, 94, 99, 177.
    See also Customer retention
Schultz, Don E., 242

Sears, Roebuck and Company, 44–45
Shareholders, 49, 98, 114
Shulman, Robert, 7, 39, 200
Simple CRM, 247
Software, 43, 244–46
Sprint, xii
Staff expenses, 59–60, 64
Stanton, Jim, 25
Sterne, Jim, 64, 101
Stevens, Ruth P., 248
Stock market value, 63, 98, 138
Stockholders. *See* Shareholders
Strategic alignment, 161–62
Strategic decisions, 198–205
Strategic initiatives, 97–99
Strategic planning, 26. *See also* Point-
    of-decision perspective
Strategic profit management,
    223–38
    by customer segment, 224–28
    for customer value, 226–28
    for the investment portfolio,
        228–33
    possible applications of, 235–38
    Strategic progress, 233, 234
Strategic value, 66, 226–28
Synergies, 13–14, 50, 169, 242

Target Marketing, 101
Targeting
    investment options for, 206
    optimal point in, 199–205
Technology, 16
    implementation and, 244–46
    marketing measurements and,
        42–43
Telemarketing. *See* Outbound
    telemarketing
Television advertising, 40–41
Test marketing. *See* Market testing
Test vs. control, 214, 215–16
Third-party influencers, 55, 57, 139
Time period

for corporate-level profitability,
128, 129–32
measuring effects of, 212
TiVo, 41
Total return on investment (ROI), 66
Total sum model, 16, 96, 99
Tracking, 39–40, 41, 44, 57, 139, 156
Truth in results, 17
Twain, Mark, 163

Uncertainty, in future value
projections, 130, 131, 138
Unilever, 5
United Kingdom, 6
Up-front expenses, 58, 59–60, 61–62

Variable expenses, 25, 26, 58, 59–60
Video recorders, 41

Vulnerable customers. *See* Customer
vulnerability

Wanamaker, John, 5
Web Metrics? (Sterne), 64
Websites, 62, 156, 219, 220, 229, 243.
See also E-mail marketing;
Internet
calculating financial value of,
101–4
measurements in, 39
Wyner, Gordon, 216

Yahoo!, 41
Yankelovich Clancy and Shulman, 7

Zero return on investment (ROI), 54
Zyman, Sergio, xi, 3, 125, 209

ABOUT THE AUTHOR

James D. Lenskold is a seasoned strategist and long-time marketing ROI champion. He is president of Lenskold Group, a provider of marketing consulting and implementation services focused on accelerating profitable growth for clients. Lenskold publishes, speaks, and consults on marketing ROI and multichannel marketing strategies. He began his career at AT&T developing and implementing marketing strategies for customer acquisition and retention. Prior to starting Lenskold Group in 1997, Lenskold helped found and grow a technology company.

A graduate of Rutgers University and Rutgers Graduate School of Management, Mr. Lenskold lives in New Jersey with his wife, Karen, and their children, Bethany and Meghan. He serves on the Board of Trustees for Training, Inc. National Association, a nonprofit organization dedicated to improving the lives of unemployed and underemployed individuals through training and constant improvement of workforce development practices.

Information on Lenskold Group can be found at lenskold.com and additional marketing ROI information and resources can be found at customerpathing.com.

The American Marketing Association is the world's largest and most comprehensive professional association of marketers. With over 45,000 members, the AMA has more than 500 chapters throughout North America. The AMA sponsors 25 major conferences per year, covering topics ranging from the latest trends in customer satisfaction measurement to business-to-business and service marketing, attitude research and sales promotion, and publishes nine major marketing publications.

For further information on the American Marketing Association, call toll free at 800-AMA-1150.

Or write to:

The American Marketing Association
11 South Wacker Drive
Suite 5800
Chicago, IL 60606-0872
URL; http://www.ama.org